ENTREPRENEURSHIP, PRIVATE AND PUBLIC

Ruth C. Young
Joe D. Francis
Christopher H. Young

University Press of America,® Inc.
Lanham • New York • Oxford

Copyright © 1999 by
University Press of America,® Inc.
4720 Boston Way
Lanham, Maryland 20706

12 Hid's Copse Rd.
Cumnor Hill, Oxford OX2 9JJ

Library of Congress Cataloging-in-Publication Data

Young, Ruth C.
Entrepreneurship, private and public / Ruth C. Young,
Joe D. Francis, Christopher H. Young.
p.   cm.
l. Entrepreneurship. 2. New business enterprises. 3. Success in
business. 4. Small business—Management. I. Francis, Joe D. II.
Young, Christopher H. III. title.
HB615.Y69 1999 338'.04—dc21 99—29458 CIP

ISBN 0-7618-1446-9 (cloth: alk. ppr.)
ISBN 0-7618-1447-7 (pbk: alk. ppr.)

CONTENTS

iii

PREFACE

Like so many other sociological research, the work of this book had its origin in serendipity.

We started a research project on innovation in manufacturing. Little empirical work had been done on this subject. We started out looking at small firms because they would necessarily have begun with a product, and we hypothesized that many of their founders would have designed something new.

Our first survey was not a sample. We simply took lists of local firms, called them up, and asked how old they were. If the firms were founded within the last ten years, we sent out an interviewer. The schedule consisted of some open-ended questions and many structured ones. These questions were based on information gathered from a small number of firms we had visited together with a list of topics in hand—like marketing, for example—and asked all about the business.

We had to do this exploratory work ourselves since previous research was so scattered, so fragmentary, so mixed together with case studies and applied approaches that it really did not provide a sound basis for systematic research. Therefore we included as many questions as we could about all aspects of the business: the entrepreneur's background, buying, selling, and business management.

Lucky for us that we did! For as we went over the first set of surveys to prepare them for coding, what particularly caught our eye were references to connections with large firms. We got very excited. Perhaps the interfirm connections would provide clues to the firm's functioning, its place in a regional structure, and to the structure of the economy itself. This little thread might, if pulled, unravel the whole fabric.

It did. We found in the five following surveys that most small firms were suppliers to a few large oligopolistic firms—that a clearly defined network of buying, selling, subcontracting, and work experience existed in a small region. There were many other nuances, but these are the basic facts: A region consists of a network of interacting large and small firms.

We have conducted five more surveys since the first, which was based in Ithaca and surrounding counties. Each successive survey became more structured since we had more data from previous surveys on which to base the next set of questions. Each survey since the first has been a sample. The second covered Monroe County; the third, the five counties of New York's Southern Tier and three from Pennsylvania's Northern Tier.

With the results of these surveys in hand, and with limited funds, we next went after data from the rural areas of a region for comparison: we did a small survey in the eight countries surrounding Rochester. Then we wondered what effect a large government facility would have on the surrounding area and surveyed four counties around Rome as were the others, Laboratories. Finally we mailed a survey to a sample provided by the New York state Department of Economic Development that includes the rest of the state not already surveyed.

Many of the small firms use computerized technology and many invent new products.

At the same time as the six surveys done in successive years, we undertook a survey of economic development offices, mainly in the counties but we included some from city and town offices and from regional, state and federal agencies. In all we conducted 100 interviews.

To the eleven hundred people, economic developers and founders and officers of businesses-- we give our sincere thanks for spending more than an hour with us of their busy day. We also wish to thank the teams of interviewers for their work.

We wish to thank Betsy Kiakowski for computer work and Letha Padgett, BeverleyWells and Nancy Pierce for a great deal of secretarial assistance. Finally, we thank Eugene Erickson and David Brown for all their support.

We finally wish to thank Donald Freebairn for his economic counsel. Since I often disagree with him, the errors are mine.

We have used material from several previous publications. Chapter 2 uses material from Ruth C. Young, Joe D. Francis and Christopher H. Young. 1993. Innovation, High-Technology Use, and Flexibility in Small Manufacturing Firms. *Growth and Change*, 24, pp. 67-86, Winter. Chapter 3 uses material from Ruth C. Young, Joe D. Francis and Christopher H. Young. 1994. Small Manufacturing Firms and Regional Business Networks. *Economic Quarterly*, 8, 1:77-82, February and Ruth C. Young, Joe D. Francis and Christopher H.

Young. 1993. Flexibility in Small Manufacturing Firms and Regional Industrial Formations. *Regional Studies*, 28, 1:27-38, July. Chapter 7 uses material from Young, Ruth C. and Joe D. Francis. 1997. "Secrecy as a Factor in the Spread of New Technology: Photonics in the Rome Labs." *American Geographical Society: Focus*, 44 (1): 7-9.

Funds for this project were provided by a Hatch grant (159412), "Survival of Manufacturing Business in New York State," a regional research grant (159450), "Rural Economic Development Alternatives in the New Competitive Environment," and by the National Research Institute.

Permission from the following has also been granted: Blackwell Publishers, Malden, Massachusetts; Carfax Publishing Limited, Cambridge, Massachusetts; and *Focus*, Lexington, Kentucky.

Private Entrepreneurship

Chapter 1

Introduction

Are small manufacturing entrepreneurs replacing large industry, serving it or simply surviving independently or are they following large? How does the federal and state government help or hinder small manufacturing business? Several things are going on in different countries and doubtless in the United States. We present data on New York State and do not know how we may or may not generalize from it. But government help exists in all states. All states have regional oligopolies and small business and all states have industry involved in high technology and trying to innovate. Thus, if different from each other, regions of the country need to explain how their basic relations do so. They certainly have some comparable pressures and trends. New York State industry sells widely to other states and nations and is not isolated. Thus for these general trends and for the interaction with other states and relations, this example is a relevant one. The question of the social context of private entrepreneurship and its relation to public agencies is a universal one about which there are conflicting claims but little information. Entrepreneurship is especially important in the modern world, but how does it fit into modern society? What is it like, how does it function?

Most economic theory and prediction assumes stability or that there's a single direction of change. An economist I know says that economics is very good at predicting when nothing changes, when trends continue, but it is not good at predicting changes in direction or turning points. For this reason we, as sociologists report on two sets of institutions that change constantly; small manufacturing companies and local economic development organizations both started and run by entrepreneurs. By that we mean independent, active, decisive, risk takers who do not consult a bureaucracy every time they move. They decide for themselves, take a risk and go ahead with plans. We will focus on the social context of entrepreneurship in these two types of organizations. A sample of 1000 firms from New York state, were drawn (omitting 10 New York City counties) and the economic development organizations in the 52 upstate counties as well. The purpose of the economic development organizations is to change their environment. Small manufacturing business is flexible, innovative, uses high technology and is changing. A product is said to last no more than 5 years. Many change much more often. In looking at these institutions, we will examine how theory fits. Often it does not. Almost half of New York State's small manufacturing firms innovate, 70 percent use modern computerized technology, yet most firms are suppliers to other firms, often to large firms. Almost a third of the firms sell thirty percent or more of their output to their most important customer, 50 percent sell 20 percent or more.

Entrepreneurs spring up everywhere, not only in New York State,-- but where they get only extended family help and no bank or government help as in Taiwan where they are tied to large firms as suppliers and get engineering and financial help from them as in Japan, and as in Romania where they are partly owned by large industry while large industry is partly owned by the government.

Various theories have been spun out to account for what small firms do. Piore and Sabel (1984) after studying Italian firms, say that large scale economic change is taking place, that small firms everywhere are replacing large due to an increase in technological capacity and a diversity of demand. Or as Romo et al (1988) have said about New York State, large, concentrated firms in an area give rise to supplier firms and also have a heavy influence on the local government. Harrison's theory (Lean and Mean 1994) says that small businesses are followers, not leaders; they are backward compared with large. All three present a great deal of information that support their views. But information in Harrison is based on studies in five different countries with very different public policies toward business and different industrial structures. Piore and Sabel concentrate on one district in Italy; though their conclusions are disputed even there; one district does not make an industrial society. Comparisons between small and large firms—when does a small firm become large?—seem artificial and pointless. The main question is relations between them and the structure of small business. We also take small manufacturing businesses as those firms with 100 employees or fewer.

Harrison has said that there are very few independent small firms. This study is a sample of 1000 small manufacturing firms in New York State. Many have survived for decades. All are completely independent. Most of them sell to a larger firm, many locally. But few sell a majority of their products to any one company, large or small. A minority of these firms have a contract with a large company; many more have a regular relationship, but no contract. As one of these said, "If we produce a good product at a good price, we are in. But if our foot slips, other firms are waiting in the wings."

In addition to selling to a large company, if there is one, they sell to a variety of other firms, to retail trade and to government, both to a lesser extent. They are mainly suppliers but market their products judiciously and in varied ways. Forty-five percent of them export from the United

States and 77 percent from New York State. About a third get help from local, state or federal government in the form of loans or guarantees of loans. Many more also get advice on a variety of topics.

A vast majority of small firms produce custom-made products and alter specifications on products constantly; only a minority mass produce. Most train their workers to fill several jobs and make them responsible for the quality of their products. They work as teams. Their owners are in charge of research and technical innovations, as well as marketing and customer contact. This specialized role of the business serves to fill a need large firms have for small, for products they do not want to produce themselves, and in which small firms specialize. Small firms constantly alter specifications and work closely with their customers with whom they have complex relations.

These small firms are neither leaders nor followers but are doing specialized jobs that make them important to large industry. Extension specialists tell us that firms want their suppliers to be not more than an hour or two away. Most small firms sell to one of a few concentrated firms in their own county. Such a firm, though, may not be its most important customer. But as we have pointed out, they export from both the state and nation. This does not mean that large firms do not import parts from abroad. They do. But it does mean that some parts that are technical and may change a lot are best supplied by small firms with skilled workers. Another issue is that within an industry firms may not remain small. An industry might begin with a variety of small firms. But within a decade or two, the majority of production might be from a few large firms. This means that time affects structure, as does national policy. So do industries.

For these reasons, we offer a study of 1000 small firms in New York State. All are totally independent manufacturing firms that have complex relations with large firms along with many other customers. Only a third have a contract with their most important customer. This picture of specialization and complexity of relations differs in important ways from the usual small-large arguments. Small firms are a key to understanding economic structure. Their relations to large industry and to the government are key ingredients in the structure of regional economies.

This book will describe the social context of entrepreneurs in small manufacturing firms (100 employees or fewer) in New York State. It will also describe the role and social context of public entrepreneurs who supervise and activate a variety of public programs for helping business. These are relatively new to New York State but such an essential part of a picture which is not complete without them, since more then about a third of small firms get help from them. Yet research has omitted them from consideration.

In saying we will describe the social context of private and public entrepreneurship, we are not saying we know or can predict who will become entrepreneurs. We have little evidence to examine for this purpose and what we have is not indicative. Private entrepreneurs have a slightly higher proportion of well educated persons, notably because industry has become so heavily a user of high technology. Entrepreneurs came from all kinds of previous jobs, highly skilled to unskilled. Likewise public entrepreneurs tend to be college educated, but they, too, come from all kinds of previous jobs. Therefore, what we will describe is the social context in which they arise, the nature of their business and how it fits into society, the support it gets, and the nature of the organization public entrepreneurs engender and how it relates to the society around it.

The book will attempt to answer several questions in New York State.

1) What is the nature of regional economic structure? How are large and small firms interrelated and tied to local governments?

2) How completely does this describe the activity and determine the fate of a local entrepreneur?

3) How modern and how innovative are small firms? One theory (Harrison) has said that small firms are part of the past, left behind modernization which has taken place in large firms. Another theory (Piore and Sabel 1984) say that small firms are more modern and have left large firms behind.

4) How do small firms finance themselves? On whom are they dependent: on large firms they supply, on extended family, on government, or are they responsible for themselves?

5) We do not have information about survival, but survival has been shown to be closely related to growth. What accounts for firm growth?

6) If tied into regional structure, are firms confined to it for supply, for subcontracting, and for sales, or do they export from the county, state and nation?

7) What is the nature of federal, state and local government intervention in the business picture and how do businesses relate to government help? Does this help make those that get it dependent on government? We will describe the relatively new forms that government help has taken and the public entrepreneurs who carry it out. Public entrepreneurs exist all over the state and do different jobs. Why are they different and how does this fill different local needs?

The book will have two main parts. One will describe the private entrepreneurs that start small manufacturing firms, how they operate, what their firms are like, how they relate to large firms, to regions outside the state and nation, and to government organizations, how they grow and survive. The second part will deal with the public entrepreneurs, the array of government help in the state, how it is organized, how it is flexible and how it differs from county to county and still gets its job done. In short, the book will describe the regional structure of small manufacturing firms, the nature of their operations, their relations to large firms and to the web of public entrepreneurs who have arisen in New York to give them help.

Most small manufacturing firms in New York State are suppliers to other manufacturing firms, many of them large firms and many of them oligopolies. These small firms are modern and users of high technology. Almost half of them innovate and almost three quarters use computerized technology. In other words, the small manufacturing firms of New York State are enmeshed in a network of modern, innovative, high technology buying and selling and subcontracting.

They are intimately related to the firms to which they sell. The vast majority of them sell to some or all firms that have just-in-time inventory control, and have to supply their products on short notice and most of them produce custom-made products. The products they supply often change specifications. Their negotiations with their most important customers tend to be complex. Almost 50 percent sell 20 percent or more to their most important customer. It is an act of entrepreneurship to run a small firm, starting, managing, financing, working both on technology and marketing and undergoing constant risk.

As large firms slim down and try to be efficient, they demand supplies on short notice, they demand custom made goods and change specifications often. Thus the small firms are supplying highly skilled products that the large companies no longer wish to produce, if they ever did. But our suspicions about slimming down and recent use of just-in-time inventory are well placed and have undoubtedly increased the use of the small supplier. The small supplier also buys parts and is part of a network of supply. The small firm is nonetheless very independent. By definition it is not owned in part or whole by a large firm. It is largely financed by the owner throughout its existence, and the owner puts in many hours of work. He has a crew of highly skilled workers trained to fill several jobs and made responsible for the quality of their work.

Since the large companies do not have any financial interest in the small and since the small do not pay high wages or provide as many benefits as large, costs to the large firms are lower. Only a third of the small firms have contracts with their main customer, and thus when the large firms change products or are in a depression and no longer need the goods the small firms provide, they can easily be dispensed with at no cost to the large firm. The owners of small firms thus fit the picture we all have of the entrepreneur taking an independent and adventurous attitude, working hard and taking risks.

Thus, the small firms lead a precarious, risky life. The only backing or support they get is from federal, state and local government sources, help, advice, grants and loans. The people who do this are also entrepreneurs, public entrepreneurs who run local economic development organizations and extend their services widely in their cities and counties.

If small firms are supplying more of the jobs now than they used to, they are still tied into large companies that they supply. Thus we have one industrial economic network, not two separate systems. The small and large firms are interdependent. But even though they depend to a considerable extent on large firms, small firms maintain independence by having a number of customers, large and small. While this book is about small firms and government efforts on their behalf, it is also about large firm-small firm relationships, about the industrial economic network that provides a social context for private entrepreneurs and about the work of public agencies and public entrepreneurs that help them.

We interviewed all of the county-level development agencies in the 52 upstate counties, as well as some town and city agencies and federal and state agencies involved. Throughout New York State we conducted interviews with or received a mailed questionnaire from over 1000 firms in six successive surveys. Firm owners were our targeted group, though for some firms information was supplied by other firm members. These small firms are the focus of our study along with the government agencies from which they get all kinds of support and help. About a third or more apply for a government loan or grant and a quarter or more get one. In addition, they get help with site selection, buildings, equipment, business plans, personnel and all kinds of advice. If a local government agency does not know about something a firm is interested in, it finds out. A survey of local development agencies supplied information on the government background for economic development and small firm survival.

These simple facts undermine a number of theories about regional development and the development and nature of small firms, and about the universality of what are seen as dominant trends. The relation of the small firm to the network of regional firms undermines any theory that says that small firms will save our economy. Since they are so interdependent with large firms, they will be affected by the tide of events. Thus regional economic theory has to take into account these networks. Rural-urban relations are changing. Cities are still important, but they do not have their former meaning when they served as ports and railroad centers for heavy shipments of coal and steel. Now smaller, lighter products less tied to natural resources can be shipped around easily by highway and air. While industrial space in cities has become expensive, computers and communications in general have brought rural areas into economic functioning. Thus the former hypothesis which may have been true at one time, no longer is-- that innovative and high technology industry sought city location until the products and their production become routine and could go to rural areas where labor was cheaper.

The picture of small firms functioning in New York State with the interdependence with large firms and with the help of government agencies is different from development in other countries and perhaps other areas of this country such as Silicon Valley in California and Route 128 around Boston. But consideration of the present development and place of small firms in New York State not only undermines many universal theories but brings up concepts, interrelations and truths that must be asked before the development of any other region or country is fully understood. Thus while it does not pretend to be a universal pattern, the pattern of industry in New York State tells us that universal patterns of economic development are a figment of our imagination. We will describe one pattern and raise questions that have to be asked in other cases.

Why do small manufacturing businesses exist? How do they operate, how are large and small interwoven to form communities, how interdependent are they or are they not? Why do large businesses buy from small? There are a number of factors that could be causing the increase of buying out by large corporations in recent years, though they have always used suppliers. One is copying of Japanese methods of management, using just-in-time inventory control, thus putting storage costs onto smaller firms. The large firms buy what they need and expect delivery in a short period. This eliminates costly storage of supplies. Under recent recessions, large firms are downsizing, tightening up, so that they contract out for goods and services they formally provided themselves. They also contract out for special custom goods that they do not want to produce themselves; these orders can be discontinued if their product changes. Thus small business has perhaps become more important as suppliers to large than it used to be. Large thrust their inventory problems on small business and large business stays thin and sleek. Thus small business has been increasing employment, while large has been getting efficient.

Today in New York State sets of large businesses, oligopolistic in nature, surrounded by their small suppliers form regions. Large firms like suppliers to be close, within an hour or two trucking time. While small business also sells to other small and large corporations, to retail, to government and institutions, and sells outside the state and nation, the framework of the industrial economy are these regional sets of oligopolies and their suppliers. A region here consists of a web of firms interacting with each other closely, working together to solve problems and produce specialized goods for each other. Small business is high technology, uses computerized processing, it is innovative, and custom producing. It is nonetheless tied into large industry as suppliers. This sounds like an industrial economy of an older era, with large firms dominant. It is different. For one thing, large firms contract out for more goods and services. They have slimmed down and buy out, saving space, salaries and benefits in rough times.

For another, small firms are modern and specialized. The small firms are high technology; a majority of them use computerized processing. Between a third and half produce new products. Most produce custom goods in close cooperation with large firms. Despite their modernization, they are suppliers. Other than the interdependence of large and small firms, there is one more fact that characterizes these modern economic regions of New York State. The firms around which the small firms cluster tend to be oligopolies. These oligopolies, a few in a region out of the greater number of large firms, tend to have most of the region's small firms supplying them. But this does not mean that they dominate the small firms. Most small firms sell elsewhere as well, and only a portion have the large firm in the region as its most important customer. But this is only the beginning. Most small firms export from the state and from the country. Many sell retail. Many sell to firms outside the region. While the large oligopolies may have stimulated the founding of small firms, the small firms do not rely solely on them for their sales. Thus their supply relations to large firms in and out of the area are very important as well as their other types of sales that diversify their markets. Oligopolistic large firms and their small competitive suppliers work together as basic elements in local manufacturing regions. Extension agents and economic developers tell us that more and more large corporations are buying from fewer and fewer small companies, and they want them to be close, within an hour or two's trucking time.

The first thing we can say is that there is no universal pattern of how large and small manufacturers are tied together. In Taiwan small business must put up its own money. It cannot even get money on loan from banks. If loans are advanced, it is from extended family members. The government does not enter into the matter at all. In Japan, small firms are suppliers to large. The large firm may own a portion of the small, and the small of the large. Engineers from the large advise the small, even design a product for it to produce. Sometimes, a large will contract with the small, even though it does not need the goods, to keep the small firm in business. The central government has great influence, of course on large industry. In Eastern Europe other patterns of government influence and ownership prevail. The government may own or invest heavily in large industry, which in turn finances small. Therefore, there is no universal pattern of relationships between large and small firms. It has been said that two things influence small business, the way the business is run and the type of government support or influence it enjoys. The latter is very important.

But we will consider the theories that have been advanced as universalistic. One of these is Piore and Sabel's (1984) theory of flexible accumulation. A key ingredient in this theory is that various economic forces have come together to cause a new industrial divide that calls for small firms acting independently but in a collegial manner. `Microelectronics and information technology play a key role in allowing more flexible production and closer co-ordination between markets and producers targeting new market niches. Firms are supposedly becoming more responsive to changing tastes and to the tendency for consumer products to support the construction of personal identities' (Sayer and Walker, 1992). For many reasons called the new industrial divide, demand is being made for more diversified market products, and the claim is that small flexible firms are supplying them, and supporting each other.

Those who reject the theory argue that it is really a mythology (Amin and Robins, 1990); or `romantic' (Sayer and Walker, 1992); that we have never had most production in more than a minority of firms, that small firms have always existed and that flexibility does not always work. Yet the theory has tenaciously hung on. But, have the great changes that the authors call the second industrial divide (Piore and Sabel, 1984; Storper and Walker, 1989) really led to a restructuring of industry according to demand into a series of small flexible firms linked together in some collegial way? This is the main thrust of the theory.

Storper and Walker, 1989, have reformulated the theory as we have cited it above. They say that, consequently, we find new high-technology industrial districts, such as Silicon Valley, scattered across North America, and revitalized craft districts in Northern Italy. But if instead we find flexible manufacturing coupled with the hierarchical bonding of large corporations and their suppliers, this would refute the theory.Northern Italy and Silicon Valley have been given as prime examples of the theory at work, but in both cases the theory has been challenged and large industries shown to still be alive in those regions.

Harrison sees small companies as being out of date, left behind. Dualism (Averitt 1968) proposed as a theory in the 1960's also sees small firms as being left behind technologically, while the large progressive firms steam ahead. We show this to be untrue today. Another factor which figures importantly in the structure of large-small firm relations is the question of modernization and of innovation.

A theory advanced by Oliver Williamson (1985) says that large firms will absorb small when transaction costs between the two are greater than the costs within the merged firm. How this is supposed to be measured, is a question. But the present study shows that many firms survive as small firms over a long period of time, supplying large industry. Large industry tells us of small industries that were started by their employees, with which they now contract for services formerly provided within the company. There are all sorts of costs and considerations other than transaction costs that enter into this equation. One New York State firm has an innovation program such that employee ideas that are considered good, are financed in a new small company if the firm does not want to set them up internally. After a time, the large firm may sell off the business, or it may reabsorb it. One such firm was reabsorbed not for transaction costs but because it was selling to the same market as the parent firm. Likewise large firms are shedding branches that produce differently than their main products because they don't know how to manage them. Thus transaction costs are only one reason why firms stay the same, merge, or go out of business.

Several questions about industry come to mind. One question is the arrangement of firms. There are three possible arrangements of firms. Florida and Kenney, 1991b, p. 143, have pointed out that the arrangements among large and small firms are critical, 'the organization of R and D, the organization of manufacturing, and the integration of the two'. In the first arrangement, there is nothing but small firms interacting with the market. In the second, we have large firms interacting exclusively with the small. In the third (the present case), we have large and small interacting with each other, and the small with many other customers as well. The first case is supposed to be that of Italy and Silicon Valley, though they are both debated. The second is Japan, particularly the automotive industry and the third, our region.

Another factor is whether the firms have retail sales, as is the case in Italy and Silicon Valley but less so in the United States rust belt. A third is how new is the industry. Silicon Valley computer companies are relatively new. Often new industries begin as a competing set of small firms, but in ten or twenty years have settled into an oligopoly. A final factor is the nature of the parts being bought by the large firm. Supply relationships between automotive firms and their suppliers tend to be more exclusive than between other firms in Japan and in the United States. Parts for cars are large and specialized and not useful in other kinds of manufacture. Smitka, 1989, tells us that other types of firms in Japan have less exclusive supply relationships than the automotive industry.

These and other factors should be considered in attempts to explain differences among these foremost cases, but they have not been. Aside from such contextual variables impinging on industrial firms, we look at several regions of the US rust belt to see the nature of the formations. Here we have large and small firms linked together in complex supply relationships. We will show that the small firms often have leaders who have local work experience, they often produce parts similar to their former employer, they seldom compete with him and a third of the firms sell products to a former employer. While they are linked to the local large firms, a great majority have large and small customers around the state and out of state, and are completely autonomous and do not have contracts, unlike the Japanese suppliers to the automotive industry. Thus, these regions of the rust belt in New York have flexible small firms acting as suppliers to large firms and supplying a number of customers in addition to local core firms. This differs from the other three cases often cited, but could be different for a variety of cultural and industrial reasons.

Romo et al (1984) have provided another approach to large and small firm relations. They say that industrial districts are composed of a cluster of small firms supplying a group of several large firms in concentrated industries. Concentrated industries are those where a high proportion of output comes from a from a few firms. They also claim that these large firms dominate the region politically. This claim will remain untested in this study, though plausible, but we will show that large and small firms do relate to each other as Romo et al suggested in New York State. We will suggest that Romo's hypothesis about large - small firm relations fits better than the other theories: the dualism theory, flexible manufacturing, Oliver Williamson's (1985) theory of transaction costs, or the Japanese model of dominant firm linked with suppliers.

The theory that prevails with regard to the economic development organizations is sociological theory that organizations founded at the same time fit society as it is at that time and do not change as society changes. But economic development organizations are exactly the opposite. They are dissimilar from the beginning and not only change over time, but their mission is to change their environmental structure. We will examine these from three view points: the formal structural of the organizations, their natural structure or how they operate from day to day, and their external relations. We will see that these organizations have some formal characteristics in common but are different from the beginning and change over time and change their environments. We will show that both sets of institutions are changing in complex ways.

Chapter 2 will give the basic facts, how firms start up, the nature of the entrepreneurs, how they are financed, what benefits they provide employees, how they market their goods, where they get their technical information and how we got our information from six surveys.

Chapter 3 will deal with questions of innovation and use of high technology. It will measure their characteristics, show them to be separate, show their relation or lack of it to industry level measures and show the relation of innovation and use of computerized technology to other firm characteristics.

Chapter 4 will show the firm acting as a member of a network of firms, show large-small firm relations and regional structures.

Chapter 5 will discuss the cause of firm growth. Part 2 will contain chapters 6 to 12 on public entrepreneurs. It will include Chapter 6, Local organizations and public entrepreneurs, Chapter 7, Federal and state development of funds, Chapter 8, The beginnings, structure, and the government context, Chapter 9, The developers and their activities, Chapter 10, The wider networks, Chapter 11, Projects, Chapter 12, Pressures on counties and Chapter 13, How the public entrepreneurs work.

Chapter 2

Starting Up and Financing the Business
The Basic Facts

Small manufacturing firms are small miracles. They are generally started with a founder's own money and many hours of hard work. They are also a big risk. Many of them go out of business. In the United States small firms with 100 or fewer employees comprise 90 percent of all manufacturing firms and 25 percent of the employment in the SIC categories we sampled. It is small firms like this that are the targets of public effort. In the latest sample this consists of 674 firms out of a New York statewide sample of 1404, or 48 percent that replied to our mail questionnaire. The firms were in fact very small. Sixty-six percent had 20 or fewer employees. Forty-six percent had 10 or fewer.

Among these small firms there was remarkable agreement on a number of things. Seventy-six percent sold to other manufacturers and 72 percent bought parts from other firms. For 59 percent of those answering, the most important customer was a large company. Thus they are embedded in a network of manufacturers in which large companies figure importantly.

Seventy-six percent custom produce. Sixty-nine percent have improved or upgraded a product and, when talking of their most important customer, 65 percent say that specifications change. Seventy-three percent say that those doing the work have responsibility for its quality and 83 percent have cross-training of workers so that they know several jobs.

Sixty-eight percent of them had some or all of their customers on just-in-time inventory, and when speaking of their most important customer, 78 percent provided goods on short notice. Yet, 74 percent exported from the county and 77 percent from New York State. All chosen in the sample were independently owned and 78 percent initially financed their own company.

This picture of small manufacturing businesses tied into a network with large, serving them so well, yet independent and self sufficient is a brave scenario, one quite different than theory conveys.

Let us look at the sample of firms in greater detail. A great majority of the respondents were officers of the company. Four hundred and ninety-eight were presidents and 113 other officers, totalling 602.

In 73 percent of the cases, the president answered the mailed questionnaire and most of the rest of the respondents were officers of the company. Those founded in earlier years tended to have an officer reply, as in later years founders are probably no longer in the company. Seventy-eight percent were male, 11 percent were female and for the rest, it was not possible to determine, they simply gave initials.

The firms started from 1654 to the present. Every year increasing numbers survive to the present. We do not know how many failed. We are told that most companies that fail do so in the first six years. Eighty percent of these companies are at least ten years old. From our table of starting dates, it appears that the same proportion drop out each year, either fail or are absorbed into other companies. Most probably go out of business.

Table 1. Number of Businesses in the United States and in the Statewide Sample Over Time

Year	Total Number of Firms in US Census at Intevals	Number of Firms in the Statewide Sample Started in the Same Years
1921	192,059	74
1931	171,450	100
1939	173,802	127
1947	240,807	164
1958	363,303	232
1963	311,931	277
1967	311,140	309
1972	320,710	384
1977	359,928	454
1982	358,061	524
1987	368,897	617
After 1987		57

They produce a great variety of products. We tried to eliminate food products and printing and publishing companies from the sample, since food companies do not have a large interchange of parts. Neither do printing and publishing, which included, for example, shops that print wedding invitations. Of the other SIC categories, seventy-one produced lumber and wood products. One hundred fifty-two firms produced machinery except electrical and 35 electrical and electronic. Eighty-seven produced fabricated metal products and 18 transportation equipment. Twenty-eight produced instruments and related products and 51 miscellaneous manufacturing. This latter category includes jewelry, toys, musical instruments, buttons, pencils, needles, brooms and the like. Therefore, our sample provided by the New York State Department of Economic Development was comprehensive and wide ranging. The array of original products was very like the present array. Seventy-seven percent produced a physical product, and 4 percent software and physical. Only 1 percent produced only software. The rest did not disclose enough information to be classifiable, but we had asked for a sample of manufacturing firms (see Table 2).

Some questions were not asked in this final mail survey which was shorter than the face-to-face interviews. Therefore, we will use data from previous surveys in these cases. We cite data from the Southern Tier (two-state) sample, data from Monroe County and the four-county sample around Rome Labs.

According to our Southern Tier (two-state) sample, a majority of firms are started by a single founder (52%). Eighty-five percent are started by two founders and 98 percent are started by no more than three persons. The founder came from a large company 45 percent of the time, and a majority (54%) started the company in response to a need or service provided by a former employer. Thirty-two percent were either owners or top managers in their former company, but they held a great array of jobs: accounting, advertising, sales, foremen, machinist or other skilled work, down to unskilled jobs.

For 52 percent the employer's company was in the same industry as the present company. Forty-five percent were still working for the former company when they started the business, but only a small proportion got help from the former company. Thirty percent still sell to a former employer. Their present main product is related to that of a former employer. Fifty-eight percent of the time the product is the same or similar, 12 percent more, it is modified or a part is used and only 25 percent have a product that is different.

Seventy-one percent thought their previous job experience gave them knowledge of the industry, 57 percent knowledge of the product, and 51 percent knowledge of a process. Fifty-two percent say that it provided them with management skills and 53 percent knowledge of the market. Thirty-seven percent say that it gave them knowledge of finance. These figures show that they regard their former experience as important. The largest percentage left the company because they wanted to start their own business (46%) and the rest for a variety of reasons. Forty-five percent still have a single owner and 37 percent more have two; that is 82 percent have one or two owners. Thirty-one percent of these co-owners are related by marriage and 61 percent more are kin. Small proportions of co-owners were co-workers, went to school together or were friends. Fifty-three percent of owners formerly worked in a company in the same county, and 29 percent more in the state, totalling 82 percent that worked for more or less local firms.

The owners come from all kinds of educational backgrounds though 9 percent have a master's degree or a doctorate, and 25 percent more a bachelors degree. Seventeen percent have two years of training beyond a high school diploma and 41 percent high school only. Only 8 percent have less than a high school education. This is quite comparable to education in the state of New York, except that 10 percent more had a college degree or higher. (In the statewide sample sixteen percent more had a college degree or better.) But of all owners 57 percent have an engineering or science background; 14 percent have a business education (see Table 3).

Most small businesses are initially financed by the owners. They get help from others, especially family members. When they need more money, again they are financed by owners or by the businesses themselves with internal funds. The second time around bank loans also increase, repayable by the owners, and security rests on the owner's property. Nonetheless about a third of the businesses statewide get some type of government loan or grant. Table 6 shows that in Monroe County 37 percent of businesses asked for loans and 24 percent got them.

Table 2. Numbers of Firms in the Standard Industrial Classification in the Statewide Sample

		Originally When Started	At Present
SIC		Number of Firms	
21	Tobacco products	0	
22	Textile Mill Products	13	15
23	Apparel & other Textile products	25	21
24	Lumber and Wood products	72	72
25	Furniture & fixtures	13	15
26	Paper & allied product	20	18
28	Chemicals & allied products	22	22
29	Petroleum and coal products	6	6
30	Rubber and misc. plastic products	15	17
31	Leather & leather products	15	15
32	Stone, clay & glass products	38	40
33	Primary metal industries	24	26
34	Fabricated metal products	82	87
35	Industrial machinery & equipment	156	152
36	Electronic & other electronic equipment	31	35
37	Transportation equipment	15	18
38	Instruments & related products	25	28
39	Miscellaneous manufacturing industries	47	51

Entrepreneurship, Private and Public

Table 3. Education in New York State and in the Statewide Sample

	New York State 1987	Our Sample
	Percentage	
High school or less	30	32
Some college or Associate's degree	22	23
Bachelor' s degree	13	26
Professional degree or higher degree	10	14

Total number 674

In the Southern Tier and the Rome area 45 percent asked for them and 38 and 35 percent respectively got them. This lower percentage from Monroe County is probably due to its higher economic status. Its economy "has been among the most economically robust in the state." (New York Time, November 16, 1997.) The Monroe economy has spread to its adjacent counties. The economic developer in one of them stated that his businesses did not ask for loans because they didn't need them. Most get loans from a small number of sources and only a few from a great number of others.

First let us take a look at how firms are initially funded. Table 4 shows the initial sources of finance for four samples, for the Monroe county sample, Southern Tier (two-state) sample, and the Rome sample and the statewide sample.

In the statewide sample, 78 percent financed their business with their own money. Sixteen get financial help from their families. Forty-one percent get bank loans. Bank loans had to be secured by the SBA, by a home mortgage or by business property. Very small proportions got help from many other sources. Their replies were a bit different when they were asked how they were financed <u>after</u> the start, when more money was needed. Many were still self-financed. This time a sizable proportion were also financed by internal company funds. The question in Monroe County about use of internal funds was not asked.

Table 4.   Financing the Company at the Start

	Rome	Southern Tier	Monroe County	Sample
		Percentage		
Owners' money	68	72	75	78
Bank Loans	36	26	44	41
Family Money	23	12	16	22
Total Number	111	117	123	674

Note: Percentages do not add up to 100 since firms can have more than one way of financing.

Family money had shrunk; the proportions decline that got help from the family. Bank loans increased greatly. From 58 to 76 percent in the various samples received bank loans and backing by the SBA also increased. A small number were financed by issuing stock. Again, they were financed by many other sources, but only small proportions of them got money from any given source: venture capital, other companies, federal and state funds, and revolving loan funds which were often local. Both initially and later in their evolution, companies finance themselves in one way or another. All bank loans and most government loans have to be secured and repaid. Thus the businesses definitely stand on their own feet. Things might be different in non-manufacturing companies -- retail shops and services, but manufacturers are mainly self reliant (see Table 5).

Their financial investment in the company is matched by their hours of work. In the state sample, 69 percent worked more than sixty hours a week at the beginning. Only 28 percent were paid a salary. Others were paid living expenses and a very small number a percent of the profit. At the time of the interview, 80 percent are paid a salary and 13 percent shared the profits, and a small number received living expenses. Their work week has also declined; now 30 percent work 40 hours a week or less, 36 percent work from 40 to 60 hours, 32 sixty, and over. These figures are similar to the answers in other samples.

Table 5.   Financing the Firm - Later

	Rome	Southern Tier	Monroe County	Statewide Sample
	Percentage			
Owners' money	41	17	47	51
Bank Loan	65	59	76	58
Family	10	6	4	9
Internal Funds	26	74	37	*
Total Number	111	117	123	674

Note: Percentages do not add up to 100 since firms can have more than one way of financing.

* Not asked

What kind of work do owners do? Seventy-four percent do research and development. CEO's are also heavily involved in marketing. Thirty-five percent have an engineering staff; for 65 percent of these this amounts to 1, 2 or 3 people.

The companies were very small at the beginning. Eighty-six percent consisted of no more than ten people, and 66 percent had no more than five. At the time of the interview, a varying number of years later, only 36 percent had ten workers or fewer, and only 21 percent had no more than five. Thus, most firms that stay in business grow over time (See Table 6). Of the non-production workers, 53 percent of the firms had at least one employee who was an engineer, scientist or highly skilled technician; 26 percent had one or two and 27 percent had three or more. The founders classified themselves as having both technical and management skills 74 percent of the time, management only 22 percent, technical only 3 percent and as being unskilled, 1 percent of the time (Table 6). Thus science, engineering and technical abilities are important to managers as well as employees.

How well do these companies treat their employees? Let us look at the lowest wage. Ten percent in the Southern Tier (two-state) sample pay the minimum wage or less. Thirty-five percent pay from this minimum wage to $5.25 an hour and 52 percent pay more than $5.25. Five dollars and 15 cents is proposed in Congress as the new minimum wage. For the highest wage, only one company pays less than $6.00 an hour. Sixty-seven percent pay $10 an hour or more. Fourteen percent pay $15 an hour or more. (Table 6). Let us compare this with the United States as a whole. In 1993, goods producing industries (agriculture, mining, construction and manufacturing) paid 2.4 percent of all workers $4.25 or less. The median wage for these industries in 1993 was $9.22. Unfortunately, we do not have exact comparisons, but the proportion of our sample paying the minimum wage or less to at least a number of their work crew seems high. Whatever its value, 68 percent of the firms paid the minimum wage to no more than three members of their crew (see Table 7).

**Table 6.   Comparison of Three Surveys, Rome Labs, Monroe
County and Southern Tier (2-State)**

	Rome	Monroe County	Southern Tier (Two-State)
		Percents	
Hours of Work Week at Beginning-60 hours or more	66	69	69
at time of survey			
40 or less	30	28	25
41 to 60	36	56	29
over sixty	32	15	20
Payment to Owners at beginning Paid a Salary	22	27	28
at time of Survey Paid a Salary	80	73	80
CEO's do research and development	79	74	74
Size of Firm - number of employees			
at the beginning			
1 to 4	59	80	66
5 to 10	22	11	20
more than 10	19	9	14
at time of survey			
1 to 4	28	32*(Production Workers)	16
5 to 10	11	15*(Production Workers)	20
more than 10	61	54*(Production Workers)	64

Table 7.   Comparison of Three Surveys and Statewide Sample--Financial Detail

	Rome	Monroe County	Southern Tier (Two-State)
	Percentage		
Owners classify themselves as technical or management	77	46	74
technical only	4	15	3
management only	19	37	22
unskilled			1
Lowest wage			
$4.25	7	14	10
$4.26 to $5.25	31	32	35
no more than $5.25	62	54	52
Highest wage			
$6.00 or less	1	6	(1)
$10.00 or more	52	74	67
$15.00 or more	11	18	14
Percent of Firms Applying for Loans	45	37	45
Percent Who Got Loans	35	24	38
Total Number	123	117	111

For benefits, we compare our Monroe County and Southern Tier (two-state) samples with national large and small companies, with production, service and manufacturing plants. Here we have large difference when comparing them to large firms and to non-manufacturing firms.

Do small manufacturing firms (those with fewer than 100 employees) differ from their counterparts in other industries -- as well as with all kinds of medium and large firms -- when it comes to providing benefits to employees?

The table shows that in the samples of small manufacturing firms, holidays, vacations and health insurance are given in proportions similar to all medium and large firms, as well as to all manufacturing firms. These benefits, however, are given in somewhat greater proportions when compared with all small firms; over 90 percent of the sample provide vacation time, compared with 77 percent in small firms, and over 80 percent have health insurance, compared with 65 percent of all small firms.

In this sample, fewer small manufacturing firms offer life insurance and pensions when compared with medium and large firms; 41 to 59 percent provide life insurance, compared with 94 percent of medium and large firms, and 26 to 30 percent have pensions, compared with 81 percent of medium and large firms. The proportions in this sample regarding pensions and life insurance coverage are similar to the proportions for all small firms that offer these kinds of benefits. Therefore, workers in small manufacturing firms enjoy vacations and health insurance benefits in greater proportions than do employees in all small firms. Percentages for life insurance and retirement benefits provisions, however, are similar.

A greater number of small manufacturing companies give bonuses compared with medium and large companies (64 or 66 percent to 27 percent). Forty-two or 28 percent of the sample provide job-related tuition assistance, compared with 69 percent for all employees in medium and large firms and 59 percent for production workers in medium and large firms.

The sample of small manufacturing firms studied found that some benefits are provided in proportions similar to all large and medium firms, while life insurance and pensions are similar to all small firms. Even among those firms with fewer than 100 employees, total size of the workforce is related to the provision of life insurance, profit sharing and tuition payments, although not to pensions and bonuses. Basically, a firm that provides any one benefit is likely to provide several others, so a pattern begins to develop.

Table 8. Small Medium and Large: Variations in Employee Benefits

	Vacations	Holidays	Health Insurance	Life Insurance	Retirement or Pension	Educational Assistance	Bonuses
				Percent providing			
All medium and large establishment, 1989 (100 or more employees)*	97	97	92	94	81	69	27
All small establishments, 1985 (under 100 employees)*	77	**	65	49	26	**	**
Large establishment production and service employees, 1989*	95	97	93	93	80	59	26
All manufacturing establishments*	**	**	89	**	70	**	**
Monroe County manufacturers Small firms	95	97	87	41	26	42	64
Southern Tier manufacturers Small firms	92	91	82	59	30	28	66

*Source: 1990 EBRI Databook on Employee Benfits
** Data not available

Questions now arise as to why small manufacturing firms are less likely to provide life insurance and pensions than other benefits where they compare favorably with large companies. Perhaps the reason has to do with the company's expectation for survival or lesser expectations for life-time employment among employees. The greater proportion that pay bonuses suggest that bonuses may be a substitute for pensions and life insurance in firms that do not always last for lifetime employment.

According to our latest statewide sample, only 30 percent of the firms mass produce, but 83 percent do a short run with modifications and 79 percent produce in batches, that is limited quantities without modifications. Seventy-six percent sell to other manufacturers, 61 to wholesalers but less than half to institutions, directly to retail customers, to services, to the government or to defense. Only 32 percent sell to defense. This pattern of producing specialized goods in small quantities and selling to other manufacturers is consistent with other evidence about the firm. But note that about one third mass produce and a considerable number sell to other sources than manufacturing firms. They typically sell to a variety of firms and thus are not totally dependent on one large firm. Note that a large proportion sell to customers on a just-in-time basis or on very short notice.

How much do they sell? Table 9 gives the value of sales per year. Only two firms have no customers. Fifty-one percent sell goods worth up to a million dollars a year. Thirty-five percent sell between one million and 5 million dollars worth. Only 11 percent sell over five million dollars worth of goods. We have data only on all United States firms, rather than manufacturing. But in the United States 22 percent have receipts totalling less than $100,000 and 78 percent more. This compares with 7 percent of our sample with less than $100,000 and 90 percent with more. Seeing that the United States data contains firms of all sizes large and small, and all types of firms, not just manufacturing, and our data only small manufacturing, these differences are more remarkable. Our small firms do a considerable volume of business.

Table 9.   Volume of Sales, Statewide Sample

Volume of Sales	Percentage
None	0
Under $100,000	6
$100,000 to $250,000	16
$250,000 to $500,000	12
$500,000 to $1 million	17
$1 Million up to $2.5 million	21
$2.5 Million up to $5 million	13
$5 Million up to $7.5 million	4
$7.5 Million up to $10 million	3
Over $10 million	4
Missing Data	4
	100
Total Number	674

Sixty-one percent of the chief executive officers are involved in marketing in the Southern Tier (two-state) study.   A sales staff is present in 24 percent of the firms and in 19 percent the vice-president does sales.

In the statewide study 86 percent market by word of mouth.   Thirty percent have marketing representatives, 36 advertise at trade or technical shows and 30 percent in trade magazines.   Forty-four percent have manufacturers' representatives.   Though they use a variety of measures, personal contact is of overwhelming importance.   Fifty-four percent have 50 customers or more.   At the lower end of the distribution only 22 percent have 10 or fewer customers.   Thus, their marketing efforts are widespread (see Table 10).

**Table 10. Comparisons of Marketing Practices of the
Surveys: Rome Labs, Monroe County and
Southern Tier (two-state)**

	Rome Labs	Monroe County	Southern Tier (two-state)
		Percentage	
CEO involved in marketing	71	73	61
Vice President in marketing	31	14	19
They have a sales staff	26	22	24
Areas of Marketing Word of mouth/ direct contact	70	72	86
Trade/technical shows	38	30	36
Trade magazines	29	16	30
Manufacture's representatives	44	35	44
Former job contacts	32	20	*
Telemarketing	8	16	*
Distributors	23	16	*
Number of customers 10 fewer	14	11	22
50 or more	68	54	54
	111	117	123

* Not asked

Sources of technical information (Southern Tier [two state] study) are in wide variety and show again the networking of these companies. Trade shows and technical and professional journals rate the highest, but customers, sales representatives and buyers have nearly as high a proportion choosing them. Thirty-eight percent use their competitors. Thus, they are enmeshed in many types of contacts when they seek information (see Table 11).

In a cross-national study, Stevens (1997) confirmes the effect of information passed around the network of firms linked by buying and selling on innovation.

How do the firms compare with the nation on survival? Table 1 gives the number of sample firms started at 5 year intervals since 1931 that now survive. It also gives the total number of firms in the United States census for each of the 5 year intervals. In the United States in 1987, there were 2.15 firms for every firm in 1931 or before. If New York really resembles the United States, this means that in New York about four out of the six firms started, went out of business before 1987 or were absorbed by other firms or grew very large. In the United States the number of firms almost doubled from 1939 to 1945 -- from the Depression to post-war. Then from 1945 on the number stayed approximately the same. That is, firms that dropped out for any reason - failure or absorption or large growth were replaced by new firms. In our sample, they were not. The ratio of 1987 to 1931 is six to one. Is this drop out in our sample due to failure or absorption or growth? We do not know but speculate that they mostly go out of business voluntarily or due to failure.

How do these firms survive? We have only the word of the SBA. They allow for a default by 1 1/2 to 2 percent of their loans compared with 1/2 of one percent allowed by banks. Philips (1989) estimate on their sample of United States small manufacturing firms that 47 percent survive six years or more. Twenty-seven percent of those with no growth survive, 67 percent of those with growth of 1 to 4 persons, 74 percent of those with growth of 5 to 9 employees, and 76 percent of those with growth by 10 or more persons. These estimates conform to what the regional SBA officer estimated. We have said that 2 out of 6 of our firms survived as is since founding. This is comparable with the other estimates. We will go into this more in a later chapter.

Table 11. Sources of Information

	Rome Labs	Monroe County	Southern Tier (two-state)
		Percentage	
Trade and Technical shows	56	41	54
Professional journals	55	52	53
Technical journals	49	40	53
Customers	38	33	50
Sales representatives	41	21	44
Distributors-buyers	33	21	43
Technical sheets supplied by comparative manufacturers or others	46	39	40
Other business like new competitors	-	28	38
We've invented it ourselves	34	26	36
Universities	8	8	12
State or federal government	12	3	11
Professional or scientific conferences	23	26	10
Large company, former employer	14	9	10
	111	123	117

The greatest problems and needs were only asked in the Rome-Utica survey. They emphasized taxes (52 percent) and government regulations (56 percent). But many other problems were deemed serious: need for money (38 percent), marketing (38 percent), the business climate (40 percent), employees (31 percent), and decline of the area (26 percent). The latter was probably stimulated by discussion of closing of the Rome Air Base and the moving of the Rome Labs.

In 1989, we started a research project on innovation. We got a list of small manufacturers in Tompkins and surrounding counties from the New York Department of Economic Development and called them up to see when they started their firms. Those that had started within the last ten years we interviewed. The reasoning was that new, small firms would have to have a new product and in many cases, they would have invented it. This turned out to be the case. New firms were a good place to look for new products. We included a wide inventory of items in the schedule. When we were coding the schedules, the names of large firms popped out at us. They were buyers and sellers, former employers and present collaborators. They were important in the small firm's life. We did not use the information from that study in the later analysis as it was not a sample and we did not envision using it as such when we started. It was exploratory.

We revised our plans. Our next survey would include innovation, but also large-small firm connections, or the place of the small firm in the industrial community. The next survey was conducted in Monroe county the next year. The following year we conducted one in the New York-Pennsylvania border region in five New York counties and three Pennsylvania running along Highway 17; these were in New York Steuben, Schuyler, Tioga, Chemung and Broome; in Pennsylvania Tioga, Susquehana and Bradford. We had interviewed economic developers in the region who told us that the Pennsylvania counties were oriented to Highway 17; these were. A chain of mountains runs along their southern border, and, according to one developer, "someone comes north over the mountains about once a year." The eight Highway 17 counties seem to form a region.

The next year we sent a shorter mail survey to the counties in the central New York region around Monroe county. The final face-to-face survey was in the four counties around the Rome Air Base, to see what effect the Rome Labs had on regional structure. These four were

Oneida, Madison, Otsego and Herkimer counties.   We finally interviewed only in the southern section of Herkimer, since it went North a considerable distance into rural regions not remotely connected to Rome Air Base. The Rome Labs are one of four research centers for the Air Force, all instructed by Congress to serve industry, as well. Finally we conducted a statewide mail survey with a shorter schedule covering the areas of the state not already included in other samples. We secured 48 percent of this sample, some 674 schedules of a sample of 1404. Of course, we did not know which of these in the sample were out of business, so the proportion of existing businesses was probably higher.

In Monroe county, we conducted face-to-face interviews lasting about an hour with presidents and founders of 117 or 69 percent of 168. In the eight counties in Southern New York and Pennsylvania -- we secured 123 of a sample of 166 firms or 72 percent, again with face-to-face interviews with presidents and founders, lasting about an hour. We did the same thing in the four counties around Rome Air Base, securing 61 per cent of the three counties we fully interviewed and more in southern Herkimer county. In the region around Monroe county, we secured 42 percent of the mailed sample.

We improved the schedule as we went along, mainly by eliminating questions and improving answer categories, but keeping the schedules essentially the same.   In the two mail surveys, we shortened the schedules to the most important questions.

In each sample there were a number of firms that had gone out of business before we could interview them.   For instance, in Monroe county we lost 44 such firms. We analyzed each survey as it came in, and while preparing and launching the next. For their differences in questions and answers, it seemed better to keep them separate.

Each survey we did in the field had a separate team of interviewers. In Monroe county, we had three local college graduates. In the New York Pennsylvania border study, we had six Cornell graduate students. And in the Rome survey, we had a group of interviewers recruited for us by the local unemployment office containing a range of persons of different occupations and educational backgrounds. Questions on the different schedules were not always in the same order.

Despite all this diversity, results were very similar.   Answers to questions from the different field and mail interviews done in different years by different interviewers came within a few percentage points of each other on nearly all the questions. This gave us renewed confidence in our results despite the obvious deficiencies in the methods. We used the results of these surveys, omitting the first survey which was very similar. Thus this book is based on three field surveys and two mail surveys. Together they contain 1000 schedules from all over New York State over a five-year period. We are talking here of upper New York State, omitting the five New York City counties and the five more in the New York SMSA, since New York City is a national city and part of a region with Connecticut and New Jersey.

Discussion

In the 1000 schedules from all over upper New York State, we have found basic facts about how small manufacturing firms start. They are founded by persons who have had other local employment, often in large companies and nearly always in industries similar to the one they founded. They are started by one to three people often tied to each other by marriage or kinship. They are slightly better educated than other New Yorkers, and have had a variety of previous jobs.

They often begin while working on another job. Only a small proportion get a salary at first and most work very long hours. They seldom get help from previous employers. Once launched, when they need money for expansion, it often comes from the firm or from bank loans. But a third of them apply for a government loan and about one third of them get one. Later in the firm's life, they are paid a salary and work shorter hours.

A vast majority of them are linked to other firms, selling to them, and buying parts from them. A majority of these are large firms. A vast majority custom produce and change and upgrade products. This calls into question two theories. One is the flexible manufacturing theory (Piore and Sabel 1984) that claims that large industry is breaking down into small firms that deal more effectively with a diversifying market. Rather small and large seem to be working together. Secondly, it calls into question Harrison's theory that small firms are fading and suppliers are mostly large firms abroad. Third, it calls into question Oliver Williamson's theory that high transaction costs cause large firms to absorb small. Perhaps some few are so absorbed, but most continue to survive and sell to large firms despite transaction costs. A vast majority supply customers on short notice, and put responsibility for quality on those producing and cross train workers to fill many jobs.

We offer an hypothesis that the reason small manufacturing firms continue to exist is that they do custom and changing jobs for other firms, particularly large firms and that they are particularly organized to do this. Therefore, they are located near their buyers. The larger firms do not want to do these custom and changing jobs for themselves, but keep to standard products.

The chief executive officers are in the vast majority involved in research and development and in marketing. They typically have a background in engineering or science, and may employ at least one engineer. The chief executive officers are also involved in marketing. Nearly all market by direct contact or word of mouth, though they use many other means, notably by trade and technical shows and trade magazines.

They seem often to pay at least a few employees in the lowest wage brackets. They do not pay life insurance and pensions as often as large companies, but pay bonuses much more often, which may be sort of substitute. As nearly as we can tell, they often go out of business. Therefore, with the investments and hard work they put in and the high risk they endure, and the independence they must show, the fact that they are in business at all, seems a miracle.

Three main questions will be dealt with in the following chapters. One is to what extent they are innovative and users of high technology and why. Another is their place in the local industrial community and their escape from it. Finally we will consider firm growth.

Chapter 3

High Technology and Innovation

A question raised by Piore and Sabel (1984) and Harrison (1994) is whether small firms are advanced or backward. Do they have high technology such as computerized production and do they innovate? The answer to these questions can help establish their functioning and their relation to large firms. Since Schumpeter (1939, 1947) first claimed innovation to be of fundamental importance in understanding economic change scientists have been puzzling over it. Innovation has a part to play in firm growth as has the use of high-technology, with which it has often been confused. Innovation also appears to have a role in firm start up. In the first survey, we sought out new small firms thinking we would find innovations there, and we did.

But what is innovation and is it another word for high-technology? How can we measure them and distinguish one from the other? Are they characteristic of whole industries, or more particularly of firms?

Schumpeter defined innovation as "the setting up of a new production function" (1939:87). "Innovation combines factors in a new way or ... it consists in carrying out New Combinations" (1939:88). He distinguished innovation from invention in that an invention must be "put into business practice" to become an innovation. Many inventions do not reach this stage. He also distinguished it from science or technology, which were not necessarily involved. He defined an entrepreneur as a person who effects an innovation; again, he is not necessarily an inventor nor is he necessarily a capitalist or risk taker. Albert Shapero, though interested in innovation, focused on the entire entrepreneurial event and said that though innovation is widely associated with entrepreneurship, he did not include it as part of the definition (1979; Shapero and Sokol 1982).

Definition and identification become very difficult. Schumpeter thought innovation of fundamental importance in economic change. Since not all firms of a different type or size adopt innovations simultaneously, he thought that when some do so, it is disequilibrating to the economy. This calls attention to firms rather than industries as being of prime importance. He saw innovation as revolutionary and evolutionary with the rise of innovating firms and the decline of older noninnovating firms in a process of "Creative Destruction." "Capitalism, by nature, is a form or method of economic change and not only never is but never can be stationary" (1947:82). He refers to "the process of industrial mutation that incessantly revolutionizes the economic structure from within, incessantly destroying the old one, incessantly creating a new one. This process of Creative Destruction is the essential fact about capitalism" (1947:83).

Philips and Kirchhoff (1989) (1989 and 1994) have written about "dynamic capitalism", reasoning from Schumpeter and pointing to weaknesses in equilibrium theory that cannot account for entreprneuership - that rationality is not perfect - that markets are not perfectly competitive and are heavily made up of oligopolies and monopolies and that economies of scale affect markets only where perfect markets exist. All of this leads us to consider dymanic capitalism in discussing entrepreneurship.

Recently attention has been focused on technological change. An Office of Technology Assessment (OTA) document (1984) on the subject states the following: "Thus the dynamic nature of the U.S. economy results from the birth, growth, maturation and decline of various industrial sectors.... This industrial revolution ... is driven by technological innovation, the process by which society uses new products and manufacturing processes. This process consists of activities surrounding the generation, research, development, introduction, and diffusion of new or improved products, processes and services..." (1984:17). The authors go on to say that since the innovative behavior of firms is very difficult to measure, two traditional measures of scientific activity are generally used as proxies to classify industries by innovative capacity or activity: relative research and development spending levels; and relative levels of scientific, engineering and technical personnel in the industry's total work force.

The report then goes on to describe five such attempts to classify industries (that is, industries as defined by the 4-digit Standard Industrial Classification code). Three were versions worked out by the Bureau of Labor Statistics (Riche et al. 1983), one by researchers at Brookings (Armington et al. 1983), and one by researchers at Berkeley (Glasmeier et al. n.d.). Others have also attempted to classify industrial sectors as high or low technology (Felsenstein and Bar-El 1989).

Thomas (1985) and others he cites doubt the validity of industry-based as compared with firm-based definitions of high-technology or innovation. The OTA report itself also offers this as one of the criticisms of these attempts to define innovation. The apparent reason for excluding innovations, and the use of industries rather than firms is a desire to use sets of available data that include only industries and not firms and do not measure innovation directly. Castells (1989) also notes the inadequacy of industry-level measures of innovation and high-technology while citing Glasmeier et al. extensively. The various studies raise the question of the validity of this strategy as well as the question of whether high-technology industry--if indeed they have isolated such industries--is also innovative. Oakey (1984) distinguished between process and product innovation and thought the effects of process innovation to be marginal.

Several theorists have also proposed that technology diffuses. In a comparison of Britain and Austria, Alderman and Fisher (1992) note that, as diffusion proceeds and reaches a saturation level, regional convergence is likely to be observed. In innumerable studies, sociologists and geographers have found that the spread or diffusion of phenomena follows an S curve. At the beginning the phenomenon will spread slowly. At some point it will take off rapidly and the curve will make a steep and rapid climb. As the saturation point is approached, the curve will level off. The proposal is that technology diffusion follows such a path. McArthur (1990) has also made the comparison of widely-diffusing versus new technology. He has also made a distinction between process and product innovation. He thinks the relation of process innovation to small firm growth is marginal and that it is product innovation that spurs growth if it is at the leading edge (1990). Others also have discussed technology transfer (Roberts 1991). If technology does follow a curve of diffusion, then whether it is innovative or is associated with product innovation probably depends on where it is on its curve of diffusion. At a later stage, why should it be innovative?

Studies of the relation of external linkages to technical information also imply a process of diffusion of technology. Among those describing such linkages are Gibbs and Edwards (1985) on diffusion of innovations, Beesley and Rothwell (1987) on the role of subcontractors, MacPherson (1985) on the role of outside consultants' use by innovative firms, and Scott (1990) on the importance of interfirm linkages in the development of "technopoles" or high-technology industrial districts. Also relevant to this claim of diffusion are Birley (1985) on the role of networks in the entrepreneurial process, and Lorenzoni and Ornati (1988) on constellations of firms and new ventures. Freeman (1991) has also summarized the roles of industrial networks and providers of technology and information on the firm. All of these studies raise the question of whether what is called high-technology is an early phase on the diffusion curve rather than an absolute, and whether high or any other kind of technology can really be equated with or used as a stand-in for innovation.

In addition to the question of firm versus industry definition and technology versus innovation, Doeringer et al. (1987) have raised another issue. Post-Fordist industrial analysis tends to classify customization, flexibility and responsiveness to customers' needs together with innovation as characterizing contemporary small firms. Piore and Sabel (1984) and Storper and Walker (1989) see new small firms that are the wave of the future as flexible, innovating and using modern technology. Storper and Walker define flexible manufacturing in terms of (1) constant alteration of goods partly in response to tastes, partly to open new markets; (2) a wide range of goods for highly differentiated markets; (3) flexible use of increasingly productive, widely applicable technology; and (4) creation of regional institutions that balance cooperation and competition among these so as to encourage permanent innovation. An older framework devised by Smith (1967) distinguishing types off entrepreneurs as craftsmen or opportunists also suggests individualized production, but Woo et al. (1991) have criticized empirical attempts to use this typology. In a study of small firms, Doeringer et al. (1987) discriminated three types of firms: mass producers, innovating, and customizers, essentially pulling apart what the post-Fordists identify as aspects of the same phenomenon. Thus we have two possible variables potentially important to firm analysis and growth and to industrial change, and we would like to know their relations to each other, and whether they are the same or closely related: innovation, and high-technology. Customization did not relate to firm growth, probably because it is so widely present in these small firms; 76 percent customize their products. It also was not related to innovations or high-technology.

First let us look at the methods of production of the firms. In the statewide sample, we recall that 74 percent of the owners said they had technical and managerial skills, and most had a background in science and engineering, though they were also actively engaged in marketing through direct contact. They were the hub of the firm. Fifty-three percent of the firms employed at least one engineer. Of these 26 percent had 1 or 2, 27 percent three or more. In addition to the fact that the great majority custom produce, 62 percent say that at least one of their products constitutes the standardization of a custom product.

We remember that forty-three percent use a just-in-time inventory system and 88 percent sell some or all of their products to firms that do so. This means careful management to be able to produce on short notice, but not to have too much goods in storage. They must coordinate closely with firms from which they buy and firms to which they sell as well as their subcontractors. Forty-two percent have at least one product other than the main one.

Table 1.   Cost of One Machine in Statewide Sample

	Percentage
0 to $50,000	50
$51,000 to $150,000	27
$151,000 to $250,000	8
$251,000 to $500,000	5
$501,000 ro $1,000,000	2
Over $1,000,000	3
Total number	674

Table 2.   Type of Machinery Used in the Statewide Sample

<u>Percentage</u>

Only hand tools	2
Standard machinery	65
Especially made or custom made machinery	30
Not answered	<u>3</u>
Total number	674

Tables 1 and 2 show the proportions that spend various amounts on tools and the types of tools they use. Fifty percent use tools worth $50,000 or less, 27 percent more tools from $50,000 to $150,000. Only 19 percent buy more. Sixty-five percent use standard machinery. Only 2 percent use hand tools. Thirty percent use especially made or custom-made machinery. For 71 percent of the firms, their own employees install and repair their machinery, in 21 percent of the firms the seller or manufacturer of the machinery installs and repairs it. Installing and repairing your own machinery has been offered as an indication of high-technology firms, but the great majority of these small firms do so. For eight percent of the firms it was outside electricians or technicians, or some combination of employees and seller or outside technicians that installed.

We have said that 76 percent sell to other manufacturing firms. They sell to a number of other buyers in smaller proportions: institutions, services, the government or defense. While 62 percent produce in short runs with changes, 55 percent in batches without change, only 37 percent mass produce. Thus they are largely specialists, customizing, serving industry, on short notice, and producing accordingly.

The methodological strategy was to use several measures of the two main concepts to see if these were related to each other and not to measures of the other concept. Research often errs because of the measurement of complex, controversial concepts with simple and single indicators that may have a good deal of "noise"--that is, relations to concepts other than the one at issue. It is often difficult to convincingly defend the validity of such single measures. For this reason multiple indicators of each of the two main concepts-- innovation and high-technology use were used. They were subjected to a principal components analysis to see if the several measures of each would load on one factor and only one factor. Then, using factor scores that provided more robust measures than single variables, we show them to be related to a group of firm characteristics, that, again, are unrelated to scores of the other factors measuring the other concept. When this procedure was followed on four separate data sets yielding similar results, support was achieved for these results and the procedure that yielded them. A number of measures of the two concepts, innovation and high-technology use, were included in all studies, permitting a principal-component analysis to be performed on each data set. In all cases varimax rotation was used.

The principal components analysis performed on the last statewide sample yielded two factors, innovation and use of high-technology. The innovation factor has high loadings on several variables: some product is a new original invention; the company has designed a new product; it has modified a product; it has upgraded a product. Thus we are concentrating on product innovation, not process. The high-technology factor has high loadings on the use of a programmable computerized process in production, they produce a programmable product, the cost of the machinery used is high and they employ an engineer or scientist. Both had a moderate relation to the presence of ongoing research (.36). Proportions having these practices are shown in Table 3. The varimax rotation ensured that the factors were not overlapping, but the loadings of the variables supported this; all but ongoing research were high on one factor and low on the other.

**Table 3. Proportions of Firms Using Various Computerized
Processes Statewide Sample**

<u>Percentage</u>

Computer aided design (CAD)	35
Computer numerical control (CNC)	25
Computer aided manufacturing (CAM)	23
Shop floor or personal computers	25
Programmable controllers	22
Production planning and	
inventory control	28
Statistical process control	19
Local/area computer network	13
Material working cases	3
Computer integrated manufacturing	
systems	6
Flexible manufacturing systems (FMS)	8
Data collection boxes (barcode scanners)	
readers	8
Automated material handling systems	10
Automated in-process inspection	6
Pick and place robots	3
Other robots	3
Automated in process inspection	8

In addition to the variables used in the principal components analysis, we also asked about the use of various computerized programs in the firm such as pick and place robots, computer aided design (CAD), computer aided manufacturing (CAM), computer numerical control (CNC), automated in process inspection and materials handling, data collection devices (bar code readers, scanners) material working lasers, statistical process control, computer integrated manufacturing systems and the like. Table 3 shows the proportions of firms with each of these. The number of these each firm used were added up to a score (sumtech). Sumtech was correlated .61 with the high-technology factor score and .16 with the innovation factor. The principal components analysis is shown in Table 4. The table shows the factor loadings, the communalities (or the proportion of the variance explained by the variables in the factor analysis) and the variance explained by each factor.

Table 4. Principal Components Analysis, Statewide Study

	Component 1 Innovation	Component 2 Use of High-Technology	Communality
Product modified	.80	- .04	.64
Upgraded a product	.79	- .06	.62
Company has designed a new product	.75	.14	.59
Product is an original invention	.66	.21	.49
Use a computerized process in production y	.00	.71	.51
Produces a program-mable product	.10	.52	.28
Ongoing research present	.36	.36	.25
Cost of machinery	-.10	.67	.46
Employ an engineer or scientist	.36	.58	.46
Variance explained by each factor	2.79	1.52	

A third factor appeared in the Monroe and Southern Tier studies, doing custom work. But it was different in the two studies because different variables were available and was omitted from the state wide survey since it was inconsistent on all of the surveys. Sixty seven percent of the Southern Tier firms did custom work, 79 percent of the Monroe County firms and 76 percent of the statewide study. This indicates that custom work is present in most of the small manufacturing firms in the state and offers a possible reason why the factor did not emerge clearly in addition to data problems.

The Factors

First of all one would like to know the frequency of innovation and the use of high-technology. Is technology such a rarity that it indicates innovation? Is innovation a rarity? Or are they both common place enough to indicate that they are part of a diffusion or development process that has gone a long way already. In Monroe county 39 percent of the companies designed a new product, in the Southern Tier sample 31 percent, in the Rome sample 49 percent and in the statewide sample, also 49 percent.

In Monroe County 55 percent used a computerized production process, in the Southern Tier 58 percent, in the Rome sample 45 percent and in the statewide sample 42 percent. The common existence of these characteristics over the whole study suggest that they are widely present and available and not on the leading edge. New York appears to be into a diffusion curve, at least among small firms. The fact that custom work was so widely present also suggests something about the nature of small companies. By various criteria the two factors, innovation and the use of high-technology appear to be largely unrelated. But what kinds of firms are high on each of the two factor scores computed? What do they tell us about what is going on?

The innovation factor is related to a number of other firm characteristics that indicate the nature of these flexible firms. They produce more than one product; they have a trade secret; they have standardized a custom product, and to a slight extent they are custom producing. Products of innovative firms tend to grow out of a product the founder's last employer produced, but they tend not to compete with a former employer. The chief executive officer is involved in research and development. The employees of firms high on innovation work in teams that complete a subassembly, the employees producing it have responsibility for the quality of the product and they are cross-trained to fill several jobs. High-technology scores are related to only a few of the variations in production, if so to a greatly reduced extent . Both factors are related to education of the founder.

Table 5. Correlates of Innovations and High-Technology Factor Scores, Statewide Study

Correlates

	Innovation	High-Technology
They produce at least two products	.33**	.02
Product is related to that of former company	.14**	.07
They have a trade secret	.43**	.17**
They have standardized a custom product	.33**	.02
They buy parts	.16**	.10*
Machinery is specialized	.16**	.07
They custom produce	.11*	.03
Education of founder/owner high	.23**	.22**
Owner's previous job was in a large corporation	.09*	.09*
CEO does research and development	.39**	.02
A team completes whole sub-assembly	.20**	.07
People producing parts one responsible for their quality	.21**	.12*
Cross-train workers so they know several jobs	.09*	.04
They produce in batches	.19***	.01
They have applied for a government loan	.12**	.25**
They got the loan	.09*	.20**

*Significant at .05 level

Producing custom goods is related to little else: producing in batches or short runs, having at least some customers that use just-in-time inventory control and selling to industry. This may be because custom production is so widespread, as we have indicated. Most firms have custom production. One might speculate that custom production is a main attraction of the small firm for the large one; the custom production firm produces special goods the large one needs but does not care to produce. The large firm can best produce standard goods for the mass market and leave specialization to the small firm.

Relations of the factors to methods of marketing and to customers reinforce their separate character. Table 6 shows the proportions of firms that operate in different locations.

Table 6. Locations of Contact Firms in the Statewide Sample

	In this County	Elsewhere in New York State	Elsewhere in the US	Abroad Number
		Percentage		
Largest customer	36	28	35	8
Second largest customer	31	25	35	5
Subcontractors	44	34	26	5
Buy parts	51	50	57	26
Have competitors	62	67	72	45

* Numbers do not add to 100% because many firms operate in several locations.

Innovation in firms is negatively related to the proportions of sales to its most important customer and to its second most important, to whether this customer is in the county or in New York State, and is positively related to its location outside of New York in other states (Table 7).

**Table 7. Correlations of factors with export
in the Statewide Sample**

	Innovation Factor	High-Technology Factor
	Correlations	
Export from the county	09*	10*
Export from NY to other States	28**	17**
Export from the US	34**	16**

*Significant at 05 level
**Significant at 01 level

Innovation in firms is positively related to a number of types of marketing: to use of factory representatives, to distributors, to advertising at trade shows and in trade magazines. It is related to selling to customers, positively, but negatively to selling to industry.

Use of high-technology in firms is related to a different array of sales and marketing techniques. It is related to use of factory representatives, and to a lesser extent advertising in trade journals, and is not related to other measures of marketing. It is not related to the proportion of sales sold to the first or second customer.

High-technology is negatively related to selling to industry (r=.-19) and positively to selling to customers directly, (r=.28), whereas innovative firms are only marginally related to selling to customers (r-.08) and not related to selling to industry.

The two types of firms seem to fill different niches. The innovative firm markets its new and flexible products, and sells widely to customers and is not so dependent on a single large firm. The high-technology industry is tied to industry, and does not make such a marketing effort. Thus, they seem to be producing and selling differently to different niches. High scores on both, however, are related to export from New York and from the United States (Table 7).

Relations to Industry-Level Measures

Table 8 shows the correlations of the five industry-level measures of high-technology reported by the Office of Technology Assessment. These were industry-level measures based on the Standard Industrial Classification (SIC) code using variations in SICs in proportions of research and development expenditures and of scientists, technologists and engineers in each SIC to indicate a high-technology industry.

Three of these measures (BLS1, 2, 3) were devised by the Bureau of Labor Statistics (Riche et al. 1983), one by economists at Brookings (Armington et al. 1983), and one at the University of California's Institute for Urban and Regional Studies (Glasmeier et al. n.d.). Tables 8 and 9 shows their relation to each other and to the three factor scores derived from the Southern Tier study.

Many of the industry-level measures are highly related to each other, as one might expect, most very highly. In the Southern Tier study, only one of the industry-level measures is related to any of the factor scores. The correlation of BLS3 to the innovation score is r= .22, significant at the .05 level. This is one out of 15, or less than 7 percent of the possible correlations, little more than expected by chance.

In Monroe County results were similar (see Tables 8 and 9) with respect to the industry-level measure correlations. In this data set the only significant relation between any industry-level measure and any factor score was the correlation of r = .25 between the Berkeley measure and the high-technology factor score, significant at the .05 level.

These results mean that there is virtually no relation between classification of firms based on the proportions of research spending or scientists, engineers, and technologists used by the SIC categories to which they belong and firm-level characteristics. That is, within any SIC category, there is much variation on all of these characteristics on the part of firms, and one cannot predict firm outcomes by any classification of SICs. This provides a reason why studies of high-technology industry have often yielded poor results. Schumpeter's distinction between firms and industries is stil! valid and important whether or not such characteristics of firms do or do not serve as the spring board of economic change or economic evolution.

Table 8. Relations among the Five Industry-Level Measures of High-technology and the Firm-Level Factor Scores, Southern Tier-Northern Tier

		Pearson's r						
	1	2	3	4	5	6	7	8
1 BLS1	--	.24++	.53++	.50++	.76++	-.00	.08	-.02
2 BLS2			.46++	.49++	.32++	.10	.12	-.04
3 BLS3				.69++	.70++	.08	.22+	-.04
4 Brookings					.69++	.16	.14	.05
5 Berkeley						.06	.17	-.03
6 High tech factor score							-.00	-.00
7 Innovation factor score								.00
8 Flexibility factor								--

+ Significant at .05 level
++ Significant at .01 level

Table 9. Relations among the Five Industry-Level Measures of High-technology and the Firm-Level Factor Scores, Monroe County

		Pearson's r						
	1	2	3	4	5	6	7	8
1 BLS1		.33++	.52++	.51++	.90++	-.19	-.03	.05
2 BLS2			.63++	.65++	.37++	.07	.05	-.04
3 BLS3				.87++	.49++	.07	.16+	.10
4 Brookings					.56++	.10	.12	.10
5 Berkeley						.25+	-.03	.09
6 High tech factor score							-.00	.00
7 Innovation factor score								.00
8 Flexibility factor								--

+ Significant at .05 level
++ Significant at .01 level

Rural and Urban Firms

One other question remains. Do urban firms produce more innovations and/or use high-technology to a greater extent than rural firms? This was the belief about urban specialization. The urban firm used more research and development and developed new products until they were perfected and did not need special laboratories, services, and qualities of workers. Originally urban, they were simplified and standardized, then went to rural areas with cheap labor for production. This was laid out by Norton and Rees (1979) according to hypotheses generated by product cycle theory and the spatial decentralization of manufacturing.

But there have been changes in recent years. Dillman (1991) notes that in rural areas "the passing of remoteness as one of the great unheralded macro trends of our extraordinary time." Remoteness has been reduced by highway and air transportation and by "telematics" or "the joining of telecommunications, broadcast media and computer technology for developing, sending, receiving sorting and utilizing information." A firm no longer has to be near a bank to use its services. This need to be near urban areas with railroads and ports was characteristic of the heavy industry of an earlier era - steel and coal. It is no longer characteristic of the modern firm.

The move out of the city has also been stimulated by the expense of city sites and increased labor costs. For example, a reason given by a bank that moved to rural New York was to reduce training costs increased by the high turnover of employees no longer expected in a rural area where employees would be more stable due to lack of competitive opportunity.

Changes have also taken place in the technical structure of manufacturing. Computerized processing is used by more than half of the firms in our sample. Moreover, manufacturing is no longer mainly the processing of raw materials. Scott (1988) says "increasing disintegration of production processes is *ipso facto* associated with a widening network of inter-industrial linkages. . ." He goes on to point out that "where linkages are small in scale, unstandardized, unstable, and in need of personal intermediation," they will be associated with high distance-dependent costs and small plants will tend to be located near their main linkage partners. Large plants, standardized, stable, and easily manageable will be more free to detach themselves from linkage partners and locate at greater distances from them. Thus the changes in manufacturing from primary goods conversion to a series of linkages, and of computerized processing have changed the nature not only of a particular firm, but of its relationships with other high-technical suppliers, the cessation of need to locate near primary inputs, and the high-tech nature of linkages. See also Storper and Walker (1989: Ch. 5).

Oakey (1984) has pointed out another characteristic of high-technology firms that are so important in today's economy. Their products have a short 5 to 10 year-life span. They do not standardize their products, they continue to depend on skilled workers, their "raw materials" are commonly complex and specialized components. Therefore it is probable that they agglomerate and that small business expands under these conditions. Pratten (1991) stated that 90 percent of the firms he studied sold to industry and mentioned their unique products and the niches they filled. But they do not need to locate close to railroads and ports.

Thus times have changed since the product cycle hypothesis was first proposed. Changes in transportation and communication and information handling are dramatic. Changes in industrial processing, use of complex linkage materials and niche building of small industries make their location choices different than those of large plants producing standard goods.

Change in industrial management also bear on industrial location. Scott (1988) also points that just-in-time inventory systems involve suppliers who deliver goods as needed. Hence they need to be close (Scott 1988). Other management changes are the slimming of large factory systems, and the casting off of branches different than the main factory. This slimming of the company together with the buying out of innovative and customized goods (Doeringer et al. 1987) mean the use of small firms as suppliers. But any location is now suitable for this set of firms.

Norton and Rees (1979) tested the product cycle hypothesis on a statewide basis and found things changing. They found that rapid growth and innovative industries had shifted from the core (in the North and East) to the periphery, the American South and West. They referred to this as "heralding a strikingly new relationship among its regions."

Phillips and Kirchoff (1989) and Phillips, Kirchoff and Brown (1989) found that high-technology firms from 1976 to 1986 have been the growth area of American industry, and that small, high-technology firms grow as much in rural as in urban areas. They attributed this to the "vertically disintegrating" large firms and the increased use of processing and information technologies that increase the ability of small and medium firms to compete with large.

In our statewide sample there were only two counties that were in a primary metropolitan statistical area (PMSA). All others were either rural or in a metropolitan statistical area (MSA). The PMSA differs from the MSA by containing a large urbanized county or cluster of counties that demonstrate very strong economic and social links and must have close ties to other portions of the larger area. The MSA must contain a total population of 100,000 or more, at least one city with a population of 50,000 or more or a Census Bureau defined urbanized area of at least 50,000 inhabitants. Thus the distinction is mainly one of size or population density. Comparing the MSA counties with the rural, no differences were found in distribution of either innovative or high-technology firms. Both were found in both types of counties without any distinction. New York State may be different than other states with its highway systems penetrating and tying together all areas. Every county level economic developer shows a map with his county at the center and showing large urban areas within reasonable driving time. But this accessibility may be true in many parts of the country. It is also helped by the nature of contemporary manufacturing as compared with the days of coal and steel. But hypotheses about firms starting in cities with specialized services and going to rural areas for cheap labor are no longer true in New York.

Summary

Schumpeter's theory of industrial innovation was based on firms, not on industries. Some firms innovated and thus upset the equilibrium. First is the problem of measurement of innovation, and distinguishing it from use of high-technology, mostly computerized technology. This we did, by factor analysis of our data where we came up with two factors, innovation and use of computerized technology. Correlates of both factors supported our analysis.

Innovation was related to a number of facets of production, indicating variation or flexibility, and more importantly to a number of different work patterns and options. Use of high-technology was related to the sum of computerized processes used and included the cost of machinery, whereas innovation was related to the complexity of machinery but not to its cost. Both factors were related to the education of the founder or chief of staff. But what of Schumpeter's first concern? Neither innovation nor use of high-technology was related to a number of measures that supposedly measured them on an industry wide basis. Both are firm level characteristics, bearing out Schumpeter's hypothesis about industrial innovation and the nature of economic change. They also change the nature of the main question, whether small firms are backward or on the leading edge to one of how small and large firms are related.

Chapter 4

Networks

There are a number of theories of large-small firm relations and thus of regional economic structure. One of these is flexible accumulation, first advanced by Piose and Sabel (1984). Flexible accumulation has been argued in a long series of papers and books, four of them consisting of critical rejections, and others raising many problems. Among these are: "Flexibility revisited: districts, nation states and the forces of production", Gertler, 1992; "The end of mass production", Williams et al., 1987; "The New Social Economy: Reworking the Division of Labour", Sayer and Walker, 1992; and "The reemergence of regional economics? The mythical geography of flexible accumulation", Amin and Robins, 1990. In addition, there is a long list of papers arguing the case (Aoki, 1984, 1986, 1991; Gertler, 1984, 1989, 1992; Aoki et al., 1986; Schoenbeger, 1988, 1989; Christopherson and Storper, 1989; Sayer, 1989, n.d.; Florida and Kenney, 1990a, 1990b, 1991a, 1991b; Saxenian, 1990).

A key ingredient in this theory is that various economic forces have come together to cause a new industrial divide that calls for small firms acting in a collegial manner. "Microelectronics and information technology play a key role in allowing more flexible production and closer co-ordination between markets and producers targeting new market niches." Firms are supposedly becoming more responsive to changing tastes and to the tendency for consumer products to support the construction of personal identities" (Sayer and Walker, 1992). For many reasons called the new industrial divide, demand is being made for more diversified market products, and the claim is that small flexible firms are supplying them, and supporting each other.

Those who reject the theory argue that it is really a mythology (Amin and Robins, 1990); or "romantic" (Sayer and Walker, 1992); that we have never had major production in more than a minority of firms, that small firms have always existed and that flexibility does not always work. Yet the theory has tenaciously hung on, have the great changes that authors call the second industrial divide (Piore and Sabel, 1984; Storper and Walker, 1989) really led to a restructuring of industry according to demand into a series of small flexible firms linked together in some collegial way? This is the main thrust of the theory. Computerized processing, flexible work methods, along with just-in-time inventory control constitute changes, but limited ones with limited explanations unless they are found in small firms linked in a co-operative way.

Storper and Walker, 1989, have reformulated the theory as we have cited it above. They further state:

> Flexible production methods appear to be on the way to becoming dominant in the economics of the United States and Western Europe . . . Flexible production is marked by a decisive geographical concentration of production and by the resurgence of the industrial district. All flexible production industries are marked by organizational fragmentation in which dense, unstandardized, transactional relations between firms are particularly important. Firms concentrate geographically in order to reduce the costs and difficulties of carrying out these transactions and to maximize their access to the cultural and informational context of the production district itself.

They say that, consequently, this theory leads us to expect to find new high-technology industrial districts, such as Silicon Valley, scattered across North America, and revitalized craft districts in Northern Italy. We do not expect to find flexible manufacturing coupled with the hierarchical bonding of large corporations and their suppliers.

Scott, 1988, differs in some ways from other post-Fordists but describes a dense web of interlinkages among small specialized establishments as vertical disintegration of large establishments takes place:

> In this manner the outlines of an interconnected complex of industries takes shape and if vertical disintegration is also accompanied by horizontal disintegration (i.e., increasing number of establishments per quantity of total output) then the labyrinth of interlinkages is likely to become particularly convoluted . . . Each unit of production performs a series of specialized tasks within the complex and each in turn continually adjusts its internal operations as the whole complex evolves through time. No single unit can unilaterally create the conditions of its own existence, since each is dependent for its own existence, since each is dependent for its survival upon the successful reproduction of

the entire social division of labor and concomitant external economies. Hence, we can only comprehend these sorts of disintegrated production complexes in their totality. They are not just simple aggregations of individual units of productive decision making and behavior but also, and more significantly, they are integral totalities whose configuration is governed by structural laws of motion as a whole (pp. 41-2).

In his article on "The technologies of Southern California" (Scott, 1990) he says, "they [technopoles] can be seen as a phenomenon that has been activated primarily by the dynamics of interestablishment linkages and by local labor markets." He defines technopoles as "high-technology industrial districts". He goes on to say, "These dynamics are, in turn, rooted in flexible structures of production, stimulating institutional fragmentation of significant parts of the system . . ." (ibid., p. 1,602).

Another question about the role of small firms is raised by studies of suppliers to the Japanese automobile industry and Japanese automobile manufacturers in the United States. In both cases, working relationships are very close, and in Japan the supplier and customer sometimes have invested in each other. They may design products together, the large corporation's engineers may help and advise the small company, and a great part of the supplier's output may go to a single customer (Aoki, 1984, 1986, 1991; Kenney and Florida, 1989, 1992; Smitka, 1989; Florida and Kenney, 1990a, 1990b, 1991a, 1991b). Smitka, however, describes the automobile industry as perhaps the extreme case of close relationships and describes much variation in supplier relationship in other Japanese industries. But in all cases we are talking of large firms with small firms as suppliers. The question is raised, however, as to why flexible manufacturing has not taken place in Japan in the form of a congress of small firms. The phenomenon is supposed to be worldwide. Why not Japan? Why are large firms so important to Japanese industrial structure? A number of theorists have vainly asked this question.

Middle America--the rust belt, from the Eastern Seacoast to Chicago--is supposed to consist of mass production industry without any touch of flexibility. There are supposed to be, overall, basically two kinds of industry: mass production or Fordist; and small, flexible production. These two types are supposed to stand for the two types of manufacturing, even though a number of critics have described them as being far from the truth, in Japan, in Britain, in Canada and in other places. If the rust belt is supposed to be the scene of mass production of the Fordist type, finding a change there comprises a critical test. Of course, Harrison (1994) does not feel that small firms are of any significance and thinks that large firms supply each other across international boundaries, thus he does not account for regional structure.

What other theories of regional location are there? An outstanding one is Romo et al.'s, (1984), hypothesis that a region consists of a few, large, oligopolistic firms and their periphery of small firms. This is like the older mass production model, but for its intertwining of political and economic forces. It does not say anything about flexible firms.

Without arguing their industrial divide theory which is complex and `romantic" (Sayer and Walker, 1992), let us concentrate on the supposed outcome. If microelectronics and information technology have been targeting new market niches, it is not in upstate New York where most small manufacturing firms are suppliers to large firms. Here, large firms seem to be using microelectronics and information technology, along with other relatively new business practices, such as just-in-time inventory control, to slim their businesses and budgets in response to recession pressures and competition. For example, one large firm now contracts with an outside organization (founded by its former employees) for public relations. Rather, these small firms help make the large firms more efficient and more responsive to market ups and downs. Thus, the studies presented here comprise a critical test in that flexible firms exist and supply larger firms rather than comprising a set of collegial firms opening new market niches.

Storper and Walker's, 1989, paradigm consists of four propositions; one is that the firms use more programmable computerized equipment. This is true to a majority of firms both large and small in our sample. A second proposition is that they use smaller, more specialized work places. All but 10% or 15% of the firms are small. A third is that the firms place greater attention to demand variations. We will show that most firms are suppliers to other firms. Since only a minority are engaged in retail trade, demand variations do not impinge on them to any great extent. We therefore approach the last proposition--that the firms use a collective and institutional order in place of hierarchical control exercised by the mass production firms.

There are three possible arrangements of firms. Florida and Kenney, 1991b, p. 143, have pointed out that the arrangements among large and small firms are critical, `the organizations of R and D, the organization of manufacturing, and the integration of the two". The three arrangements are shown in Figure 1. In the first, there is nothing but small firms interacting with the market. In the second, we have large firms interacting exclusively with the small. In the third (the present case), we have large and small interacting with each other, and the small with many other customers as well. The first case is that of Italy and Silicon Valley, though both are debated. The second is Japan, particularly the automotive industry, and the third, New York State.

However, there are many other factors that could explain differences among these sets of firms. One is cultural or national. Japanese industry is not plagued by anti-trust laws. It has been anti-union for a long time. Long-time employment and worker loyalty to the firm are the outstanding characteristics.

The second factor is whether the firms have retail sales, as is the case in Italy and Silicon Valley but less so in the United States" rust belt. A third is how new is the industry. Silicon Valley computer companies are relatively new. Often new industries begin as a competing set of small firms, but in ten or twenty years have settled into an oligopoly as currently seems to be the case with some parts of the industry. A fourth factor is the nature of the parts being bought by the large firm. Supply relationships between automotive firms and their suppliers tend to be more exclusive than between other firms in Japan and in the United States. Parts for cars are large and specialized and not useful in other kinds of manufacture. Smitka, 1989, tells us that other types of firm in Japan have less exclusive supply relationships than the automotive industry.

These and other factors should be considered in attempts to explain differences among these foremost cases, but they have not been. Aside from such contextual variables impinging on industrial firms, we look at several regions of New York State to see the nature of the formations. Here we have large and small firms linked together in complex supply relationships, as in the third part of Figure 1 Chapter 1. We will show that small firms often have owners who have local work experience, they often produce parts similar to their former employer, they seldom compete with him and almost a third of the firms sell products to a former employer. While they are linked to the local large firms, a great majority have large and small customers around the state and out of state, and are autonomous, unlike the Japanese suppliers to the automotive industry. Thus, these regions of the rust belt in New York have flexible small firms acting as suppliers to large firms and supplying a number of customers in addition to local core firms. This differs from the other three cases often cited, but could be different for a variety of cultural and industrial reasons.

Our sample and the book concentrate on very small companies. We will quote from the statewide sample but the other regional studies in Monroe county, the Southern tier and the Rome area give similar results. Sixty-five percent have 20 or fewer workers. These firms are embedded in a network of selling to, buying from, subcontracting with, and having competitors in a network of large and small companies within their own county.

They also have relations with a variety of local, state, and national agencies that provide loans. From 37 percent in Monroe County to 45 percent in Rome and the two state sample apply for loans and from 24 percent in Monroe, to 35 percent in Rome and 38 percent in the two state sample get them. Thus at least in this respect they are tied into government as Roma et al (1988) predict.

As we have said, seventy-six percent sell to other manufacturing firms. Fifty-nine percent of their most important customers are large firms. Seventy-two percent buy parts from other firms. Eighty-six percent say that they market by direct contact. At least seventy-two percent have competitors in the county, in the state, or elsewhere in the country. Fifty-eight percent subcontract to other firms. thus, they are part of an interrelated industrial structure in which large firms play an important part and they have much contact with each other. In addition to these facts, seventy-six percent say that they custom produce, that is they produce special products to order. This makes them very attractive to large firms.

Table 1. Percentages of Firms That Applied For and Got Loans

	Rome Area	Two State Area	Monroe County
		Percentage	
Applies for loan	45	45	37
Got loan	35	38	24
Total Number	111	123	117

Firms not only sell to large firms. Their founders often come out of jobs in large firms. Twenty percent of the founders had a previous last job in a large corporation. In one quarter of the firms, their product is in the same industry as the founder's last firm of employment. In forty-five percent of the cases, their product is related to the founder's last firm of employment: it is the same, similar, modified or a part is used. A quarter of the sample firms sell to a former employer, but only thirteen percent compete with one.

Though seventy-six percent sell to industry, firms also sell to a diversity of other customers. Fifty-two percent sell wholesale, but only 42 percent sell retail or to retailers, thirty-two percent to institutions such as hospitals or libraries, thirty percent to service industries, thirty-nine percent to the government and twenty-six percent to defense. Thus though they depend on industry, they also broaden their sales base. This is unlike Japanese small firms that work hand in glove with large firms and sometimes each owns part of the other. Their relations are very intimate and if the relationship collapses so, very probably, does the small firm, whereas United States firms have a variety of options. Thus we see that small firms are embedded in a network of buying, selling, subcontracting and competing with other local firms with which they have many contacts.

There are two major questions. One is the type of relationship they have with their most important customer. The other is the web of local relationships among firms and the extent to which small firms are or are not dependent on these. Although many have a major customer in their own county, seventy-two percent export to other states and forty-five percent export from the United States. We have also seen that substantial proportions sell directly to retail, to institutions, and to the government. Thus the basis of structure may be in the county, but not the ultimate fate of the firm.

Storper and Walker claim that small contemporary industry is flexible and uses a collective social and institutional order in place of hierarchical control exercised by the mass producers. It uses more programmable, computerized equipment, smaller more specialized work places and puts great dependence on demand variations. We have seen that the latter claims about small firms are true. Fifty percent or more are computerized, they innovate, change specifications for products often and do custom work. But do they use a collective social order in place of a hierarchical?

Let us look at their relationships to the largest customers to ascertain their intimacy. Sixty-four percent say that their relationship undergoes wide fluctuations. Only twenty-three percent have a contract, though sixty-four percent feel they are a designated, certified or preferred supplier. Thus they have close but not guaranteed relations.

As for quality control, 73 percent say they both inspect, twenty-five, we inspect and only two percent say they inspect. Thus responsibility is on the seller motivated by the customer. Sixty-three percent say that some or all of what they sell to this customer consists of special products rather than standard. Thirty-seven say all of them are special. Seventy-one say that specifications on the product change from time to time and seventy-one percent also say that they at least sometimes perform custom work. Fifty-six percent say that the customer is on just-in-time inventory control and eighty-three percent say that they are expected to produce on short notice. Forty percent say that rather than simply placing orders, they have complex negotiations about product alteration, quality control or the like.

Thus their relations are complex, constant, and intimate and are not by any means guaranteed. They tend to have regular long term relations though not to have contracts. Many demands for variations and custom-made goods are put on them, and they have to be responsible for quality as well as prompt service. They have complex negotiations and as one of them said, "If we produce a good quality product at a good price, we are all right. If not, other companies are waiting in the wings." The small companies seem to perform specialized tasks for the large companies that probably do not want to perform them themselves.

Williamson's (1985) hypothesis is that companies merge to save transaction costs. We do not have data on costs but we do know that 40 percent of firms have complex negotiations with their most important customer. Seventy-one percent do custom work for the customer, and 83 percent are expected to produce on short notice. Fifty-four percent of the customers use just-in-time inventory control in Monroe County. The question was not asked in the statewide sample. Results are similar in the Southern Tier region and in the Monroe sample. It does not seem likely that these firms remain independent because of lower transaction costs.

Eighty-six percent of the firms sell by word of mouth. But many other informal relations also exist. One example of this came up at a meeting I was attending to appeal for funds. A proposal was made by a junior college and a computer company for funds for a building they would use to show the suppliers of one of the city's major corporations how to use computers. When asked, they said they would show other firms too, but that they would start with firm A's suppliers. The array of business located in different areas--electronics, photonics, etc.-- suggest that, as in Silicon Valley, employment of high-technology personnel with different skills is one reason for such location. But regardless of such possible relationships, there is a strong network of buying, selling and subcontracting relations among large and small manufacturing firms. This raises questions about small firm location. Industrial extension workers tell us that large corporations like to have suppliers within a few hours of them, and indeed one such company told us that it required suppliers to locate in the same town.

Table 2. Relationships with the most important customer

	Rome County	Monroe County	ST-NT Region	Statewide Sample
			Percentage	
They have a regular, ongoing relation	94	98	91	--
Sales are very consistent (rather than fluctuating)	63	67	62	36
They are a designated supplier	87	74	78	64
They have a contract	67	32	29	23
There are other suppliers	65	53	58	
They sell a special product (rather than a standard product) to the customer	58	68	69	63
Specifications change from time to time	66	74	65	71
They do custom work for this customer	58	76	66	71
They are expected to produce on short notice for this customer	89	62	84	83
Orders require complex negotiations (rather than a simple sale)	55	60	48	40
They deal with one person on a regular basis	85	62	80	--
They have social contacts with the customer	37	24	20	--
They satisfy quality control requirements by inspecting themselves	40	31	17	25
They satisfy quality requirements by both seller and buyer inspecting	19	53	73	73
Total sample size	103	117	123	674

To what extent are the contacts local? To what extent do they form local networks that are the skeletons of regional structure? We have already seen that large and small firms are connected in buying and selling relations. To what extent do they form a basis for regional industrial structure?

Storper and Walker, 1989, speak of regional change, and Piore and Sabel, 1984, see the region of the future as composed of a network of small firms with some kind of overarching structure. Romo et al., 1984, take a different position--that a regional economy consists of a small number of large, core, oligopolistic firms and a periphery of their suppliers and service firms. They see this industrial structure very much intertwined with the political structure. Scott, 1988, also sees relationships with large firms as of central importance, but diminishing.

What role do core firms play? We have three sources of information on core companies which can be used to address these issues. Respondents were asked to name former employers and also their two most important customers. They were also shown a list of the twenty-six local establishments with 1,000 or more employees in Monroe County and the twenty-four with 500 or more in the Southern Tier region, and a number in each of the other counties, and asked whether they buy from or sell to each, or all of varying numbers of large firms in the counties in the statewide sample.

Of the sample firms in Monroe County, 80% sell to one of the twenty-six largest establishments. In the Southern Tier (ST) region, 68% sell to one of the twenty-four largest. In Monroe County, 76% sell to one or more of the four firms to which the largest number of sample firms sell and in the ST region, 58% sell to one or more of the top six. The top four firms in Monroe County are Eastman Kodak, Xerox Corporation, Rochester Products Division of General Motors and Bausch & Lomb. In the ST region, the six are the IBM Corporation, Dover/Universal Instruments, Dresser Rand, General Electric, GTE Products and Corning Glass. Their concentration ratios are listed in Table 3, and range from 51% to 92%.

Table 3. Concentration ratios of principal products of core firms

SIC		Percentage produced by 20 largest firms
3229	Pressed and blown glass	92
3545	Machine tool accessories	37
3571	Pumps and pumping equipment	51
3573	Electronic computing equipment	71
3592	Carburetor, piston rings and valves	89
3624	Carbon and graphite products	90
3728	Aircraft parts and equipment n.e.c.	74
3811	Engineering and scientific instruments	59
3851	and systems	74
3861	Ophthalmic goods	91
	Photographic equipment and supplies	

Former employers for 23% of the Monroe County sample firms' chief executive officers were among the top twenty-six firms, and 16% in one of the four core establishments. Of the firm's two most important customers, 28% were in the top twenty-six, and 21% in the top four core companies. The same facts are true for the ST region, where proportions selling to the six largest were somewhat smaller, as one might expect with smaller firms and a larger region.

In the statewide study forty-eight percent of firms in Onondaga County sold to the top 5 firms and in the Erie-Niagara area 41 percent sell to the top 5. This is especially remarkable since Monroe, Onondaga and Erie-Niagara are heavily industrialized. The core firms there seem to underpin the industrial structure of the region even though, as we have pointed out, the small firms have developed opportunities to sell their products to a variety of customers in a variety of locations.

In Onondaga and the Erie-Niagara regions we do not have information on concentration ratios but the companies are not only large but many are well known and multi-branched: General Electric, Cooper Industries, B.G. Sulze Inc., Crucible Materials and Welch

Allyn Inc., Fisher Price Inc., General Motors, Stripit Inc., and E.I. du Pont de Nemours.

With our sample sizes we have no way of assessing the importance of indirect ties. Granovetter, 1973, has pointed out that such `weak" ties can be important. If firm A sells to firm B that sells to core firm C, of how much importance is core firm C to firm A? We do not know, as we would have to in order to assess the importance of core firms.

However, the sample of small firms is not exclusively dependent on large local firms. Aside from this lack in our information, we have shown that the majority of most important customers named in either region are not among the core group or top twenty-six, or twenty-four in Monroe County. Indeed, in Monroe County 44% of the most important customers are outside the county, and 28% outside the state. Of the second most important customers, 38% are outside the county and 27% outside the state. In the Soutern Tier region relationships are spread out farther; 74% of the most important customers were outside the county and 42% outside the state. Of the second most important, 83% are outside the county and 45% outside the state. We have also noted the use of out-of-state suppliers. Thus, while the core companies are of considerable importance--perhaps more so than we are able to show for lack of information on indirect ties, our sample firms sell elsewhere and buy elsewhere. Even though a large majority of the firms sell to one of the core establishments, these establishments are the principal customers for only a minority of firms. Thus, core firms are of pervasive but not exclusive importance, as is often the case in the Japanese automotive industry. They may comprise the organizing reason for the existence of most small firms and exert important present influence, but small firms by no means rely on them exclusively.

The question arises as to how spread out are the network ties among companies in the eight counties of the Southern Tier region. First, the region is a region insofar as supplier ties between sample firms and large firms of the region across county and state lines show this. These ties go throughout the region and across state lines. Secondly, two counties, Broome and Steuben, tend to have small firms from around the region supplying their large companies. These two counties have the largest number of large firms in the Southern Tier, eight in Broome and five in Steuben. Broome has a population of 212,200, Steuben

99,100 and Chemung has 95,200. Thus, the deciding factor for a county's attraction seems to be its share of large companies or its industrial strength, not merely its size. Table 4 show the proportions of all supply relationships to each county in the Southern Tier. Broome and Stueben together account for 78%.

Table 4. Proportions of all supply relationships of sample firms to largest firm in each county in the Southern Tier

County	No.	Percentage
Broome	135	54
Chemung	31	9
Tioga, NY	20	6
Schuyler	0	0
Steuben	82	24
Bradford	53	15
Susquehanna	17	5
Tioga, PA	7	2
Total	345	100

Third, supply relationships tend to be greater (in addition to relationships with firms within the county) to firms in adjacent counties than those at a greater distance, with the exception of the two industrial centres. Table 5 shows the proportion of all supply relationships within the same county, to adjacent counties and to counties one county beyond the adjacent, and to those at a further distance: 34 percent are to large firms within the county; 38 percent to counties adjacent; 16 percent to counties one county away from adjacent; and only 12 percent farther away. Thus, two factors seem to influence supply relationships: the pull of firms in the two major industrial centers, and distance.

**Table 5. Locations of ST supply relationships to largest firms:
proportions to firms in same county, adjacent counties,
in counties one county away and further**

County	No.	Percent
Same county	129	34
Adjacent county	145	38
One county away	62	16
More than one county away	45	12
Total	381	100

Discussion

In these two regions of New York State and Pennsylvania, both large
and small firms exist. The majority of small firms are suppliers to
large, and in each area few core oligopolistic firms play a large role in
buying from small. The Romo et al., (1984), model seems to fit best.
In addition to the supply role, small firm owners gained work
experience in local firms and subcontract and buy supplies locally.

The flexible structure hypothesis is rejected. A majority of small
firms use computerized processing. A majority appear to be flexible;
they change products and they do custom work. And they do these
things while meeting the demands of just-in-time inventory control on
the part of customers. Therefore, as the post-Fordists describe the
progressive, flexible, responsive small firm, they fit their
characterization to this extent, though not in the sense of independent
producers unrelated to large firms.

While we can make a case for the regional significance of core
oligopolistic firms and their small firm suppliers as an organizing
element of the regional industrial economy, this very real network does
not keep small firms totally dependent or captive within the region. It
is impossible to figure out how important the demise of the large firms
would be to the success of survival of the small firms, but the latter do
have other outlets for their products inside and outside the region.
They are not as dependent or interdependent as Japanese automotive

suppliers in any way. Nor are they independent firms divorced from large firm contact as is proposed in Italy or Silicon Valley.

We return to the original question: why do small manufacturing firms exist? A principal reason is that they supply custom goods to other manufacturers, especially large ones, under conditions of changing specifications and on short notice in order to meet demand of just-in-time inventory control. They fill special needs of larger firms that those firms do not want to meet themselves. We are told by large firms that they are tending more and more to buy goods and services out, trading more with fewer suppliers with whom they have close working co-operation. Thus, the flexibility of small firms services the relationship, and the small firms fill a special niche in the industrial economy. This is why a regional economy consists of core firms and suppliers.

Thus, the theory of flexible manufacturing, consisting of a series of small firms interacting only with each other is rejected for these regions. There are a majority of flexible firms in these regions--firms that use computerized technology, perform custom work, innovate and change and adjust projects. They are part of an interdependent network of firms that supply job experience, subcontract with each other and buy and sell to each other. But they mainly serve the large firms of this and other areas. While they ship out, most have a relationship with the core oligopolies of the regions. Therefore, for the rust belt, the flexible manufacturing model does not hold in the sense of transforming a region into a multiplicity of small firms, without large ones. This is critical test because it means that flexible firms can be an important part of a regional economy presided over by large firms. Romo el al's theory of oligopolies and their suppliers best fit the New York case, though we enlarge it by stating that half of New York small firms are high-technology and 25 to 30 percent innovate. Thus the high-technology and innovative small firms are part of a large-small network.

Figure 1. Models of intra-firm arrangements

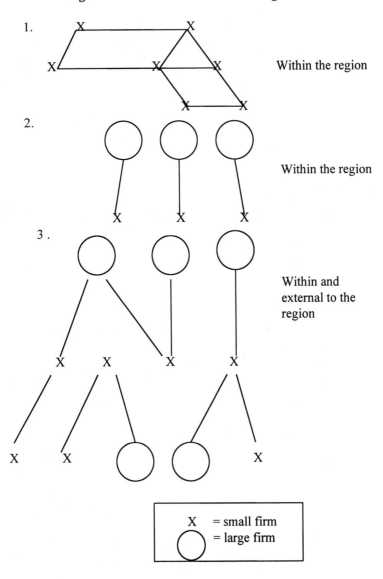

1.   Within the region

2.   Within the region

3.   Within and
                                                                        external to the
                                                                        region

X   = small firm
◯   = large firm

Chapter 5

Summary of Private Entrepreneurship and the Question of Firm Growth

A high proportion of small firms throughout the state sell to one of a small number of oligopolies located in the same county. They also export from the state and nation. But their basic structure is as suppliers to large firms. Seventy percent of these small firms use computerized processing (or are high-technology) and about a third are innovative.

These results together undermine the theory that small firms are replacing large firms (Piore and Sabel). They also undermine Harrison's theory (1994) that supplies come largely from large firms in Europe or Asia; some get supplies from abroad but many come from small firms in the same county.

The nature of relations between these firms and their customers also undermine Williamson's theory of transaction costs, that firms merge to save money. We have shown that firms stay apart over many years when they have very complex and changing relations. Maybe some merge, but which ones do is not predictable from the nature of the small firm. Neither do small firms submit to the domination that Japanese suppliers undergo.

In New York State most small firms are suppliers to large manufacturers. They buy parts, sell parts and subcontract for parts. They are members of networks. Chief among the firms they supply are highly concentrated firms in the same county. This does not mean that they are captive of these firms. Seventy-seven percent sell outside New York State and 45 percent sell outside of the United States. A majority supply industries, but a substantial but lesser proportion also sell retail, to institutions, and to government including defense.

This is not a picture of small firms left behind large, or small firms leaving large behind in progress. Nor it is a cause of merger when products are custom made and negotiations complex and delivery time fast and when specifications change.

No longer do firms start in cities where labs and specialized personnel are available, and move to rural locations when their production is standardized and labor cheaper. They are equally distributed over urban and rural counties. They may be denser in urban areas, but they are equally innovative and high-technology in rural counties. Rural counties have no different proportions of innovative and high-technology firms.

Why do we see the industrial economic structure consisting of networks of small and large firms participating in a series of supply and demand? Why do they particularly supply a few concentrated (oligoplists) firms in a county, and to a lesser extent the nearer the firm to the county seat? For one thing, they supply specialized custom made, changing products at short notice, about which they have complex negotiations. These intricate relations are easier to carry on within a region. Industrial extension personnel and big businesses tell us that more and more large firms are buying from a smaller number of suppliers who are only a couple of hours away.

There are two major factors, unrelated to each other that characterize these small firms; high-technology use and innovation. In innovative firms, the highest relationships are that the CEO does research and development and that they have a trade secret. A group of other correlates suggest a flexible firm. Thus, innovative industry is flexible and wide ranging, while high-technology firms are less related to marketing efforts, but to the most important customer, a large firm, and to selling to industry. High-technology firms are classed as such on the use of a computerized production process.

An innovative company also has the kind of workforce that is often suggested as being good for industry in general; people are trained to do more than one job; they are assigned responsibility for the quality of work and a team completes a whole subassembly.

The other main fact of this research is a hint at two directions a firm can take. Innovative firms sell to a large company, high-technology firms sell widely and out of the area. But they do not describe types of firms but directions a firms can take.

These two aspects of companies clearly go in different directions but a given company may be high on one or both of these factors. At any rate they free modern, small firms, from being thought to be backward and simple, undeveloped. Computerization of work processes seems to be diffusing judging by its prevalence. That it does diffuse is also borne out by economic developers who tell how one factory gets machines and other business owners visit to find out about them.

Since about a third of companies are innovative and over 50 percent are high-technology we concluded that New York State companies are modern. Since the two characteristics of companies are both widely distributed in both rural and urban counties any thought of rural companies being less technologically qualified, backward companies is erroneous. This may have been true at one time. It is no longer.

Most of these companies do custom work and adapt to the demands of the companies to which they sell. Most provide customers with goods on short notice and many have complicated negotiations with their major customer. This is true of firms of all ages. This seems to rob Williamson's transaction cost theory of merger of any ability to predict even if one could realistically measure transaction costs.

These facts seem to indicate that industry has undergone major changes. Rather than converting raw materials, most factories buy parts and sell parts. There are production networks that demonstrate that industry is changed, perhaps forever. Transportation improvements, telematics, and non-dependence on raw materials have changed modes of production and location of firms. Firms now can locate where it is feasible without many of the constraints: in rural areas, in places without paying costs of obtaining natural resources, near highways and airports.

Thus the study of small firms tells us about economic structure in general. A very high proportion of firms in a given county tend to sell to firms in the county and nearly 50 percent to one of the top 5 or six firms. These latter tend to be concentrated. That is, a large part of the output of the industry comes from 20 or fewer producers in each 4 digit SIC. We may say they are oligopolies. The economic organization of cities and their surroundings is based on large concentrated firms and their suppliers.

All of these small firms are independently owned, most by one or two owners and their kin. Most of them financed themselves as a firm and even later when they become eligible for loans. Eleven percent of the owners are women. Many of these have inherited the business from a father or spouse. Here is a place where women are shut out, perhaps by not being able to save money for the start, perhaps by not being part of the network that exists. Why is a puzzle. Some women start many other kinds of retail and service, that do not require the same technological skill, experience or knowledge or network ties.

Firm Growth

There are many questions. What is necessary to start a business and keep it going? These are questions we started with but since that time eight years ago when we did the first study many questions have been answered and we now have a good description of how industry operates in a locality with large and small firms interdependent with the area dominated by oligopolies. However small, a firm likes to carry business out of state and nation, and this maintains a measure of independence. Small do not exist without large, but that said, they are not completely dependent on large. This is a happy turn of events. Small firms are not tied to large to such an intimate degree as in Japan. And we have no way of knowing for sure, but American firms are very innovative and technologically advanced and most grow if they stay in business. Why not? They are rooted in a free society.

The OECD Employment Outlook for 1995 says that approximately 40% of all United States firms survive six years after founding. Firms that grow have a much higher rate of survival; 66 percent of growing firms survive. Even low growth firms have a higher survival rate than non-growing (Phillips and Kirchhoff, 1989). Manufacturing firms have the highest survival rate over six years, 47 percent. Therefore, firm growth is important in investigating the question of survival.

Phillips and Kirchhoff (1995) estimate that 75 percent of firms that drop out do so for voluntary reasons: death, retirement or desire to seek a more profitable business and the like. Only 25 percent are estimated to drop out for financial difficulties or bankruptcy. With these facts in mind, that we do not have firms that grew over 100 employees or firms that dropped out, let us examine what happened with those we studied. The firms in question began as small firms. The average number of employees when they were founded was 8. From that time to the present, these firms increased employment by a mean of just over 14 employees, with some firms increasing employment by over 300 employees. Only a handful of firms did not grow at all.

Several variables were used to predict (in a two-step regression) the volume of sales and the change in employment by these firms. Change in employment was explained by volume of sales, the innovation factor, the high-technology factor, and negatively the total number of workers when the firm started. The volume of sales was regressed on the high-technology factor, initial business planning, marketing efforts, having a patent on a product, and the location of the most important customer (see Table 2). We must note that having a patent is a constituent of innovation; perhaps it is institutionalized innovation. Companies do not always want a patent on an innovation. They would rather have a trade secret unavailable to rivals. Therefore, having a patent represents a stage of innovation.

Change in the number of workers resulted from economic success, and to a lesser extent, high-technology production. As expected, the volume of sales has a positive impact on the increase in the number of workers. We found that firms that used high-technology in production were more likely to have increased their workforce. Innovativeness had a marginal impact on increase in the number of workers. But having high-technology, a patent, marketing through factory representatives, might be regarded as institutionalization of the use of resources. In other words, they may be indicators of a successful business but not causes. The causes may be some overall quality of management. The number of workers that a firm had in the beginning had a slightly negative impact on the increase in the number of workers. Explanation of this fact rests on the limit to growth in larger firms that do not grow beyond 100 employees by definition.

This result led us to further investigate the reasons behind economic success. We found that a combination of production processes, management and sales strategy all had a positive impact on the volume of sales. Firms with their most important customer in the county tended to have lower volume of sales, while firms that marketed through manufacturing representatives tended to have higher volume of sales. High-technology firms also had increased volume of sales. If a firm applied for a loan, their current volume of sales was greater than those that did not. This result implies that systematic accounting of resources as well as construction of a business plan leads to business success.

Entrepreneurship, Private and Public

Table 1: Correlations between Variables				
Variable	Innovation Factor	High Tech Factor	Total Worker at Start	Change in size of workforce
Volume of Sales	.20	.46	.27	.56
Innovation Factor	1.00	.00	.00	.19
High Tech Factor		1.00	.19	.28
Total Workers at Start				-.24

Table 2: Standardized Parameter Estimates		
Response Variable Predictor Variables	Change in Workforce from Start to Present	Volume of Sales
Volume of Sales	$.64^3$	
Innovation	.06	
Total Workforce at Start	$-.42^3$	
High-Technology	$.07^1$	$.29^3$
Largest Customer in County		$-.20^1$
Has a Patent		$.25^2$
Markets Product Through Manfanufacturing Representatives		$.23^2$
Applied for a Government Loan		$.21^1$
Adjusted R^2	.49	.39

[1] = significant at .05 level
[2] = significant at .01 level
[3] = significant at .001 level

A word about marketing: the proportion sold to the first customer did not predict either variable nor did export. A variety of marketing measures were related concerning the spread of marketing beyond local sales to a wider audience. Local sales were negatively related, suggesting that getting wider recognition and not being subject to the rise and fall of the local economy was important.

Taken together, these results describe the type of small firms most likely to succeed in a regional economy. Successful firms combine business moves with technical skill to create efficient production processes. Those firms tend to have networks of marketing representatives who sell their product regionally and nationally.

Thus small industry and large are interdependent. Though small firms have other outlets than sales to industry, it is a mistake to look at small firm growth as an independent phenomenon with no connection to what is happening in large firms. On the contrary large and small firms share the same economic fates. This increases the problem for a location when a large firm closes or moves. This closure or move also affects suppliers and their suppliers in addition to the workforce of the company moving. It affects the whole economy of the region.

Another question concerns the spread of industry to rural areas and the role of cities. Transportation and telematics tie firms to concerns in cities. The nearer the firm is to a city the more likely it supplies large firms in the county. Or conversely, a city consists of a group of large companies and their suppliers. Oligopolies are very important; half or more of the firms sell to the top 5 or 6 firms. Yet small firms are not subject to control by large as we see it in Japan. Seventy percent export from New York, and 45 percent from the Untied States. Factories sell to large firms but also to small, to retail, to government including defense, and other institutions though to a lesser extent. So the web of firms is local to an area, invigorates the economy but leaves firms free to get out of state and out of industry customers that keep it healthy.

How do these networks arise? We know that firms exchange information widely. We know owners have typically had previous job experience, often in a large firm. They have been successful enough to save money needed for startup and hardworking enough to get business off the ground. A portion sell to previous employers, and many produce a product related to that of a former job. Thus private entrepreneurs are hard working, experienced, especially in technical matters, and self reliant and are not afraid to make innovative decisions. They also are brave and adventurous since there is no guarantee of success. Many go out of business each year for a variety of reasons, some voluntarily and some involuntarily.

Firms grow if they are successful or have a high value of sales, high-technology and are innovative. Firms that have a large value of sales seem to have institutionalized certain characteristics. They are high-technology users. They have a patent; they sell through factory representatives, do not have their largest customer in the county and have applied for a loan. Most people would regard these as desirable characteristics for a company to have that wants to succeed. But we point out that these are merely indicators of success, not causes. They mean the owner for whatever reason has made some good choices and has managed his business well. But is does not mean that an extension agent will help a business to grow by urging this behavior on it. Further study would be required to see causes and effects. The cause might be good management that leads the owner to file a patent, apply for a loan or the like. The adjusted r^2 of volume of sales (or its predictability) was only .39 (of a possible 1.00). This leaves much territory for further explanations.

Public Entrepreneurship

Chapter 6

Local organizations and public entrepreneurship

In 1969 New York State passed legislation that made it possible for local governments to set up Industrial Development Agencies to issue Industrial Revenue Bonds and carry on industrial development. New York was the second last state to do so. This brought about the eventual establishment of Industrial Development Agencies in every county of the state and in many cities and towns. It also stimulated the organization or mobilization of a number of other local development organizations with the same goals. This new set of local development organizations is mentioned here for two important reasons. First, they constitute a new public-private partnership between government and business on a local level. Government-business relations are often assumed by theory to be confrontational or antagonistic, seldom resulting in joint or cooperative efforts. Thus these local development organizations embody a new type of relationship on a local basis. Secondly, we seldom have the opportunity to study an entirely new type of organization early in the organization's history. These new organizations have, for the most part, existed fewer than twenty years, and thus provide a rare opportunity for looking at a set of completely new organizations as they start and in their early years. Yet now they appear to have become institutionalized.

Local economic development organizations are set up by a county, city or town, or private groups therein. The Industrial Development Agencies, which comprise the majority, issue Industrial Revenue Bonds. The state has empowered city, town, and county government to vote Industrial Development Agencies into existence. The local legislature appoints a board of directors of seven people from broad sectors of the community, mostly business, and this board hires staff, if they have any, and they have to approve bonds issued. These agencies have municipal powers – the right of eminent domain, the right to levy taxes, and to forego paying taxes on property they own. This feature is important since the IDA holds title to any property for which it has issued a bond until the bond is paid off.

Other local development organizations are private, not-for-profits, with membership, or they are special industrial development arms of the local chambers of commerce. These various organizations are often also Local Development Corporations set up to process New York Job Development Authority loans. They are all typically small organizations; many have only one or two staff members, and the largest number their staff in the teens. A large urban county may have several organizations, but each will be quite small. The local organizations also gain support from a variety of regional agencies or regional offices of state and federal agencies. This part of the study focuses on 61 county-level local development organizations in upstate New York, omitting the five New York City counties and the five New York SMSA counties, since this greater New York City area is different from the rest of the state, and subject to different and national forces. The study will also describe the network of other agencies, city, town, county, or regional, that often cooperate and keep in close touch. While they depend mainly on government resources, they make interesting use of these and act in enterprising, innovative, imaginative ways, taking risks, to provide integrated and comprehensive help to a business that has to meet the economic pressures of the marketplace regardless of bureaucratic constraints.

Virtually all agencies report that job creation is their chief goal. Lending agencies peg amounts of loans to the number of jobs to be created, and this sets the stage for the developers to define economic development as job creation and preservation. Economists and business people may see business as profits, products or productivity, they may focus on innovation, quality, competition, or efficiency. Developers see business as jobs. Job creation guides their efforts and choices.

Meyer and Rowan (1977) add to the primary roots of organization beliefs what they characterize as "rational myths" – rational, widely held beliefs that are not yet empirically verified. One belief on the lips of developers is that the agency should be a "one-stop shop." Above all, their task is one of coordinating and integrating available help to meet a business's needs in one program so that the owner or manager can deal with a single agency and not go to a confusing multiplicity of agencies on his own, but rather is presented with a total comprehensive program. Another commonly held belief is that the economic development organization should not do for business what business can do for itself. However, developers have different perceptions of what business can do for itself, and there are certainly actual differences in needs and resources from place to place and business to business.

Seemingly created by the same social forces, and certainly by the same law, organizations nonetheless operate in a variety of ways. Stinchcombe (1965) has offered a widely cited perspective that organizations take on a certain form when they are founded because of the structure of the environment at the time of founding, and that when the environment changes, the organization does not change to meet new forces, but stays the same as at the time of founding. Rather, new organizations arise to meet new environmental pressures. His paradigm does not deal with the range of variation existing in a set of organizations that arise at the same time, perhaps each existing in a slightly different environment, nor does he allow for any change or growth. We will see much variation in organizations, and we will see that they have greatly expanded the tasks they perform from the narrow one for which most of them were founded. Perhaps organizations only seem the same, and seem unchanging because the microscope has not focused on them sufficiently closely and in sufficient numbers. Differences can be illustrated by two conflicting interpretations of the enabling law made by the heads of two counties agencies: one, when asked about agency activities, referred to the law saying that all Industrial Development Agencies could do by law was to issue Industrial Revenue Bonds, and he seemed surprised that we could even ask what else they did. Another read passages from the same law saying, "See, according to the law the agency has very broad powers. It can do anything it wants." Thus, a set of agencies, created by the same law and founded within a few years of each other, interpret their charter very differently and engage in very narrow or a wide range of activity in accordance with these varying interpretations of their mandate.

This part of the study consists of hour and a half-long interviews with the staff of 61 county agencies, plus more with state, federal, and some regional, town and city agencies. The interviews were conducted in 1986 and 1987. By 1990, all were still in existence and at least two new county agencies had been formed. We will describe and interpret the structure of these organizations, their similarities and differences, the bureaucratic world they deal with, and the activities they carry on in behalf of business. The task is to show how public policies work out in a new way in a new type of local organization bridging two worlds, and how a set of new organizations are organized and carry on their work, in some ways varying and in some ways similar.

While the New York State legislature passed laws enabling counties, cities, towns, and villages to establish Industrial Development Agencies (IDA) in 1969, it took a period of years before nearly all counties had such an agency, and longer before some of them became more than paper entities. But the process gradually stimulated a great deal of activity on the part of such agencies as well as other public and private economic development organizations.

The fees charged for issuing bonds, the payback from Housing and Urban Development (HUD) loans, grants from the Economic Development Administration (EDA), and local funds allocated by county governments were used to pay administrative costs, to buy land and build buildings and provide infrastructure for industrial parks, to start industrial incubators, set up revolving loan funds, to launch programs for recruiting firms to come into the county, and to pay for research and consultation on the direction the county should take. Most agencies spend the major part of their time helping existing businesses expand and survive and helping local start-ups. Most recruit business from outside, but such recruiting uses a small part of their time and resources.

Agencies differ in the types of help they provide business, but they typically include site selection, and many keep inventories of sites and buildings available. They typically keep in touch, formally or informally, with the industries in their county, and frequently have organized programs of visitation. They usually state that they are ready to help new or old firms with any problem they have. This often includes help with regulations, permits, or zoning, sometimes even sponsoring special legislation. A major task is putting together financial packages. For a business to raise funds for expansion or remodeling, for example, it is often necessary to put together the total amount needed from a variety of sources: the owners' own funds, bank loans, and local, state, and federal loan funds. Since all of these have different types of complicated applications, and their requirements change frequently, it can require a good deal of expertise and often several months to put together the right package. Help also sometimes includes assisting with business plans, though less frequently, and putting businesses together with various types of experts or consultants needed. These agencies will undertake as trivial a problem as housing for new executives, or help with visas, or as large a one as building or buying a spur railroad needed to supply a factory or ship its output. They sometimes help with leveraged buy outs, intervene with plants threatening to move, or help intercede with unions. In border areas particularly, they help with the organization of Foreign Trade Zones. No problem is too large or too small for them to tackle.

These organizations are often quasi-governmental, set up by county legislatures and allocated public funds, but they operate autonomously. They may also be private, supported by member contributions or part of or related to the Chamber of Commerce. Sometimes they are part of or related to the county planning office. But, as we describe their functioning, their activities, and their staff, it will become apparent that though they are not businesses, neither do they resemble a typical government bureaucracy. Their decisions are made on their own; they don't need permission from government officials, and they have the capacity and will to respond quickly to need or opportunity. They are willing and able to take risks. They undertake any task that comes up, try to meet any need, and this leads to a great variety of activities and programs. They are always trying something new.

Let us see how an agency might operate in behalf of a new business coming into the county. Its entry into the county is due either to the marketing and recruiting efforts of the agency or to initiatives on the part of a corporation. The first task the agency might help with is finding a place to locate. It may help plan and arrange financing for a building and equipment and needed infrastructure; it will, if it owns the property, either sell or lease land or buildings. If it issues a bond for some or all of the money needed for buildings and equipment, it holds title to the property until the loan is paid. Therefore the company does not have to pay local taxes in this period, and also is forgiven taxes on building materials used. The agency will put the business in touch with local professional help needed, accountants, lawyers and the like. It will show the executives around, help them with personal problems like housing. It will put the business in touch with the state

Department of Labor which will recruit and screen needed labor, and set up training programs with the help of the local Private Industry Council, through which federal training funds are made available. Together the agency and the Council may contact community colleges that will provide either college or in-plant training as needed. It will mediate between the business and local agencies or officials about regulations, zoning permits or licenses. After the business is established, the agency will keep in touch with it and help it deal with problems as they come up, such as remodeling or expansion. If the agency did not organize it, a business might not in reality know of or be able to organize itself to take advantage of the various local, state, and federal helps that exist. If these industrial development organizations were not necessary to begin with, they would have become so for the reason that as such agencies have proliferated, any county that does not have one providing instantaneous and efficient help cannot compete well.

In fact, we will argue that these local development organizations comprise a new set of local institutions that act as conduits for state and federal funds, adapt their use to local needs, resources and opportunities while they perform a broad and detailed role in industrial development beyond mere accession of funds.

The Public-Private Partnership

Anyone who thinks that the United States lacks industrial policy should take a look at the many policies, programs, and activities that an array of federal, state, and local governments carry on in behalf of industry. And this is what we propose to do in New York State where we will examine them through the work of the local industrial development agencies that utilize these programs. While we will examine a wide variety of activities of a range of actors, we must remind ourselves that these are a small part of the total complex we can label industrial policy. But in this study we confine ourselves to policies that help industrial development directly and the local development agencies that carry them out, channeling federal, state, and local aid to private industry.

Federal and state programs that are well designed and have good intentions sometimes fail or help only a fraction of those at whom the program is targeted. Local economic development agencies of New York State, mostly dating from the early 1970s, provide us with possible answers to questions of program failure. They perform three tasks that may be necessary to ensure success. First, they mediate, translate, negotiate between government programs and private enterprise. They provide a stable, publicly accountable organization which has well-defined powers with which government programs can negotiate, rather than directly with private individuals or businesses, and they also provide an accessible agency for local people to deal with. Secondly, they gather information on programs and on their own areas and use this to coordinate a variety of helps into an integrated plan of action for a business. Finally, they adapt programs to the local situation, knowing the actors, using local resources and their own wits to supplement federal and state aid, and bring about a usable and practical solution suitable to a particular local problem. Thus this new public-private partnership may be the harbinger of the way other programs need to be organized to become effective.

Local economic development organizations in counties, cities, and towns in New York State have created a new public-private partnership. Their formation stimulated a great deal of other local economic development activity. The local agencies are bridging organizations, standing between public agencies and private enterprise, helping business put public loan funds to work to solve a wide variety of complex problems encountered by private industry in opening plants, expanding, remodeling, heading off decline, and competing under changing economic circumstances.

That a group of organizations should perform a task of standing between and bridging government and private enterprise makes good sense once we know they are there and see what they do. But such a state of affairs is surprising in view of much theory about relations between the economy and government. In the case of state-run economies, economy and government are the same; or are they? In China and Russia we hear of a good deal of negotiation, adjustment, diverging interests, arbitrary rulings of government over forms and amounts of production, private evasions of government rulings, changes in direction, poor quality, and low productivity. It is not easy for government and the economy to work in harness. Sometimes theory views government and the economy as being totally separate.

Politicians talk of what the government can do to, or for, private enterprise. Both theory and popular belief see their separateness, not their connections. Sometimes they are viewed as confrontational or antagonistic.

Herman (1981) and others in recent years have been at pains to point out connections at a national level, such as the flow of government officials into private enterprise and the drawing on top levels of corporate management for cabinet posts, lobbying and PACs, and many other relationships. But joint public-private projects and relationships have not heretofore occurred or been studied often, and usually only as case studies. Quasi-governmental agencies such as the Tennessee Valley Authority exist but are rare. The idea of bridging institutions, making possible a public-private partnership is a relatively new idea. Therefore, the study is useful for what it can add to this continuing dialogue. What are and should be relationships between government and the economy? Is it possible to preserve the common good for which government exists while it works to assist private enterprise? We will describe this new relationship. It will raise questions as to what relations government and the private sector should have, and how they should be monitored.

Public policies enacted to help individuals or organizations always have a set of directives and constraints that a legislative body believes will ensure the carrying out of a specific and relatively narrow purpose or program. A policy is devised to suit most cases, the general case. But few individual or corporate users exactly fit the terms set down in law, and one program seldom solves all problems. Furthermore, public agencies are constrained and uncomfortable in dealing with individuals and private organizations. They like to deal with other organizations like themselves – isomorphic with them, organizations that are controlled by or are part of government, whose authorities and duties are set down in rules and regulations known to all, that are predictable, stable, and publicly accountable, and that are sure to be there next year. Private enterprise, on the other hand, finds it difficult to deal with government bureaucracies – their rules are too inflexible, do not fit a particular case, their hierarchies of authority too slow to respond, they have difficulty dealing adequately with new, different, changing problems, and their solutions are only partial. Government agencies have a well-defined mission, and private industry seldom has well-defined problems that stay the same over time. The local economic development organizations stand between bureaucracies and the private sector, and work with business on a one-to-one basis with an enterprise's whole problem.

These agencies try to be one-stop shops and provide all that is needed to deal with a complex problem. They help a business put together an assortment of loans and other material and managerial helps needed to solve the problem. These come from a variety of federal, state, and local government sources, and from private organizations such as banks, venture capital, professional accountants, lawyers, and real estate developers, and from the local economic development organization's own resources when other sources fail. They try to coordinate a wide variety of information and help into an integrated plan for each business to suit its peculiar needs in a responsive and timely fashion. Thus policies work which might fall on barren ground without a local agency to act as intermediary, a source of information, and a facilitator, a public entrepreneur.

They stand between government bureaucracies that are publicly accountable and businesses operating in a competitive marketplace. What are necessary constraints for a government agency would cripple a business trying to meet market conditions. The local economic development agency makes possible a partnership between actors from two very different worlds. Scott (1981) states that what he terms rational organizational theorists (Weber, Boulding, Kerr) agree that "organizations are called into existence by the increasing need to coordinate and control complex administrative and technical tasks. Enlarged political states, expanding markets, and improved technologies both require and are made possible by the development of organizational forms that can manage complex exchanges and coordinate diverse, interrelated activities" (Scott, 1981:141). This coordinating function is just that of the local economic development agencies. The characterization may miss the mark with other organizations, but is exactly on target for these.

Organizational start-ups in general are difficult to track, especially on a comparative basis. We see what organizations do now, and assume that the functions they are performing reflect the reasons why they were started. When we want to study a set of organizations, we typically have to study them as they are now, many years after they were started, or rely on historical data. The latter can be rich, but still lack information on early formative years and early changes. Historical information can lack detail on early variation among what may now be similar organizations. Perhaps what they are doing now, in their mature years, bears little resemblance to what they did at the beginning and little relation to reasons why they got started. Perhaps present seeming uniformity has resulted from variation and change and dropping out of organizations and programs that did not work, or perhaps we are looking only at what a range of organizations have in common rather than their differences that have emerged to meet their different problems. These organizations are still young and, in general, people involved in their founding are still there.

The Theoretical Approach

Most organization theory has been devised to explain the structure and functioning of complex organizations, not small simple ones like these. The basic building block is bureaucratic theory. But small organizations do not have complex hierarchies, and layers of organization. Questions about communication channels, power, span of control, how the formal organization does or does not coincide with the informal do not make the same kind of sense as in large complex organizations.

There is some discussion of professionals that takes care of some types of small organizations such as doctors' and lawyers' offices. And perhaps others such as barber shops have not been considered important enough to warrant theoretical effort. Of course, there is a literature on entrepreneurship and small business start up but it is mostly the work of psychologists or economists who are less concerned with organizational problems.

But organization theory, though devised to explain complex organizations, nonetheless provides suggestions that might explain why local development organizations are as they are and function as they do. First, organization theory suggests reasons why such organizations exist at all. Herbert Simon (1957) devised the concept of bounded rationality. This means that there are cognitive limitations on individuals as information processors. The local development organizations gather and disseminate a great deal of information from government to business, information that imposes a practical burden on a business person's time and faculties even if it were possible to absorb it, since he may use such complex information once in his lifetime. The local development organizations are, above all, information centers.

Another hypothesis advanced by Stinchcombe (1965) is that organizations founded at the same time have similar structures suitable for the society of that era, but as society changes, the organizations remain the same. There is little evidence for his hypothesis since start up organizations are seldom studied and rarely over time. This set of economic development organizations founded around the same time, made possible by the same legislation and devoted to the same goal, will provide us with one opportunity to examine whether they took the same form.

Organization theory states that organization form varies with the environment, specifically that organizations tend to be isomorphic with these environments and "thus acquire resources and legitimacy associated with them" (Meyer and Rowan, 1977). The local development organizations face two environments, that of government and that of business. Therefore their legal forms, communications with and support from local and state government, and their public accountability make it possible for them to deal with government agencies. Their entrepreneurial nature and flexibility make it possible to deal with businesses that enjoy the freedom of operating in the marketplace (Friedman, 1962). In other words, they perform a bridging function between public and private worlds, or like the Roman god, Janus, face in two directions.

The local development organizations have a number of characteristics that organization theory would find plausible. They are small flexible organizations. Organization theory tells us that formalization interferes with the performance of complex ambiguous tasks, and serves better routine predictable tasks (Blau and Scott, 1962:116-128). Not only are most of these small, but they typically are faced with complex problems, each of which is a little different than any other and has no set solution. Furthermore, in complex urban counties where there are more industries and people and where complicated situations prevail, organizations stay small. Additional effort is secured by the presence of four or five small organizations. In such a case (Pfeffer and Salancik, 1978; Scott, 1981:193-203), organizations solve problems of interdependence, and hence avoid possible confusion, competition, or redundant efforts by various bridging strategies. They serve on each others' boards of directors, they meet and communicate on a regular and frequent basis, they launch joint ventures, and they have worked out a division of labor among them recognized by all. Thus they cooperate, but maintain independence, small size, informality, and flexibility. If blended into one larger organization, a degree of formalization would set in, along with lines of communication and control, set solutions, stability, and with these, some inflexibility and loss of ability to respond quickly and with new solutions. On a regional or state basis the local development organizations form associations for cooperation and communication.

Local development organizations vary in comparison with each other again with respect to demands of their environments. Particularly do urban and rural local development organizations vary because of differing demands and resources. But older industrial regions have activities that the less developed and newer regions do not.

Why are local development organizations quasi-governmental or public agencies, rather than being constituted as businesses like legal, engineering, accounting or management consulting firms? First, of course, are the legal constraints on Industrial Development Agencies and Local Development Corporations. But aside from these, organization theory tells us that organizations and markets are alternative means of organizing work, and that organizations have advantages over markets in reducing uncertainty and increasing the security of the organization itself (Scott, 1981:144-50). Local development organizations operate in an environment of constant uncertainty and change. Government support, if protective, may be necessary for their survival. State support, it is claimed, increases the probability of organizational survival (Aldrich, 1979:188).

Scott (1981:187) also argues that in the short run organizations adapt to their social environments but "collectively and taking a longer view, organizations gradually transform their environments." In the short run local development organizations have to be responsive to local government, local business, local needs, and local resources. But their reason for existing is to change their environments.

Scott emphasizes important distinctions between various theories of organization that he classifies as rational, natural, or open systems. At the risk of oversimplifying his thinking, rational theories emphasize the formal and normative characteristics of the organization. Natural systems theories emphasize informal structure, actual behavior, and system survival. Open systems theory emphasizes relations of the organization to its environment and the organization's complexity and availability of its component parts.

We have pointed out in the case of the local development organizations that the organization's formal structure enables it to cope with local, regional, state, and federal agencies and legitimate its position. We will look at the formal structure of local development organizations, or examine them as rational systems. Their formal structures define them as public agencies. There is some kind of public control of their boards of directors. Often local government has to take certain legal steps to establish them. They are publicly accountable. In respect to such aspects of their formal structures, they resemble governmental and public agencies. Therefore state and federal agencies that deal with them can feel confident about how things will go and either require or desire to work through them. Their activities are open, predictable, responsible, and eventually subject to public scrutiny, as are units of government with which they have a great deal of contact. Their formal aspects enable them to face and deal with government.

In Chapter 9 we will proceed to show that the activities of the local development organizations vary a great deal, that their actual behavior and day-to-day functioning does not, by and large, flow from the formal characteristics. The latter impose constraints and provide opportunities, but a large proportion of what they do and how they do it is not prescribed by the formal charter. Key characteristics are spontaneity, flexibility, ability to move in new directions, to take initiatives and to respond quickly in response to a wide variety of needs and demands from a variety of businesses and agencies. Thus in Chapter 9 we will begin to look at aspects of the IDAs as natural systems. Most of their programs, activities, and day-to-day operations are not specified in their formal charters, they are neither prescribed nor prohibited. There are few set tasks that have to be undertaken by all agencies. In their informal day-to-day operations they resemble private enterprise. As they respond to economic pressures and market opportunities, often of an unanticipated nature, in responsive, flexible ways, so do the agencies study and act in consideration of resources and opportunities. They rise to unanticipated occasions that often require personal responsibility and quick decisions, seldom possible in normal bureaucracies but common to business. They seem to exist to screen and integrate input from a varied environment.

Local development organizations are also open systems, communicating and working with the wider society in many ways, at the vortex of information gathering and disseminating, linking up many other organizations into a network. They exchange information and work with a wide variety of public and private organizations and businesses that are part of a local, regional, and state network with links to federal agencies. Their doors are open. They listen to and try to help anyone who walks in, and they work as part of various and shifting teams. They could not exist in closed-door situations apart from this network.

Thus the framework Scott and others use to study complex organizations will also help us focus on formal and informal aspects of these organizations that make it possible for them to deal with both government and business and on their open nature and extensive ties that make it possible to work in the wider community.

Above all, the directors are entrepreneurial in nature. Entrepreneurship is defined in various ways. Schumpeter (1934) and others (Lebenstein, 1978) emphasize the entrepreneur as a source of innovation and disequilibrium. Kent (1984) concludes that entrepreneurship is more than the start up of business. It "requires the element of growth that leads to innovation, job creation and economic expansion." This is precisely how economic developers have defined their jobs, and they feel comfortable with a definition of their job as a public entrepreneur. Several observations from the organization literature help us here. One is that in formal organizations, organization roles determine individual attributes. Most of the developers view their role in similar ways and it follows from their view of organizational goals (Scott, 1981:59). Natural systems theory emphasizes that characteristics of leaders follow from the situation (Fiedler, 1964, 1971). Insofar as their activities and directions differ, the developers face different problems in affluent or poor counties, urban or isolated locations, an old industrial structure or a new one. But in any case their position is entrepreneurial. In the main, developers seem happy in their jobs. They give off an atmosphere of optimism and hope. Studies of job satisfaction show that the greater the variety, autonomy and degree of responsibility in a job, the more satisfaction (Scott, 1981:155; Blauner, 1960; Sheppard and Herrick, 1972; Special Task Force, 1973). The developer's job is very varied, and he has a great deal of both autonomy and responsibility. Developers differ sharply in one respect from other professionals described as undergoing "a prolonged period of socialization and training in which they are expected to internalize standards, acquire a repertory of skills, and master a general set of theoretical principles that will enable them to make decisions and act autonomously in a responsible and expert fashion" (Scott, 1981:154). We will show that developers differ greatly in education and job experience and have only short periods of training specific to this complex job. Rather, they do share a repertory of possible activities they can undertake, but they are shaping their jobs and developing skills as they go along.

This study of the county development organizations of New York State is a study of only one set of organizations. But organization theory developed for complex organizations can be illustrated and it, in turn, makes plausible the structures and activities of local development organizations that, without it, seem strange and inexplicable. Thus, this study, in terms of research design, does not test theory, but gives it plausibility, and theory provides a way of integrating and understanding empirical facts we have discovered in the investigation of local development organizations. They are small, flexible, entrepreneurial organizations serving as centers of information, and they perform the task of putting together various types of aid into an integrated plan suitable for a particular business problem. They intercede between business and government. And they have tended to remain small.

The Study

We undertook the study of county-level development agencies as a result of an exploratory study of innovation in small manufacturing firms. As we interviewed firms, we became aware of the existence of incubators, industrial parks, and loan funds, and the importance and difficulty, sometimes, of getting help. In that study, 54 percent of the businesses interviewed received some kind of government help (Young and Francis, 1989). We became aware of a new set of actors and agencies unlike any that existed before. The new thing about these agencies was above all their intermediary role between business and government. They were neither business nor government, but helped put the two together, acting to help create new jobs by using public resources, by acting as public entrepreneurs. Thus, we decided to interview all of the agencies operating at a county level in the 52 upstate counties of New York since these agencies clearly played a role in innovation. As we went around, we found that often city and town agencies played an important part, and included a number of these. We also found regional organizations or regional branches of federal and state agencies providing important backing and support, and interviewed several of each type to understand the role they play. We also interviewed people in all of the federal and state agencies that the developers draw on. Their printed material gives a great deal of the picture of how they operate, but we thought we needed a fuller idea of how things go in fact, what their aims and goals are, and how their directions have changed over time. Thus we conducted 61 county agency interviews, 22 with regional agencies, 15 with state and federal agencies, and 12 with city and town agencies, to get a comprehensive picture of the interrelations and how help is handled up and down the hierarchy of agencies. These took place over a year's time in late 1986 through the summer of 1987.

The interviews were open-ended. An interviewer would ask the head of the agency to tell about the structure and program of the organization. About an hour later, save for a few requests for elaboration or words of encouragement, the informant would ask whether we had any more questions, and we would ask about topics he might not have covered, going over a checklist to ensure comparability. This allowed his presenting things he considered important, things unique to his agency, things we would not have known existed, especially in the early stages of the study. But it also allowed getting comparable data for the various agencies. Interviews typically lasted an hour and a half, some more, a few a shorter time. Those that were shorter often were with people in newer agencies whose programs were just getting underway. No one refused an interview; all were cooperative and helpful. These are intelligent, knowledgeable, articulate people. Because they were talking about things they had to think of every day, over and over, in a comprehensive way and make sense of in order to operate effectively, the information is detailed and makes sense. The senior author conducted all of the interviews, and the second author also participated in a number, so that we were able to exchange views and analyses as the study went along. The interviews covered all of New York State excluding the ten counties of the New York City SMSA. The latter area was omitted since it is subject to different and national influences, unlike the rest of the state. For reason of the time travel took and the length of the interviews, scheduling and interviewing took place over the course of a year.

We have three sources of information: the interviews, brochures and annual reports of the agencies, and loans and grants awarded in the county as reported by the lending or granting state or federal agency. Thus we will mainly be seeing the agency through the eyes of its director, typically an optimistic believer, supplemented by state and federal data. To some extent this bias must be kept in mind. But one of the director's main tasks is to attract and package outside funds, and we do have a check on what funds have come into the county's business.

However, in evaluating the directors' statements, we must keep in mind the fact that any project that is funded is evaluated as credit-worthy by at least one and often several participating public and private agencies in addition to the director. This is a check on failure and we did not hear of many failures. Occasionally, a project fell through because the various sources of funds could not act in time. Occasionally an agency issued a bond for a project that failed later. Sometimes they could not sell a bond for a project that did not have sufficient appeal. Therefore even in the case of bonds, there is an outside check.

Therefore the apparently low project failure rate is very likely the truth. Certainly the developers did not seem very upset when telling about them. Failures were infrequent, publicly known, and part of the job. Therefore, any shortcomings of the program are probably mainly sins of omission, things that should have been done but have not been done. But how can we judge this? Every county has an agency.

Therefore, there is no group of counties without agencies with which we can compare those with agencies. Further, a characteristic of a successful developer is to adjust his program to the local capacity, resources, and needs. Therefore, differences among counties are to be expected, and it is not easy to decide what indeed should have been done. As with many public programs, evaluation is difficult or impossible.

Summary

Local development organizations of New York State provide a means of studying a new type of government-business relationship, a public-private partnership, through which a variety of industrial policies reach business. They also furnish a set of new organizations that we can study in their early years and can compare their similarities and differences from the perspective of organization theory.

Chapter 7

Federal and State Development Programs and Disbursement of Funds

It has been said that two things affect small business: the way business is carried on and the way government efforts and funds reach business. The government's role in business is very different in different countries. In Japan, government agencies decide which corporation will institute an innovation, and government help and control is heavily present. In Hungary, the government owns part of large corporations, and these, in turn, own smaller, so that government control, and rescue, is always hoped for. Government constraints hover over small firms in France and Germany. The role of government in the United States is difficult to fully understand: it encompasses trade agreements, labor law, tax law, 700 government laboratories that contribute to research, consumer, environment, health law, and many other aspects of government help or hindrance, including defense policy.

We will understand a lot of it if we analyze federal and state help to counties, and local government, and the way counties and local government extend help to industry.

Federal And State Development Programs

A main task of local economic development organizations is to connect business with a wide array of government helps. Many federal and state departments and agencies assist industrial development directly or indirectly (see, for example, State of New York, Department of State, 1980, reprinted 1983). But a few federal and state programs are the ones most frequently mentioned and used by local developers. In briefly reviewing their activities, we will see that their way of working with local governments and local not-for-profit organizations encourages the growth of local organization and meshes with local programs. In this study, we examine how several of these programs most prominent in New York State industrial development distribute their funds. We must remind ourselves that such direct funding of industrial development programs is only a small part of what can be considered industrial policy.

In this study of New York State counties, we confined ourselves to one aspect of an industrial development policy, to questions of distribution to counties of funds from several federal and state loan and grant programs. The programs selected to be examined were named most prominently by county economic development agencies. A main task of these agencies is to try to access such funds for county development efforts and county industries.

The basis for distribution of funds does not answer questions of the effectiveness of these programs. However, whether funds were distributed in accordance with their stated purposes, or if not, on what basis, provides a start in evaluating these efforts and the policy behind them. A chief reason we cannot easily evaluate the effects of these funds on county development is that they are too entangled with other forces, and often an economic development project will draw on several sources of funding.

We can make a beginning by answering several questions.

(1) Does funding vary over time in response to economic ups and downs?

(2) Do funds disbursed by the several agencies vary in accordance with their stated purposes?

(3) What characteristics of counties are associated with disbursement of funds?

The Data

The data for this chapter were provided by the several agencies included in the study from the beginning year of their disbursement until recently as follows. They include the number of grants/loans/bonds and the dollar amounts.

} Industrial Revenue Bonds issued from 1960 through 1986. Provided by the New York State Department of Economic Development.

} U.S. Department of Commerce Economic Development Administration grants from 1962 to 1988.

} Urban Development Action Grants, provided by the United States Department of Housing and Urban Development from 1981 to 1986.
} New York State Job Development Authority funding from 1962 to 1986.
} New York State Science and Technology Foundation funding from 1983 to 1987.

Each source gave for each year the number of loans and grants and amounts of funds disbursed to each county.

We did not include Small Business Administration help, which is great, in this analysis since it goes directly to firms, and county and local organizations have little to do with it. A firm simply goes to the regional SBA office, files an application and is dealt with. They insure loans given by banks, which refer clients to them. They give a great deal of help and advice throughout the loan period, beginning with a course on filing an application. Many would-be entrepreneurs are screened out of this course which tells them how they fall short.

All of these funds claim an aim of creating jobs and alleviating poverty and unemployment. Consequently, for this appraisal, several measures of affluence, poverty and unemployment in the counties are included. Since labor quality is important to development we included the proportion of male college graduates. Because differentiation or urbanization affect so many aspects of county life we will also include two measures reflecting this: total employment and total manufacturing employment, both as proportions of the total of employment or manufacturing employment of the 52 upstate counties. We will also see whether such funding is related to political party dominance, since a previous study found party dominance to be related to various aspects of county fiscal policy and patterns of expenditure (Young et. al., 1984). The study is confined to the 52 upstate counties and excludes New York City and the five other New York SMSA counties as does the surveys of firms since these function quite differently from the rest of the state and are subject to different and national forces.

In the present analysis, the number of bonds, loans or grants is used rather than dollar amounts. The reasoning for this is that it might require an equal degree of effort to secure a small amount as a large, and we wanted the study to reflect county effort expended as far as possible. Moreover, use of dollar amounts would probably not have made much difference in the results, but use of numbers of bonds/loans/grants was considered preferable. Table 1 shows the correlation between number of loans/grants/bonds issued for each county by each funding source and the total dollar amounts, and it is uniformly high.

Table 1: Relation between Total Number of Loans/Grants/Bonds Issued by each Agency and Total Dollar Amounts.

Agency/Program	Pearson's r
Industrial Revenue Bonds	.98
Urban Development Action Grants	.84
EDA	.63
Job Development Authority	.92
NY Science and Technology	.92

The Federal and State Development Programs Studied

At the present time, the federal agencies most involved in funding local economic development projects are the Economic Development Administration, the Department of Housing and Urban Development, and the U.S. Small Business Administration. Housing and Urban Development has economic development programs of two types. One of these types is Community Development Block Grants, one program for larger cities, an entitlement program, and one for small cities under 50,000 population. Both are meant to benefit low income individuals and poorer areas. In the case of the HUD Small Cities program, economic criteria are used to rank applicants. The other is the Urban Development Action Grant program, which is the one most directly aimed at economic development to distressed areas. It is highly competitive based on HUD criteria.

Economic Development Administration

The first Economic Development Administration grants were made to New York counties in 1962. The total number of grants issued from 1962 to 1988 was 765 and at one time or another included 45 upstate counties. The number issued peaked in the late '70s and early '80s, then fell again with changing national policies. EDA grants and loans went for a wide range of development activities. They include industrial site preparation, industrial parks, planning activities, physical infrastructure (roads, water, bridges, sewage systems), and new buildings and building renovations, for technical assistance centers, and for loans to business for both working and fixed capital. Help is supposed to be directed to economically depressed areas, with special focus on alleviating unemployment.

Housing and Urban Development

The other federal agency most involved is the U.S. Department of Housing and Urban Development, especially through its Urban Development Action Grant program, again directed toward distressed cities and counties. This department also has awarded Block Grants to cities and counties, large and small, through several different programs focused on economic distress. The Block Grants may be used for public improvements, general rehabilitation of blighted areas, necessary infrastructure, and community development. But a portion generally goes directly to various types of more specific economic development projects, and not-for-profit organizations may apply to local governments for these funds. The second type, Urban Development Action Grants, are awarded to distressed towns, villages, and urban counties, and they apply for particular economic development projects. The repayment of these loans, extended to business by the local governments to whom the grants are made, goes to the local, not the federal government, and can be used in various ways such as to finance industrial parks or revolving loan funds.

The first Urban Development Action Grants (UDAG) were committed in 1978. We have lists of grants made up to and including 1986. Except for a peak year, 1984, when 51 grants were made in the state, and 1980 when there were 44, grants made per year ranged from 11 to 23. A total of 169 grants were made in 38 counties over this period. Many were for building construction and renovation, site preparation, and for equipment, often in connection with business expansion or remodeling. Grants sometimes included working capital. Sometimes infrastructure was also funded: water, sewers, an electrical plant, a waste treatment plant, a road, for example.

The greater part of the UDAG were for construction and rehabilitation of buildings for a variety of business purposes: manufacturing, retail, warehousing, office space, or for services such as hospitals. Many were general or speculative, for unknown or for a variety of prospective businesses, and also for housing. A similar number were for the expansion or location of specific businesses and sometimes involved equipment. A few were for industrial site or industrial park construction.

Industrial Revenue Bonds

Industrial Revenue Bonds are issued by local Industrial Development Agencies. The paperwork for a single bond can be bound in a volume the size of a large telephone book, and the legal costs can amount to $50,000. For this reason, bonds are not often issued for much less than half a million dollars. Only 7.7 percent of all bonds issued in New York were for less than $400,000. Occasionally, the IDA became owner of a property in reality, rather than nominally, if the business for which it issued the bond defaulted on payments. Occasionally, it has not been able to sell a bond and had to back down. Since bonds do have to be bought, often by financial institutions that exercise care in such investments, this process constitutes a natural check on the issuance of bonds for projects of doubtful success. From 1960 through December 31, 1985, 2,713 bonds were issued by the 62 counties of the state. A total of 1,652 bonds were issued in 52 upstate counties.

State Funds -- Job Development Authority

In addition to these federal funding sources and Industrial Revenue Bonds, there are several state sources of funding. The main ones used and spoken of by economic developers are the New York Job

Development Authority, the New York State Science and Technology Foundation, and the New York Urban Development Corporation. The Job Development Authority operates through a series of local organizations, the Local Development Corporations, and through them makes loans to businesses. They lend only 40 to 60 percent of the total needed; the rest comes from other public and private sources. They take second mortgage position, making the borrower more desirable to a bank by doing this. Fifty-seven percent of their loans go to businesses with fewer than fifty employees. Since they provide only part of the loan needed, working through Local Development Corporations, they intend to, and do, stimulate the working together of a network of local organizations, public and private, in behalf of business. A total of 469 awards were made in 49 upstate counties.

Urban Development Corporation

The Urban Development Corporation started working mainly in urban areas, chiefly New York City, and on housing. Later they went into large community projects, such as a stadium or convention center. In the last few years, they have gone into direct economic development and spread their efforts over the state including rural areas. However, their economic development or business assistance program is recent and they did not provide data on it.

New York State Science and Technology Foundation

The New York State Science and Technology Foundation has a different mission, to stimulate innovative technology-based business ventures. It makes loans, including funds for working capital, encouraging entrepreneurial talent, and favoring businesses with fewer than 250 employees, locally owned, and in the high-technology sector. It also funds research and development projects in universities, colleges, and nonprofit laboratories. They deal directly with loan recipients. They have organized seven Centers for Advanced Technology around the state and eight regional technology development organizations that cover the regions of the state. They provide these regional organizations with matching grants not to exceed $25,000 for the promotion, attraction, development, and expansion of science and technology-oriented activities such as conferences, registers of facilities, helping small business apply for technology grants or federal contracts, gathering and disseminating information, and supporting university collaboration. These organizations may be sponsored by colleges or universities, Chambers of Commerce, or other not-for-profit organizations. The Science and Technology Foundation also has a Small Business Innovation Research program that provides matching grants up to $50,000 to businesses which have already received Federal Phase I Small Business Innovation Research grants. A total of 223 awards were made in 29 counties.

Common Features

The various programs have some common features. One is that they frequently provide partial funding and require a recipient to find other sources as well. They frequently provide kinds of funds or work with clients that private lenders will not deal with; they try not to compete with banks. They frequently require the intervention of a unit of local government or a not-for-profit organization. When they deal only through local governments, frequently not-for-profit groups can apply through the latter. Even when lending agencies do not require it, the not-for-profits often initiate or help with applications, and agencies may wait for requests to come in, often through local organizations. Most funds are for fixed capital, and working capital is provided only in limited instances. Many are focused on economically distressed areas and on job creation, and many loans are tied to so many dollars per job to be created. They are meant to stimulate private efforts, supplement them, but not substitute for private funds. By their nature they make necessary the coordinated activity of the local development organizations and are conduits through which federal and state funds flow to business.

Many other federal and state departments and agencies offer specialized assistance of some kind, for agricultural business, for tourism, for training, for special purposes such as historic preservation, for pollution, for energy, for access roads—to name a few. The state also provides various tax incentives and services of advice and information through the Department of Economic Development and its regional offices or, for example, the New York State Office of Business Permits and Regulatory Assistance which tries to be a one-stop shop for companies in such matters. There is a network of Small Business Development Centers around the state. Knowledgeable local developers can make use of these and many other forms of assistance offered by federal and state agencies as part of a client company's total needs, and maintaining close contact with the government and its officials occupies a part of their time and energy.

A more complete description of all the major government programs available in New York State, including many more than we are studying, can be found in *A Step-by-Step Guide to Resources for Economic Development*, published by the New York State Urban Development Corporation and the New York State Department of State (1980, reprinted 1983).

Change in Funding over Time

The first question dealt with was change over time. Were there any cycles in funding, any peak years, and were they the same for all counties and all programs? Was there any relation to the business cycle or to general economic ups and downs? Examining numbers of loans, grants or bonds issued by each agency in each county for each year, it was clear that there were no regularities within agencies, no patterns common to all counties, and no relation to economic peaks or troughs. Counties often differed from each other, as did agencies, insofar as there were peak years at all, and normally there were none. This implies that both counties and funding agencies varied over time probably in response to local pressures and events or agency policies, but not to changes in the economy.

Relation of County Characteristics to Patterns of Disbursement by Agencies

Table 2 shows the relations of the several county characteristics to each other: share of total and manufacturing employment, average family income, proportions of vote registered as Republican/Conservative and as Democrat/Liberal, the proportion of male college graduates, the proportion unemployed, and the proportion living below the poverty level. The years used for the data, 1968 to 1975 anteceded disbursement from New York Science and Technology, and UDAG, and were fairly early for the other programs.

Table 2: Correlations of County Characteristics with Each Other.

	1	2	3	4	5	6	7	Pearson's r 8
1	-	.97#	.57#	-.44#	.37*	.36*	-.28	-.39*
2		-	.57#	-.43#	.31*	.33*	-.27	-.41*
3			-	-.33	.07	.43#	-.39*	-.82#
4				-	-.43#	-.08	.16	.26
5					-	.06	.00	-.04
6						-	-.49#	-.49#
7							-	.50#
8								-

#Significant at .01 level.
*Significant at .05 level.

1 = Total employment in the county as proportion of total employment in 52 upstate counties.

2 = Total manufacturing employment in the county as proportion of total manufacturing employment in 52 upstate counties.

3 = Average family income, 1975.

4 = Proportion of votes registered as Republican, Conservative, 1968.

5 = Proportion of votes registered Democrat, Liberal, 1968.

6 = Proportion of male college graduates, 1970.

7 = Proportion unemployed, 1975.

8 = Proportion living below poverty level, 1975.

Table 3 shows the relation of the disbursements to each county for each agency to county characteristic. All of them were highly related to share of total and manufacturing employment which explains a large part of the variance of each. These measures also reflect urbanization or differentiation.

Table 3: Proportion of Bonds, Grants, or Loans This County Holds of All Such Funds Held by 51 Upstate New York Counties Correlated with County Characteristics.

	Pearson's r							
	1	2	3	4	5	6	7	8
Proportion of all upstate Industrial Revenue Bonds issued by this county	.98#	.93#	.54#	-.45#	.38#	.31	-.25	-.37*
Proportion of all upstate EDA loans/ grants received by this county	.58#	.57#	.15	-.30	.48#	.03	-.09	-.02
Proportion of all upstate NY Science and Technology Foundation grants received by this county	.90#	.85#	.44#	-.38*	.29	.50#	-.29	-.35*
Proportion of all upstate JDA loans received by this county	.83#	.85#	.50#	-.48#	.35*	.24	-.27	-.34
Proportion of all upstate UDAG received by this county	.84#	.83#	.55#	-.49#	.36#	.29	-.31	-.39*

#Significant at .01 level.
*Significant at .05 level.
  Same notes as for Table 2.

Only two other variables were related to the disbursements by any agency when the effect of share of employment was parceled out. The proportion of EDA loans/grants was related to the proportion of Democrat/Liberal registered voters. In a previous study, Young et al. (1984) found that such enrollment was related to the proportion of county expenditures for public assistance and welfare and to the ratio of county debt to total revenue. These facts of public assistance burdens and difficulty with meeting the demand suggest that Democratic counties so positioned would be alert to and in need of government assistance. Together, total employment and the proportion of Democratic/Liberal voter enrollment had a multiple correlation $R^2 = .42$, or explains 42 percent of the variance in disbursement of EDA funds, adding 8 percent to the variance explained by total employment alone.

The proportion of male college graduates was related to New York Science and Technology grants when the effect of employment share was parcelled out. Together, the two variables, total employment and the proportion of male college graduates, have a multiple correlation of $R^2 = .85$, and explains 85 percent of the variance, adding 4 percent to the variance explained by total employment above. Since New York Science and Technology Grants often go directly to colleges or universities, and since college graduates tend to cluster in college towns, this makes sense.

For disbursement to counties of Industrial Revenue Bonds, Job Development Authority loans, and Urban Development Action Grants, only share of employment was related, when its effect was parcelled out of other variables, despite the avowed intent of UDAG grants to help poverty areas. For Industrial Revenue Bonds, share of employment explained 96 percent of the variance, for Job Development Authority loans 69 percent of the variance, and for Urban Development Action Grants 71 percent of the variance.

Table 4: Proportion of Loans, Grants, and Bonds Issued in this County by Each Funding Agent Correlated with County Characteristics.

	Pearson's r							
	1	2	3	4	5	6	7	8

Proportion of all loans, grants,
bonds received by county
that were:

	1	2	3	4	5	6	7	8
Industrial Revenue Bonds	.22	.20	.32*	.00	-.12	.12	-.29	-.36*
loans/grants	-.19	-.18	-.32*	.01	.16	-.36*	.63#	.47*
NY S&TF grants	.17	.13	.11	-.09	.01	.74#	-.33*	-.28
JDA loans	-.11	-.09	-.04	.05	-.02	-.12	-.20	-.02
this county	-.01	.01	.04	.00	-.13	-.01	-.20	.01

#Significant at .01 level.
*Significant at .05 level.

1 = Total employment in the county as proportion of total employment in 52 upstate counties.

2 = Total manufacturing employment in the county as proportion of total manufacturing employment in 52 upstate counties.

3 = Average family income, 1975.

4 = Proportion of votes registered as Republican, Conservative, 1968.

5 = Proportion of votes registered Democrat, Liberal, 1968.

6 = Proportion of male college graduates, 1970.

7 = Proportion unemployed, 1975.

8 = Proportion living below poverty level, 1975.

Relation of Characteristics of Counties to Share of County Funds Secured from the Various Agencies

Table 4 shows the relation of county characteristics to the <u>share of the total county funds</u> secured from each of the several agencies, allowing another perspective.   Share secured from issuance of Industrial Revenue Bonds was related positively to average family income and negatively to the proportion living below poverty level. Since bonds are issued mainly in large amounts and involve mainly large corporations, this is reasonable. The share of county funding secured from the EDA is related strongly to unemployment ($r = .63$) and also to the proportion living below poverty level, and negatively to average income and proportion of male college graduates. In neither case does it mean that counties with these characteristics got more grants/loans because of them, but merely that a larger proportion of the county's total loans came from that source. This is in line with the mission of the EDA and its stated criteria. The proportion of county funds secured from the New York Science and Technology Foundation is highly related to the proportion of male college graduates ($r = .74$). This also makes sense in terms of the stated purposes of the foundation's funding. There were no county characteristics that explained shares of county funds secured from the JDA or UDAG funds.

The Rome Labs

Another federal attempt to aid industry are the 700 government laboratories that exist for government purposes but for which Congress has passed legislation urging these to help industry.
-quote from "Photonics Spectra", March 1996-

In the case of the US, the big potential participants in technology transfer are in the vast network of federal labs that has become an integral part of the national economy since World War II. Much of this network -- most obviously the Department of Energy's weapons labs like Sandia and Lawrence Livermore -- are monuments to the Cold War years when money was no object in checkmating the military might of the Soviets. Today, with that threat extinguished -- and replaced by a strident demand for governmental austerity -- programs for transferring the labs' technology have become the major rational for keeping them in business.

The size of the governmental enterprise at issue here is truly awesome. In all, the US maintains more than 700 labs employing a total of nearly a million people, of whom approximately 170,000 are scientists and engineers. Some of these facilities -- principally those under the auspices of NASA and the National Institutes of Health -- aren't progeny of the Cold War; but the ones that are may be living on borrowed time.

At best, they must accept the prospect of funding cuts and restructuring in the years immediately ahead. At worst, they are candidates for extinction if they can't carve out new roles for themselves through technology transfer -- specifically, by making their physical assets and scientific talent available to the private sector to bolster the economy and enhance national competitiveness.

Editorial Comment

The labs include labs operated by the Department of Agriculture, the Department of Defense, Department of Commerce, Department of Energy and Department of Transportation, as well as national labs and labs of the Atomic Energy Commission. For a long time the government has wanted these labs to transfer technology to industry, especially in our post-war world. Have they succeeded in this transfer?

The Rome, NY "Superlab"

The Rome Laboratory has been at Griffiss Air Base in Rome, New York since 1951. It has recently been under consideration for closure but has survived to date. It had an initial staff of 426 people. It now has a staff of 1100. Eighty-seven percent are civilians: 6 percent have PhD.s, 27 percent have masters degrees, and 36 percent have bachelors degrees. For the year 1992, the Rome Laboratory had a budget of approximately $293 million. It became one of the Air Force's four "Superlabs" in 1990. It specializes in command control, communications and intelligence research and development, and its scientists and engineers are also involved in software engineering, computer architecture, artificial intelligence, solid state sciences, signal processing, electronics systems and photonics.

The Rome Lab does research primarily for the Air Force, but its products have great potential for private industry. Its photonics center (established in 1971) is one of the world's leading facilities exploring advanced optical components and system concepts for dramatically improved information processing speed, and for communications throughout and data storage in systems which are physically small and highly reliable. In 1989 the Lab's photonics research space was quadrupled. Photonics makes it possible to store vast amounts of information in a small place, such as an encyclopedia on a disc the size of a long-playing phonograph record. Any information on it can be retrieved in seconds. Thus this change from electronics to light marks a watershed. It has great potential. Is this being transferred to industrial production?

An Air Force fact sheet states:

> In simplest terms, photonics is the use of light, or neutral photons, instead of electricity, or charged electrons, to process, store or transmit information. Photonic devices have the potential to be lighter, cheaper to build and use, faster, carry or store more information and are less susceptible to "noise" or electromagnetic interference. From a military standpoint, immunity to interference is critical for secure, jam-resistant communications.
>
> The worldwide consensus among scientists is that photonics may lead to a technological revolution in the 21st century just as electronics revolutionized the 20th century.
>
> In the United States, electronics is a $200 billion-a-year industry and growing about 10 percent annually. On the other hand, photonics is a $10 billion-a-year industry growing at a rate of about 50 percent annually. Predictions indicate the growth rate of the electronics industry will decline, while the growth rate of the photonics industry will remain at about 50 percent annually for the near future. Some already familiar photonics applications include fiber optic telephone systems, compact disks (the forerunner of which was developed by Rome Lab), supermarket price scanners and laser scalpels used for precision surgery.
> [January 1991]

The Rome Laboratory says that "Our Corporate Philosophy is people oriented, focused on our customers and based on a commitment to quality and excellence."

All United States research and development laboratories are united in the Federal Laboratory Consortium for Technology. If someone were to approach Rome Laboratory for help it was not qualified to give, it could refer the person to the correct lab through the Consortium. Legislation was passed in 1980 requiring federal labs to be active in technical cooperation. It was amended and improved in 1984, 1986, 1988, and 1991. In 1986 legislators established royalties for federal inventors, mandated that technology transfer be considered in employee evaluations, and allowed labs to negotiate licensing agreements, exchange personnel with research partners, and allowed personnel to participate in commercial development to the extent that there is no conflict of interest. In 1988 legislation was passed emphasizing the need for public and private cooperation, establishing centers for transferring technology, establishing industrial Extension Services within states, and extending royalty payment requirements to nongovernmental employees of federal labs. In 1991 further emphasis was given to establish model programs for national defense labs to "demonstrate successful relationships between federal government, state and local governments, and small business."

Can a military lab "reach out" to local industry?

The Rome Lab has a staff whose task it is to spread to industry its photonics capabilities. It has developed college programs cooperatively with the Mohawk Valley Community College, the SUNY Institute of Technology at Utica/Rome and the Rochester Institute of Technology. The Lab's personnel travel around New York State participating in workshops and seminars. The Lab has a small business office, a contracting directorate and staff whose job is outreach to business. Is it doing all it can?

The Photonics center's staff is 33 in number, 24 of them civilians. Five have doctoral degrees, seven have masters degrees. In 1989 the newly-enlarged center was dedicated by the commanding general of the Air Force Systems Command soon after he and then-New York Governor Mario Cuomo signed a joint agreement to foster cooperative research in photonics. Pursuant to these joint aims, the New York Photonics Development Corporation (PDC) was established by Oneida County, Rome Laboratory, and the state, and occupies a small office at the Mohawk Valley Community College, just outside the gate to the Air Base. Its purpose, to serve primarily small- and medium-sized companies in New York and the Northeast. It purports to help industry by:

* Inventorying the technological needs of New York State's photonics companies;

* Communicating Rome Laboratory's offerings to these same companies;
* Assessing the case of converting their products for sale to commercial markets;
* Providing companies with application and product engineering assistance, as well as business assistance

The N.Y. Photonics Development Corporation's director is a former designer of mainframe computers, eminently qualified to do the job.

What has happened? Has the Rome Lab stimulated the photonics industry in its immediate environment, or around the state, or in the northeastern United States?

As of 1992, Rome Labs had developed cooperative research and development agreements with only twenty companies nationwide. These included some of the largest in the country: General Electric, Northrup, General Dynamics, ITT, Gruman, Westinghouse, and AT&T Bell Laboratories. Several of these are among the prime military contractors in New York State. This list was provided by Rome Lab.

Nor has the Rome Lab benefitted small firms in other ways. Even on supplying goods and parts for contractors for all kinds of goods and services used, twenty-six percent of the contracts were with small firms; the rest with large firms and universities. Nineteen percent of the contracts were with New York firms, and these with only twenty-three companies. Specifically, sixteen contracts were with eleven small New York companies out of 274 contracts existing in 1992. Was the Rome Lab providing these small companies with photonics technology? Not at all: these companies supplied goods to the Lab and to Griffiss Air Force Base.

We conducted a survey in the four counties around Rome: Oneida, Madison, Herkimer and Otsego. The Base and the Lab together were fourth in importance among large businesses in the area being sold to by the firms; but only 13 percent of the firms were doing business with either one. To break this down a bit more, eleven percent had business with the Base or Lab; two percent did business with, or worked for, one or the other. Four percent worked for the Base or Lab, and one percent bought goods or services from the Base or Lab. Only one firm was a spin-off from the Base or Lab.

We can conclude that the Labs work with only a few large companies nationwide and a small number of small companies, especially in the region around the Base. But they do not supply these small companies with the technology transfer they are mandated to deliver. Only so little, despite repeated Congressional couragement? This is the reality of the situation despite boasts by the Rome Lab about technical accomplishments for the Air Force, as published in the *Mohawk Flyer* and the *Utica Observer Dispatch* in 1992 and 1993. At that time the U.S. Government was threatening to close the Lab, along with the Air Base. This decision was recinded later because it was deemed too economically damaging to the area. Was it, really?

Spreading the Word: Not a Good Record

For the Rome Lab personnel assigned to spreading the word, this is not a good record; and the director of the Photonics Development Corporation tells a similar story. By 1993 in counties adjacent to the Lab, the PDC had put twelve companies in touch with the Lab. The director had also worked with three other firms with whom the Lab "might develop a relationship." A few other firms -- nine --- had a working relationship with Rome Lab, and two of these were spin-offs. But neither one was involved in photonics! Of the eighteen photonics firms in Oneida and Madison counties, none were spin-offs from the Rome Labs, and the story was similar state-wide. By 1994, the director of the PDC said that not much progress had been made, despite much effort. The Rome Lab had a new commanding officer more open to outside connections, but had suffered budget cuts that diminished its capacity to work with outside companies.

By the end of 1994, the Photonics Development Corporation had been busy for upward of five years trying to get the Rome Lab to work with small- and medium-sized businesses around New York State, with very limited success. There are, according to the Director, some 400 photonics companies in New York State. Overall, they are working without the cutting-edge knowledge that the Rome Lab could provide.

Is this case unique? We do not think so. In October of 1993, a *New York Times* article described the troubles that the Sandia National Laboratories, a nuclear research lab located in New Mexico, was having in making its products available to industry via the Martin Marietta Corporation. This situation could be repeated at many other national labs.

Why have these technology transfer efforts met with so little success? It is unarguable that the 700 U.S.-funded labs, engaged in research and development of a highly scientific and successful sort, could provide research and development assistance to large companies, and more especially to small companies. Small companies have few resources of their own and desperately need help. Here is this treasure trove of goodies, that doesn't seems to transfer to private industry, despite different kinds of efforts over a long period of time, and motivation provided by Congress. Why has the transfer not taken place?

Why Not? Secrecy

One answer is the secrecy in which these labs are enmeshed. When we first went to the Rome Lab and asked for a list of companies with which they worked, we were told that the Commander would not permit the list to be given out. It was secret. We appealed to our Congressman to intercede, and the list was immediately sent. Secrecy is not fertile ground for technology transfer.

The Rome Lab now has a new Commander with changed views. But progress is still slow. Why? The main mechanism created by the PDC for working with companies is a joint venture resulting in a joint patent, with research contributed by the PDC as well as the Rome Lab. But small- and medium-sized companies that need technical information do not have the capital to enter into a joint research venture of this type. There is no mechanism that exists for simply transferring information to a company that needs it. How can this be done?

Because the staff of the Rome Lab has been cut instead of enlarged, it seems that the U.S. government has given up on this approach to the spread of valuable technology beyond its own laboratories. Should it give up? If photonics is the wave of the future it should not. It should be making strenuous efforts to transfer information, education and skill, by public information pushes, by releasing patents anyone could use -- by some means, making public what has been private. Why should we taxpayers fund labs which do so little for us?

Something new is needed, a stockpile of information freely given and available, through labs, university and extension efforts -- free information and patents available for a small fee. Something similar to the Cooperative Extension service of colleges of agricultural research is needed: an industrial extension system.

Congress has repeatedly called for technology transfer from these labs to industry. The many public service programs initiated by the U.S. government toward high-technology industry speak for the importance of technological development in industry. Yet these high-powered labs, with a great store of technology easily convertible to industrial production, sit on top of this storehouse of information, transferring very little to private industry. New mechanisms are needed, along with a new attitude.

As of August 27, 1994, Rome Lab was scheduled to be closed in another round of base closing. New York's Senator Daniel Patrick Moynihan protested the close-down and after negotiations it is still open. Was he right to keep it open?

Conclusions

We started with three questions. The first was whether disbursement of funds followed economic peaks and troughs, or was related to business cycles. An examination of disbursements of each fund in each of the 52 counties over time revealed no relation at all to economic cycles.

With all of the five agencies disbursement of funds was highly related to the share of upstate employment in that county. In turn, this measure is highly related to urbanization, population, and differentiation (Young et al., 1984). Beyond this, disbursement was related in the case of the EDA to Democratic/Liberal party enrollment that, in turn, reflects pressures on county funds for welfare and public assistance. Science and Technology funds go to counties with high proportions of college graduates, reflecting its mission directed at innovation and involving colleges and universities directly.

Looking at the matter from a different perspective, that is, what share of each county's funds are derived from each agency, affluent counties derive proportionally more from Industrial Revenue Bonds, counties with high unemployment and poverty from the EDA, and counties with high proportions of college graduates from New York Science and Technology. These tendencies are consistent with the nature of the agencies and their funding policies. We emphasize that if counties with high unemployment get a greater share of their funds from the EDA, this does not mean they are getting more money overall. Shares of county funds acquired from different agencies do differ, though total amounts secured do not, in the main, do so. Affluent counties derive a high proportion from Industrial Revenue Bonds, and poorer counties from EDA funds. Those with a higher proportion of male college graduates derive a higher share of county funds from New York Science and Technology as well as more funds in total. But, from the agency's point of view, for three of them, disbursement is highly related to total employment and nothing else, regardless of the stated missions.

What does this imply for the many regional, county, city, and town agencies engaged in economic development? In the first place, every county in the state has an economic development organization and we have no way of knowing what would happen if a county did not have one. Much of their effort is helping firms and local governments to secure various kinds of funds from state and federal sources. Is this effort pointless? The results of this research indicate that their efforts might not result in more funding, but without them a county might be disadvantaged. We do not know. But they surely have great effect on the way the money is used for a great variety of possible purposes and put together in a great variety of possible combinations or packages, as we will describe. They also offer a variety of other kinds of help needed to make the funds work effectively: site selection, employee selection and training, management and business planning, zoning and other problems with local or state government authorities, and many others. Local agencies have become necessary conduits for state and federal funding programs, helping aim them at local problems in unique ways and providing the auxiliary help needed to make them work. These agencies have become institutionalized as part of local structures, even if they do not seem to alter the amounts of money received.

We also reviewed the efforts of another government attempt to aid industry, The Rome Labs at Griffiss Air Base. We considered that despite Congressional legislators, a lab staff and efforts by the State that little had come out of it in the way of technology transfer. This is important for the state, but these labs are one of 700 labs in the United States operating in a similar manner..

We will go on to see how federal and state programs work at the local level.

Chapter 8

The Beginnings, Structure, and the Government Context

State legislation and state development programs made possible the existence of many local development organizations and stimulated the activities of others. Therefore we shall look at how these local development organizations started, their continuing relations with government, and describe their formal structure as it is constrained by legislation that enabled local governments to organize development organizations. We shall be examining both formal aspects of these organizations and the nature of their ties to government.

The Start Up

The local development organizations started up over a long period of time. A few of the organizations have been operating for many years, such as the Metropolitan Development Association of Syracuse. However, the Industrial Development Agencies date from 1969 on, when the legislation was passed. Many did not start immediately, and some only a few years ago. Many did little for a number of years. Twenty-five started in the peak years between 1969 and 1973 just after the bond legislation was passed. Eleven antedated the bond legislation. Twenty-four were started in the years from 1974 to 1987, including ten in the last seven years. From the outset the organizations continued to vary in many respects, as they did in their starting date.

Around 1984 or 1985, many organizations seem to have gained new strength, possibly due to an upturn in the state and national economy, and consequently, expansion and modification. They changed direction, broadened their scope, mobilized, took on new staff or changed staff, and increased activity. Industrial arms of Chambers of Commerce have been organized. Thus, in both start-up and in a recent phase of increased activity, state-wide events and pressures have probably resulted in a flurry of local action.

In addition, in a number of regions, mobilization took place seemingly in response to local events.   Why mobilization occurs sometimes seems to be a response to a perception of a major economic problem confronting the area, or a disaster or catastrophe.   Sometimes it appears to be a new opportunity, but in any case it is a perception of a sudden change in the area's economy.   In some counties, Erie for example, mobilization and organization of economic agencies seemed to be a response to the closing down of the steel mills leaving many thousands unemployed.   The close out of older, larger industries, often branch plants (a crisis that occurred in several areas of the state) signaled the end of the older, smokestack heavy-industry based structure.   Along the Southern Tier counties, the destructive floods of 1977 were followed by various relief programs.   The flood is spoken of as a watershed in this area, and the relief programs led to a larger continuing effort.

The Tug Hill Commission, which operates in parts of a number of northern counties, was formed in 1972 to cope with a threatened land sale by a large corporation that would upset the local economy.   The Development Authority of the North Country was authorized in 1985 in response to a locally organized effort to cope with the expansion of Fort Drum and its effect on the several counties involved.   The Metropolitan Development Association of Syracuse was also originally organized in 1959 to meet a threat of a move of a large Chrysler Corporation plant, and more than thirty years later the organization is strong and active.   In all cases, the work of the agencies have widened beyond their original scope and continued well beyond the immediate crisis that brought them into being.

Another situation that gives rise to the creation of a new agency or radical reorganization of an old one is dissatisfaction with the work of existing agencies so that local leaders band together to bring about a change.   An example of this is the reorganization of the Adirondack North Country Association.   It had existed as a small organization for thirty years, though it had been involved in some important projects: getting the Northway from Albany north to the east of the Adirondacks (Highway 187) put through; assisting in attracting the 1980 Winter Olympics to Lake Placid; getting the Amtrack running from Albany to Montreal.   In 1984 it adopted a nine point program for development of the fourteen Adirondack and North Country counties and hired a new full-time executive director.   The program had multiple foci: agriculture, tourism, transportation and recreation, industrial development, forestry, crafts, education, health and human services, and international cooperation.   A group of leaders from the area went to Albany and met with the legislative delegation from the area.   As a result, the legislature made a financial grant to the organization two years running.   As we traveled over the area talking to economic developers, many mentioned their participation in ANCA and its work in favorable terms.   It appears to be helping the region to think as a region, and the local group's contact with their legislators as a group may have been instrumental in causing the latter to think and act as a delegation in the interest of the area as a whole.

An example of another type of opportunity was the opening of Highway 17, the Southern Tier Expressway, running from east to west through the counties along New York's southern border.   It was funded by the Appalachian Regional Commission in order to develop a poor area.   A town agency in Hornell, New York, became very active when it acquired transportation access to the rest of the state.   Before that, a staff member said that if you wanted to go to Corning, the main town in the county and county seat, you would hop on the noon train.   When the highway came through 4 miles north of the town, the community put through a four-lane road to it and began to develop the community. Organization start-up, reorganization or mobilization, then, often has been a response to a crisis or a suddenly acquired opportunity but continues and widens its efforts long after the stimulating event.

Thus, start-up or mobilization of an agency may be due to a state or federal policy or pressure, a local initiative, a new opportunity, or a perceived change of a dramatic nature in the local economy, or a combination of both need and opportunity.   We will see that local agencies continue to differ in many ways and we will suggest some reasons for this.

Structure of the Organizations

The Industrial Development Agencies, that comprise the majority of the 61 county agencies interviewed, are quasi-governmental.   For a new local Industrial Development Agency to be set up requires a vote of the state legislature and a vote of the local legislature in the locality at issue. The local legislative body then appoints a board of seven directors. This board of directors has authority to operate the agency including appointing staff, approving budgets, and approving all bonds issued.

Many of the IDAs and eight of the remaining twelve other agencies were also Local Development Corporations. These are organized by at least twenty-five people in the locality at issue, mostly bankers and other businessmen, incorporated, and the certificate of incorporation is filed with the state. They are then designated as a Local Development Corporation, that is, permitted to process New York State Job Development Authority loans.

Forty-nine of the organizations were IDAs, many of these were also LDCs, and eight more were LDCs only. Four of the IDAs were combined with a county government department, and two were units of county government. We will see that most of the federal and state funding agencies deal with units of local government, and not-for-profit organizations, though in some few cases they deal directly with business.

In addition to being authorized or authenticated by government, many organizations had other connections with local government. Many were housed in government offices and received funds from county government. Many used local government loans or other funds in their programs.

But most organizations, whether IDAs or not, tried to distance themselves from government. One way of doing this was by setting up organizations parallel to the IDAs not subject to government control, using the same offices and the same staff, but with different boards of directors, different charters and methods of organization, and different sources of funds and different programs. The staffs typically used all resources in the several organizations which they served in putting together programs of help. But having the other organizations set up freed them from strict control by local government and enabled them to broaden their activities, react quickly and in new ways without having to be approved by the IDA government-appointed board of directors. Sometimes the board of directors of the parallel organization was larger and more diversified as well.

Thirty-one agencies had only one organization under the same roof, twenty-seven had two organizations, three had three or more. Of those agencies housing only one organization under the same roof, twenty-three were IDAs. Two of these were integrated into planning departments. Three were Chambers of Commerce, and five were other types of organization. Thus there is a great diversity of form of organization among these agencies performing similar industrial development tasks on a county level.

Another way in which the organizations distanced themselves from local government was physically. Even though forty-nine organizations had connections with county government by virtue of their being authorized by county government or actually being part of it, only twenty-one were housed in county office buildings. Thirteen shared offices with Chambers of Commerce, and twenty-two had their own office space that they owned or rented. Five part-time executive directors operated their agencies out of their shops, offices or homes. This evidenced the desire of most of the agency executives to distance themselves and their work from government, to stand alone as, at most, quasi-governmental agencies, though clearly related to local government by various ties.

Thirty-eight of the sixty-one received some of their operating funds from the county government, but only sixteen received all of their funds from the county. Typically at the beginning, the county provided administrative funds to set up an IDA. But, if at all successful, before long the agency developed other sources of revenue. These include fees charged business for issuing bonds, from 0.5 percent to 1.5 percent, mostly in the 1 percent range. Since an agency may have issued 25 or 50 million dollars of bonds in a year, this can amount to substantial sums. Some agencies earn money from the land and buildings they own. A number raise part of their funding through member contributions, and a few receive state, town, or city funds. Occasionally there is an EDA grant, a HUD grant, or a line item in the state budget for some agency activity.

Nine agencies received funds from county government and from fees charged for issuing bonds. Seven operated on such fees alone. Five received their funding from Chambers of Commerce. Four got allotments from county government and also from contributions by individuals or corporations. For the remaining twenty counties there were fifteen different combinations of sources of funding from county budgets, fees, income on property owned, contributions, and the Chambers of Commerce.

Operating funds or capacity can be quite different than an agency's own funds. Often a county agency will exercise the bonding capacity of cities, towns, or villages within the county that have IDAs without executive directors. They will often be asked to manage part or all of the money a unit of government receives as the result of the repayment by a business of a Housing and Urban Development loan. Such repayment goes not to the federal government that extended the loan, but to the local government where the business is located and to which the federal government has made the loan which, in turn, makes a loan to the business. Sometimes Housing and Urban Development Community Development Block Grants are used for industrial parks or other economic development purposes. Thus the developer can draw on resources other than those of his agency, and the resources a developer can use may be much larger than those to which his agency has title.

Twenty-two of the organizations raise money through member contributions, and of these nine are themselves Chambers of Commerce or receive money from them. Five of these are industrial development arms of Chambers of Commerce; that is, the Chamber has a separate department and staff hired for this purpose. Thirteen have offices located in Chambers of Commerce with which they have close working relations if they are not a department of the Chamber. Industrial development is a relatively new specialty for local Chambers of Commerce. We see that they often take the lead in larger cities where they have played a strong role long before the IDAs came into existence.

In sum, though set up by acts of local legislative bodies, the IDAs act as pretty much autonomous units. Their own board, not typically comprised of a majority of government officials or legislators, has the authority to run the agency. While many receive county funds, most do not depend solely on these. Most agencies physically distance themselves from official county offices. Many of the IDAs have set up some not-for-profit agency along with the IDA. And a number of economic development organizations have no connection with county government. Thus they stand between government and business. They often have governmental authority necessary for dealing with nation and state, and yet are not part of government. They stand apart and, for the most part, operate autonomously.

Developers are constantly working with various units of government at the state and local level, and with elected officials or administrators in various state departments for a wide range of reasons. Because of the way these issues came up in the interviews, these types of cooperation may well be underreported. But all but sixteen agencies reported some kind of working relationship. Of five more, we do not know about their relations with officials or legislators. Nine agencies were parts of planning departments or located in planning departments, and ten more kept in touch with or worked with planning departments. A number of developers are themselves planners, and regional planning offices offer backup to county developers. The industrial or economic development job is different than planning, but planners offer support to the developers by way of information, assessments, evaluations, plans, zoning, mapping, etc.

Thirty-six agencies mentioned helping business with issues such as zoning, regulations, licenses and the like, and think it part of the job to help cut red tape, and to know the right person to ask. When asked about lobbying or intercession with respect to government or legal matters, seventeen reported lobbying or sponsoring state legislation, five through the Chamber of Commerce. All of the IDAs belong to a state-wide organization, the New York State Economic Development Council. This organization keeps in close touch with legislation and legislators, and its executive director reports that it is often consulted on legislation concerning economic development. In fact, present officers were instrumental in organizing the original IDA legislation. Therefore all of the IDAs are represented through its efforts, and may do no direct lobbying. The Chambers of Commerce are also very actively involved in legislative issues and organizations connected with them are taken care of in this way. The not-for-profit organizations are not allowed to lobby, but even they keep in touch. Sixteen agencies reported keeping in close touch and asking help from elected officials or administrators at a state level. When issues are about to come up in the legislature, the state representatives in a given district will often organize a meeting of developers in their constituency to seek their opinions. At least one United States Congressman also keeps in touch with developers in his district by monthly meetings. Several agencies have had special legislation proposed or passed to solve particular local problems, including budget items for incubators, race track ordinances, and special permits.   Twelve agencies have been involved in organizing Foreign Trade Zones in their counties, sometimes locating them in their own industrial parks. A Foreign Trade Zone allows flexibility for a business in arranging when to pay tariffs on raw materials or parts it imports and finished products it exports, and has been more popular, therefore, in counties bordering on Canada.

In addition to the infrastructure necessary for their industrial parks, twenty-nine have worked on other problems of infrastructure in their counties. Infrastructure development is not their primary purpose and they seldom are the lead agency for such purposes. These include a variety of types of downtown development including face-lifts, buildings, shopping malls, county office buildings, and renewal and remodeling of various sorts. These sometimes include comprehensive development or redevelopment of a downtown area or a waterfront area. These types of projects are also often the focus of city or town economic development agencies.   They include a number of transportation problems: roads, airports, ports, bridges, urban transit, bus terminals and, in fourteen cases, agencies bought or in some other way rescued spur railroads abandoned by Conrail, but deemed necessary to local factories. Two of these built new ones. They also deal with water and sewer development problems and impact assessments, as well as natural gas and energy recovery. In several cases they have gotten into housing development; in at least one case such intervention was deemed necessary to attract and hold needed labor.   Thus their relations to various levels and agencies of government are extensive and varied, and in all cases they act as an intermediary agent who is trying to intercede to make government, public officials and public services helpful to industrial development. In such efforts, they go wherever the problem takes them.

Summary

The founding of many of the local development organizations was made possible by state and county legislation. Whatever their origins, their goal is economic and especially industrial development of their areas, and they define development as jobs. Despite the common stimulus and common goal, the organizations vary greatly in structure. Some are part of local government, some are quasi-governmental, some are quasi-governmental but also operate parallel private organizations, and some are totally private. They vary also in sources of authority, sources of funds, and physical location. Stinchcombe (1965) did not define what he meant by similarity of structure, but it is difficult to imagine how organizations with such fundamental differences in basic structure could be considered the same. Nor does he define what he considers the same time, but these organizations were created in response to the same opportunities, with similar constraints, for the same purposes and within a few years. As we continue, we will note that within this span of time, a number of them have reorganized, changed programs, directions and geographic areas to be covered. The evidence here does not support the Stinchcombe hypothesis that organizations founded at the same time are similar in structure and do not change. On first look, these organizations should be similar, but they are very different.

The Industrial Development Agencies exist because of state legislation and are accountable to county, city, and town governments. Local Development Corporations exist to process JDA loans. These two types of organizations, often overlapping, comprise the vast majority of local development organizations. In addition, they utilize programs of a wide variety of other state and federal programs, work with many government agencies and department at all levels on a wide variety of tasks, and make government contact and intercession one of their main tasks.

Federal and state funding agencies set the stage for local organization by decentralizing their efforts and working through local governments and organizations. Since local governments often do not have their own developers, they, in turn, work through the local development organizations. State and federal agencies further make necessary local coordination of funding by supplying only limited portions of funds needed by a business, and by their intent on supplementing, not supplanting, local private funding efforts. In addition, the local development organizations keep in touch with elected officials, lobby directly or through other state and local organizations, are consulted by and in touch with legislators about proposed legislation, and occasionally sponsor special bills. They work closely with local government officials and departments, and with state administrators, and know whom to call for any kind of problem a business may have with government, or for any kind of help that might be available from government. When community infrastructure is necessary to economic development, they work closely with local government to develop it. Local developers spend a considerable portion of their time dealing with government in various ways and in systematically keeping in touch. They try to be apolitical, however, maintain good relations with all, and remain apart from political conflict, yet able to deal with whomever they need in the course of work for their clients. Thus local development organizations, varying in many ways, share a main task of working with government in behalf of local economic development.

Chapter 9

The Developers and their Business Development Activities

The local development organizations also face the world of business, of private enterprise. The nature of the developer himself characterizes this side of the organization. Sociologists tell us that the organizational role dictates the character of the person who fills it. If so, what he is like tells us much about the organization. We will look at the developers and we will continue to explore what the organizations actually do for business and how they do it. That is, we will look at them as natural systems, at their actual behavior in its informal aspects. What they do includes a great variety of activities, many shared by a number of organizations. But the program of each agency differs from the others, and on a project-to-project and day-to-day basis. Above all, each project has unique aspects, has to be constructed to fit the individual case and in a timely and responsive fashion. In this way the work of the organizations resembles the way in which a business has to operate to survive. Little of what the organizations do for business is specified in their charters. Their formal organization sets the most minimal constraints on them and provides only the most basic opportunity. Most of what they do is the developer's choice and creation, decided on an informal basis as problems, pressures, and opportunities arise.

What about the people who staff these agencies? One such person that I asked to describe his job said that he might be called a public entrepreneur. Others whom I asked to react to this description found it very comfortable. They also use the word facilitator. They also, of course, describe themselves as economic developers, but this does not convey as much of the essence of the job. What are they like? They are imaginative, always thinking about new ways to use resources or meet problems. They have a detailed, up-to-the-minute knowledge of the local economic resources, pressures and opportunities, and the people involved and of government programs and people. They are willing to take risks, to take responsibility, and to make quick decisions. They respond to needs and opportunities, and have a way of turning a problem, such as a vacant factory or school building, into an opportunity. They feel it's their job to learn new things as necessary, to become an expert on health regulations if that is what the problem involves. They have to be able to supervise building construction, deal with property, land, buildings, railroads,and infrastructure. They, of course, have to understand business costs, profits and losses, and business management. They have to deal effectively with government officials and agencies and know whom to call for what problem. They deal with a wide variety of government agencies and officials as well as unions, educators, and business people. Even while they work their way through a labyrinth of official and unofficial relationships, they have to avoid letting themselves or their agencies become the center of conflict. Some have backgrounds in planning, some in government, and some of the younger ones have had a career since the beginning in economic development. But more often they have a background in business, either in corporations or often they have owned or still own a business of their own. Nearly all funds, federal, state and county, are loans, not grants. Nothing of a material nature is given to business. What business gets is lower taxes, lower interest rates, and sometimes more moderate pay back terms. The shared philosophy is to help business help itself. Whether or not they have a business background or have been entrepreneurs, developers have to think and act like business people and entrepreneurs.

Many of the more successful ones have cosmopolitan experience and a cosmopolitan point of view. That is, they see local problems and opportunities from the point of view of the wider economy and society of which they are part. There are a number of developers who have retired from responsible jobs in business or government, often in cities far from the county, and thus can function from a wider perspective, but many of the younger developers have also had experience in the wider world. When asked, they will say that this experience provides contacts. But probably more importantly, it enables them to see how their county can fit into the wider economy and adjust to wider pressures. A colleague who participated in one interview said that what impressed him the most about that developer was how well his program was tailored to fit the needs and resources of the county and how well he understood these. That, despite much that they have in common, is what impresses the interviewer about most of these people, that they know their own area and tailor programs to meet its needs. Developers typically give off an aura of the right person in the right job. They love their work, and their enthusiasm is contagious and helps advance their causes. They are idealistic and convey the impression that they are engaged in an important work that helps society. The universal goal is job creation and preservation. Business is not seen as profits or products, but as jobs.

Despite their very varied backgrounds, the developers are similar in many ways. The phrase "public entrepreneurs" encapsulates a great deal about their attitudes and ways of work. The nature of the problem and the type of opportunities available to such organizations seem to call for entrepreneurs. They best fit this new organizational structure. As we went around the state meeting them, we began to think of the developers in terms of chess pieces. If one picked up any two of them and changed places (and they do move from agency to agency), both would act in similar ways in the new jobs. They might not do the exact same things as their predecessor, but the approach would be very similar, remarkably so considering the differences in their backgrounds. We have said that they make quick decisions, take responsibility, are very energetic and active, and imaginative. Whether they come from private enterprise or public service, they are best described as entrepreneurial.

Thirty-five have had experience in private enterprise; eighteen in corporations, and fourteen have owned their own business. Three more have had legal experience. Twelve have a background in planning, and eighteen in other kinds of government service. Two come from education, and nine started their careers in development. The backgrounds of three are unknown. Eighteen have had experience both in government and private enterprise. Until recently, few began their careers in development. Few formal training programs exist for economic development in universities and most drifted into it from other fields. But most of them, however they got where they are now, impress one as being very much at home in this new type of job that they did not envision or aim at in the beginning. It's as if they finally came into a job they have been waiting for and preparing for all of their lives. Their satisfaction and enthusiasm are evident and undoubtedly contribute much to their credibility and ultimate success.

We have spoken of their imaginative approach to problems and strengths of their counties and their ability to act in accordance with this knowledge. Some of their imagination is spent on organizational problems. Examples of this are the organization of a consortium of agencies within a county, the organization of inter-county marketing teams, development of volunteers who are given time from business to participate in agency work, conducting workshops about business needs for fire departments, police and other local services, and working to get the aged and women of childbearing age into the labor force in areas with a labor shortage, and in one case devising a development strategy through an internal community planning process involving public hearings and public participation. These innovative organizational approaches vary according to local problems and needs.

Others have developed innovative approaches to financing. These include selling properties to get money or buying properties to rent, issuing bonds that would give the agency funds over and above the immediate need to use for various other purposes, getting large one-time financial allocations from local or state government to set up revolving loan funds. In one case, an agency signs for loans and is responsible for their repayment, so it in turn can lend to Canadian companies. One even toyed with starting a bank.

In addition to the standard types of help widely prevalent, they have performed many other services and conceived many other plans in progress in individual cases. These include working on a fiber optics line to a super computer, providing systematic information on government contracts, organizing local industries to try to provide things previously bought outside the area, trying to organize a technical center for plastics research which various companies could use, and being prepared to give away free county lands to business. These examples illustrate the adventurous nature of the developers in solving problems and helping their counties to make progress.

Scott (1981:154) states that "individual professionals are subjected to a prolonged period of socialization and training in which they are expected to internalize standards, acquire a repertory of skills, and master a set of theoretical principles that will enable them to make decisions and act autonomously in a responsible and expert fashion." If we think of doctors, accountants, lawyers, or engineers we understand what this education and training entails. What is the socialization process for these developers that come from such a variety of backgrounds?

Within their first year on the job, most developers take a one-week Basic Economic Development Training Course offered by the New York Economic Development Council, one of several such courses offered in the country. This includes sessions offered by economic developers and other specialists on such topics as what to do with old buildings, establishing and operating revolving loan funds, the various sources of loans available to business and how to apply for and package them, and on marketing their area. Some start in a several-person agency as assistants. They also take other short training courses or workshops from time to time and most attend a day and a half-long update session each year, also offered by the New York Economic Development Council. Yet this amount of training is very little considering the variety of educational backgrounds and work experience of these developers compared with the training and internships offered other professionals. Of course, developers usually have college degrees, and a number have Masters' degrees in a relevant field such as business or planning. But these provide no direct training for this job. Other professional educations typically involve either an undergraduate degree or additional graduate training directly in the field in which they are to work, and many involve some type of internship as well. Of course, many of the state and federal programs on which the developers draw are the same, providing some common resources. But the range and complexity of the problems they deal with, and the degree of initiative and autonomy called for, make great demands on developers considering their limited opportunities for socialization into their jobs. While they have been provided with opportunities and some information, they have to deepen this knowledge on the job, and decide on their own when the establishment of an industrial park is a good idea, persuade those involved to proceed with it, and work out the process of getting it going with a network of people and agencies over a considerable period of time. It involves acquiring suitable land, access roads, water, sewer, heavy duty electricity, constructing buildings, and putting together funding packages to finance all of these. They then must find businesses to locate in the park and work out leases or terms of sale. This requires a good deal of imagination, independent initiative and skill that is not acquired in a short training course.

Working With Business

There is no standard program for an agency, only a range of opportunities and possible activities to choose from, a variety of different and sometime unique problems to solve, and the constant challenge of adapting opportunities to local needs.

Recruitment from Outside

In addition to connecting and interceding between business and government in various ways, economic development agencies perform a wide variety of industrial development tasks. One of these is recruitment of industry from outside, or marketing the area. Many people thinking of the job of economic development imagine it mainly as a matter of trying to induce industry to come from outside the area and move to or locate a branch in the area. Actually, a very small part of the developer's time is so employed despite the fact that only sixteen have no program for recruiting industry or, as they think of it, marketing their area. Either they or some other agency, such as the Chamber of Commerce, typically will have developed a multicolor, glossy brochure that can be sent out enlarging on the county's assets. Some have developed slide shows or video shows that they take about with them. Many participate in recruitment teams for a region or on a state-wide basis. Eighteen, either on their own or with the help of the State Department of Commerce, recruit abroad, especially in Canada. And occasionally a developer will make a trip to Europe or the Orient in behalf of his county.

There are a number of commercial research organizations that offer to do a research on the county, assess its potential in comparison to the nation, the state, and its own area, advise it on general and particular assets and problems, and end up with a list of industries for which it has good potential and on which it should target its recruiting; that is, they develop a marketing program. Substantial fees are charged for such efforts. It has not been possible to evaluate whether such efforts have borne fruit. The closest we have come to that is one agency that when asked assured us that the study had been well worth the money because it recommended just what the staff had itself decided should be done and helped convince the county that they were on the right track.

While some agencies do make strenuous efforts to market, have formal marketing programs, and spend substantial amounts of money on them ($150,000 for example), many others express skepticism about the results of marketing. Most, regardless of whether or not they have such a program, spend most of their time on existing industry. Of the forty-five agencies that have a marketing program, thirty of them have a formal program. This typically consists of targeting sets or types of industries, targeting geographic areas, sending out mailings of brochures and the like, following up responses and other contacts, conducting tours for those who accept invitations, and following up with help needed. Some give seminars or put on exhibitions in other places. Marketing also might include an advertising program in trade journals or attendance at trade or real estate shows. All of this can be very expensive relative to agency budgets, and it is difficult to assess results. This is probably why even those organizations that carry on a marketing program put only a small number of eggs in that particular basket.

A question that is difficult to solve is what to regard as a good enough return for marketing efforts. If a major program induces a small number of industries to come, maybe one or two, is this enough? Perhaps a few such industries will employ substantial numbers of people over many years, people who might be on welfare rolls or move out of the county but who now pay taxes and have become consumers. The problem of evaluation involves long-range issues.

Working with Existing Local Business

The main task for most developers is keeping in touch with and trying to maintain what industry they have, helping it solve whatever problems it has – to expand and to remain in the county and to remain prosperous. Existing industry gets most of the time and attention of developers. Only eleven have no visiting program, and they probably have much contact. All know a great deal about the county's economic and employment structure, its resources, and the existing businesses and industries. Twenty-five have formal visiting programs in the sense that they have a program for regular visiting of each firm in the county over a period of a year or eighteen months; or they have a special staff person who does nothing else. Sixteen more keep in touch, work on problems, but have a less organized and comprehensive program. For nine agencies, we do not know; this aspect of the work was not appreciated sufficiently at the beginning to get good information from early interviewees.

We included in the study only organizations that have programs of industrial development rather than those that deal only with retail trade or tourism. But most industrial development agencies will deal with whatever walk-in business they get; no one who walks in or calls will be simply turned away. Some deal with various types of business in addition to manufacturing, agriculture, retail trade, and tourism. All will at least talk with such people and try to refer them to other types of help in such a way that they are not wandering helplessly from agency to agency.

There is often a division of labor on the part of the set of agencies in a county where the Chambers of Commerce will mainly deal with retail trade or the tourist industry, and the Small Business Development Center will get referrals from small business. Most local development agencies give some kind of help to small, start-up business, but only a minority go as far as helping them develop business plans, which are indispensable to seeking funds from a bank or other agency. Only fourteen give no help to small business. Eighteen others only refer small business people to other more suitable agencies. Twenty-nine give some kind of direct help, sometimes in addition to referrals. Of these, only thirteen help with business plans. Though helping small business is not their major focus, that local development organizations do provide some help is corroborated the study of small start-up industries in New York State (Young and Francis, 1989). Twenty-five to 38 percent report getting such help.

In visits and other contacts, developers try to keep in touch with problems of industries in their areas. These might be expansion, threats to move, reorganizations of various kinds, labor difficulties, physical problems of suitable land and buildings, pollution control, remodeling or retooling of production, recruitment and training of employees. Sixteen of the agencies have helped with management or employee buy outs, particularly in the older industrial counties of the state. In the areas where traditional large industry was formerly the mainstay of the economy, such as steel or automobile production, many of the employers have been branch plants of larger corporations. In cases where a branch plant is being closed down or moved out, an agency will make an attempt to see if money for remodeling or expansion, or help with labor, will induce the plant to stay. They may also, if it seems suitable, and if there are adequate management people locally who could take over the business, see if they can help such people put together a financial package that will enable them to buy the business. Sixteen agencies have participated in buy outs that succeeded, four more tried one that did not work out, and two others said they encourage them.

Despite the reputation New York has for labor difficulties, such a reputation does not seem justified if one is to accept the developers' assessment. When asked if they intervene in labor problems, most developers said that they did not, largely because the county had none. In a majority of the upstate counties there are no unions. In those that have them, they have for the most part been relatively peaceful, free of strikes and stoppages. Of course, many of the newer, high-technology industries that are prospering in New York are not unionized. Where there have been difficulties in a minority of counties, developers are often willing to help out, talking to both sides, though a couple avoided such issues. However, labor problems of a different kind are mentioned. There are areas of high unemployment, and in some of these the unemployed may be poorly trained and educated for modern jobs. Other areas see labor shortages on the horizon and are wondering how to cope with these by recruiting labor from outside the county or trying to get older people and women in the child-bearing age back into the labor force. But conflict is seldom reported as a problem developers need to deal with.

For both incoming and existing industries, the agencies offer a variety of tangible kinds of help in organizing land and buildings, and infrastructure, and in assembling a variety of loans into an adequate financial package for buying, building, acquiring equipment, or remodeling. Indeed, it is for fixed capital purposes that most loan programs exist. But such tangible helps are part of a comprehensive, holistic approach to trying to help business to understand and solve its problems, and are never administered in a vacuum. In the first place, loans will not be given if the business is not sound, does not have a sense of direction, know what it is doing and how to do it, and, above all, have good management. So material help has to be given in the context of a comprehensive approach to a business's problems.

The industrial developers have a good deal to do with property. As we have already described, a number own and manage railroad spur lines. Of these, two operate the line as tourist attractions in addition to the industrial service they provide. A number help with a variety of types of infrastructure development. However, the main problem they deal with is one of finding and developing an industrial site and the needed buildings. Fifty of the sixty-one agencies have said that they help with site location, and the others probably do too. A number keep inventories of sites and buildings and keep these updated. In other counties the developer may not find it necessary to operate a computerized inventory because the sites may not be great in number and are well known to him. The public utilities also help with site selection. This is a service widely offered to new or expanding business.

In order to provide adequate sites and buildings many counties have industrial parks. Nineteen agencies own a park, and of these five own more than one. Three own land with buildings that they do not call parks, and six more own land. In twenty-five counties, industrial parks exist not owned by the agencies, but eight of these are managed by the agencies. Only twelve counties do not have industrial parks at all. These tend to be rural counties that do not think it realistic to anticipate or even may not want much industrial expansion, such as some of those in the Adirondack area. Park space is needed not only for incoming business but for local start-ups and expansion.

The more urban areas tend to have a variety of parks owned by various agencies, units of government, or private enterprise, and as one fills up, try to develop a new one. Most developers think that it is necessary to be able to offer industrial park space to industry, though all industries do not necessarily want to locate in a park. Some need much more space, for example, or less. A park offers a piece of land already judged suitable for and zoned for industrial use. It offers access roads, is typically close to a four-lane highway or sometimes an airport, and may have a railroad siding. It will have water sufficient to meet fire insurance requirements, sewage facilities adequate for industrial use, and heavy duty electricity. Many parks have flexible policies about selling and leasing. An industry may buy or lease land. It may build its own building, have one built for it, or go into a finished building or a shell building that it will finish, alone or with other industries. If the agency holds title to the property, taxes are forgiven, though in the case of bonds the agency may negotiate some payment in lieu of taxes. If a public agency holds title, building materials are not taxed. Industrial parks are so widely available that, except in some very rural counties, most economic developers feel that they cannot compete without one in recruiting industry. To be able to move into a park, usually nicely landscaped and with adequate parking space for employees along with infrastructure provided, saves a business an immense amount of time and trouble and, in some cases, money. It also is a known, problem-free entity. The agency, in developing a park, can draw on state transportation funds to develop access roads, and put together financial packages to finance the park. Therefore, agencies have to have personnel capable of coping with managing property and supervising building.

Lest the reader conceive of industrial parks as a suburban or rural phenomenon, let him note that cities feel as much need for these as other areas, indeed, more. Much urban land is zoned against industry, and many old buildings are not suitable for modern enterprises. Parks are needed to provide attractive and suitable space in areas where it is hard to find. Most county brochures contain pictures, diagrams and detailed description of industrial parks, signifying the value developers attached to them for attracting business. Ten agencies earn part of their upkeep from their property, though this is not its main purpose.

Property ownership and management is not confined to industrial parks. Agencies typically are challenged to find uses for industrial property left idle. In two counties, former steel mills, with the help of agencies, were turned into installations for repair of subway cars. Often a building will be turned over to local government for taxes, or donated by a company moving out or closing down. Or an agency will raise money to buy it, or will find a buyer. Old buildings are turned into shopping malls and incubators, or rehabilitated and divided up into smaller spaces for smaller factories if a user for the whole cannot be found. These may include also old school buildings. When a building comes vacant, the developer will think it over, come up with ideas for its use, proceed to recruit suitable buyers or tenants, and help with rehabilitation.

One of the uses for old buildings is as industrial incubator. An incubator typically offers low rents to start-up businesses that need small amounts of space. It also offers shared services, perhaps telephone, secretarial, shared office machines or receptionist, perhaps meeting rooms. There are many multi-tenant buildings that do not offer low rent or shared services, and these, properly speaking, are not incubators.

An incubator will often have a graduation policy, that is, the new business is given a period of years in which to grow sufficiently prosperous and stable, but then must move out. An incubator also has a manager, often an experienced businessman, who will keep in touch with tenants and give helpful advice. They normally avoid managing the businesses but may put them in touch with professional consultants, lawyers, accountants and the like, and sometimes secure a little free consultation for a beginning business. At times, they may delay rent payments in a bad period. Incubator tends to be a buzz word. Only fourteen counties now have one, but fourteen more are trying to get one. Two have buildings called incubators, but which do not provide shared services. Incubators, as one may deduce from their graduation policies and help to start-up firms, seldom make much profit. They are seen as useful in an urban context as a seed-bed for new business in an area where there is a large pool of firms from which to draw. They are also seen as useful in conjunction with an overall development plan, particularly in conjunction with a technical university. For instance, Rensselaer Polytechnic Institute started an incubator in an old college building, partly as a way in which ideas generated by Institute faculty and research could be developed commercially. The Institute also owns an industrial park, particularly for innovative high-technology business, and sees the two as part of an overall plan of industrial development. Developers also help business with problems of equipment, remodeling and updating, adoption of new systems, and problems of pollution control. Therefore they are in every way involved in the physical plant and problems of property.

Most of the agencies spend a great deal of time helping business find loan money, putting together loan packages from a number of sources.

Small business loans are largely a matter of bank loans, SBIR loans, and Small Business Administration guarantees. Occasionally a small business will get help from a local revolving loan fund. Most of the time of the agency is spent on other types of loans and of larger amounts. The costs of issuing a tax-free bond, involving paperwork eventually bound in a volume the size of a telephone book and amounting to perhaps $50,000 in legal fees, mean that it is not cost-effective to issue a bond for much less than half a million dollars. Despite their higher interest rates, this is a principal reason why taxable bonds are becoming popular as tax-free bonds are being phased out by federal restraints. Taxable bonds can be issued more easily and for smaller amounts, since legal fees are only a few thousand dollars.

In addition to bonds, agencies help business apply for loans from a number of different state and federal agencies. Fifty agencies report helping business put together financial packages. Their intercession is necessary because the applications are very complicated and time-consuming, the rules and regulations change from time to time, and every application has different requirements. But more than this, often the sum of money needed has to be put together from a number of different sources: the person applying typically has to put up some of his own money, some may come from a bank loan, some from a local loan fund, and some from a federal source such as the Department of Housing and Urban Development, or state funds such as the Job Development Agency, the Urban Development Corporation, the New York State Science and Technology Foundation, or the New York Business Development Corporation, as we have seen. Some loan funds have rules that make securing a loan from them contingent on the borrower's raising part of the needed money elsewhere. Some agencies tend to have used one of these funds more than others, and views about which fund is most likely to solve their problems varies around the state, but the Job Development Authority, of these, is most widely cited.

Putting together a financial loan package may take the time of an agency staff person over a period of several months. Some of the larger agencies have a specific person for this task. It may also require a team effort over this time on the part of several agencies contributing to the solution of the problem. In this respect the county agencies, along with city, town and village agencies, and regional organizations may be compared to drops of water on a pane of glass. At one time they seem totally separate entities; but if you shake the glass, they may coalesce into one large body of water. While the agencies do not blend their staffs, offices, or operating funds, they cooperate, work closely on large projects, divide up the jobs, and take care not to undermine each others' efforts. And organizing a sizeable loan fund for a large project is a task often requiring such cooperation.

In addition to federal and state funds, many agencies and local governments have organized local revolving loan funds. The reason for this is to have a greater margin of flexibility: to loan to smaller projects, to loan for working capital, and to supplement larger packages. Only eighteen of the counties have no loan fund, and of these, five are trying to get one. Thirty-one have their own loans funds, and five of these also draw on local or regional loan funds. Twenty-six of those that have such a fund have gotten some of the funds from federal sources, from a grant from the Economic Development Administration, from a Housing and Urban Development Community Development Block Grant, from the pay back from a Housing and Urban Development loan to business (that is, the business repays its loan to the local government, not the federal), and two from the Appalachian Regional Commission. Six have acquired funds from fees, property, or local fund raising, one from a bank, two from the state, and two from a court decision involving a large corporation. The agency does not always hold title to these funds; sometimes a city or local government will have title, but the agency will manage them, for often cities and other local governments will not have staff for this purpose. Eighteen have derived their loan funds from a single source, and fourteen from more than one. And these are a small proportion of the 503 revolving loan funds in New York State.

Amounts available to loan vary widely. The smallest fund has $20,000, the largest has $30 million. Five have $100,000 or less, four more have less than $500,000. Five have between $500,000 and $1 million. Four have between $1 million and $1.5 million, and five have more. For five, the amounts are unknown. Thus helping business secure financing is a major task of most agencies. It began with issuing bonds. But now it draws on many state, federal, and local sources, and requires considerable expertise to put the right package together and in time for it to be of use.

In a very few of the more prosperous counties undergoing considerable growth and expansion, financing is not regarded as a major problem. In such cases enough businesses are starting up or coming in or expanding in the county without help that the agency's role in financing is of no importance and requires no effort on their part. But despite the larger role of financing in most cases, many developers did not consider finance a major problem for business. Rather they were of the opinion that a worthwhile business could find funds if it had a good product, a good plan and, above all, good management.

We asked everywhere about venture capital. For the most part, developers do not have much contact with venture capital, and those who have more contact do not seem to have much problem with it. The reason for its lesser importance is that few businesses want to acquire capital in this manner, for they would have to give up a share of control or ownership that they do not want to yield. This is confirmed indirectly by venture capitalists. Considering the number of venture capitalists and the number of businesses each finances, their role in general is not a large one.

In addition to the economic development agencies proper, the developers usually work with the Private Industry Councils. There is one in each county whose task it is to use federal funds to arrange training needed, in a factory or in a school or community college that might even go to the factory to do the training. They also work with the New York State Department of Labor which will recruit and screen labor for a new factory that has moved into the state. They also know and avail themselves of any other help other agencies can give, such as help with access roads from the New York State Department of Transportation.

In each county, at least informally, a division of labor exists among the agencies serving the county, be they regional, county or local. Which agency performs what task may change over time, particularly as new agencies are created. The agencies may divide the area along geographic lines, with a city agency taking care of a large city, town agencies taking care of smaller, and the county agency taking care of the rest of the county, that is, the rural areas. Or, two Chambers of Commerce may exist, one for the eastern part of the county, one for the western, and both cooperating with a county IDA and other agencies.

Agencies may also divide the tasks along functional lines, each specializing in different jobs. While Chambers of Commerce, if they have industrial arms (and most do not), typically take the lead in marketing, the division of labor among organizations differs widely from county to county. The Chamber of Commerce may take no part in industrial development, it may confine its efforts to marketing, or it may provide a wide array of services to industry. Similarly, the IDA may confine its efforts to issuing Industrial Revenue Bonds or it may have a wide range of activities, as described above. We do not have enough cases for a firm generalization about why different agencies may take the lead or do the bulk of the development work in one county and not in another but there is an hypothesis that can be offered. In some counties where the Chamber of Commerce or another private agency has been dominant, rather than the IDA, developers talk of the conservatism of the county, the belief that government should not do what business can do for itself, that business organizations have always been strong in the county and should take the lead, and leaders believe the government role should be minimal.

In fact, many developers, regardless of the division of labor, say that they do not believe in doing for business what it can do for itself. An agency may help with formulating business plans, but only for those that cannot do it for themselves or afford to pay a consultant. The general aim is to help business help itself. Many treat the agency as the business of last resort. That is, if private developers will establish industrial parks or incubators, the agency does not need to do so. If private persons will not do so, the agency does. If there is an unused building, a vacant factory or school, the agency developer will accept the challenge of putting it to profitable use if no one else will do so. Thus, it follows that this theme may also give reason for the division of labor in some cases. Where business leadership is strong and politically influential, it will take the lead.

Agency functions may overlap at times, but they generally do not compete. In fact, agencies are well aware of each other's specialties and refer clients around to the proper place. They all realize the folly of having clients wander around from agency to agency in a haze of confusion. If an agency cannot be a one-stop shop, as they so often try to be, they at least try to sort things out, contact the appropriate place, often act as liaison or centrally organizing agency for combined efforts so that the various contributions work in an integrated way. It may be that our interviewing situation did not elicit complaints, but our overall impression was one of cooperation, of all having a common purpose, jobs, and working together toward this goal.

Small Business

All of the activities described can in principle benefit small business. Among these are development of incubators, programs of visitation and business management advice, help with permits and regulations, site selection and some of the loan funds. Tax-free bonds that have not been feasible to issue for less than $500,000 generally do not help. Now that taxable bonds are becoming more common, they are practical to issue for smaller amounts, and small business might benefit from them. The locally operated revolving loan funds are especially suitable, for they are often issued for working capital, in relatively small amounts, and on the basis of intimate knowledge of the business person and the business.

No developer will turn away anyone who comes in the door or telephones; they will try to provide help or referral. Many provide various kinds of assistance directly, as we have indicated. But the main sources of help for small business are the seven regional offices of the Small Business Administration, the Technical Assistance Centers funded by EDA and the universities, and the eight to ten (still expanding in number) Small Business Development Centers, funded by the SBA and the colleges where they are located.

The SBA offices provide loans or, more frequently, loan guarantees, business management assistance, information on government procurement, and they act as an advocate for small business with the federal government. A person receiving a guarantee or loan is required to have a business plan, among other things, and their various seminars, training courses, and counseling provide help with these. They can guarantee up to $500,000. They must be convinced of the soundness of the plan and especially of the management. They can lend without collateral, though they do not often do so, if the business by nature is not one that uses much equipment or physical property. They aim at a slightly higher default rate than banks. Banks typically have a maximum default rate of less than .5 percent of the dollars loaned.

Theirs might be 1.5 to 2 percent. They take somewhat higher risks and believe that they fund many businesses that could not get funding from banks without their guarantee. They also refer clients to the SBDCs for counseling. They make heavy use of SCORE groups of volunteers consisting of retired business executives they organize, who counsel businesses on all kinds of management problems. The SBA can also pay for professional consultation for a business if they deem it necessary, either a failing or successful business. It is difficult to evaluate the service. But they, like other agencies, public and private, that deal with small business try to screen out potential failures. One common method for doing so is to put an applicant through the process of formulating a business plan. When he has done so, he often sees that his idea is unworkable. They continue to monitor the business they guarantee throughout the loan period, as do the cooperating banks. But they tell of business people that do not seem to see fate frowning on their efforts until failure is inevitable, and who will not listen to criticism or advice. Nonetheless their default rate is estimated by one SBA executive at a 6 percent or 7 percent liquidation rate a year with a seven year loan duration, at roughly 40 percent overall. This is below the 50 percent estimate of the overall failure rate of small business (Miller, 1990). Venture capitalists, who typically choose more advanced and well developed prospects than these to finance, may have a portfolio of fifteen companies they invest in. A few will fail, a few more just pay off the investment, and only a couple are expected to earn substantial profits. By this criterion, they are doing well with only a 40 percent default rate on SBA loans and guarantees.

The Small Business Development Centers consist of eight to ten established at colleges and universities around the state and administered by an office at SUNY-Albany. They intend ultimately to have seventeen centers, and are in the process of establishing local advisory boards for them. They are financed by the SBA and the local college where they are located. They help with all kinds of problems, including business plans. They take referrals from state, federal, and local agencies. Each may have eight or nine full-time staff people. Each person may take ten new cases a month and carry a maximum case load of twenty-five. Cases may take only a few hours or involve the total evolution of a business. The largest our informant knew of as of that date took 213 hours, but they generally do not take more than

23 hours or 3 months.   It was estimated that the system had been processing six to eight thousand individuals or firms per year, with a growing case load. They also sponsor seminars and conferences.

Two Technical Assistance Centers also exist.   One is at SUNY-Plattsburgh, funded by the university and the EDA, the other in Niagara County.   They have broad functions, but one of their tasks is small business counseling, along the same lines as the SBDCs.   The SUNY-Plattsburgh Center takes referrals from all over the Adirondack-North Country fourteen counties, and sometimes beyond.   They have all the business they can deal with and more.

In addition to local loan funds, banks, and the SBA, the other main source of small business financial aid is the SBIR funding of research and development, by a combination of federal and matching state funds, administered by the New York State Science and Technology Foundation, the purpose of which is to encourage innovation.

Developers do not often have much contact with the SBA, though there are notable exceptions.   A reason for this is the development agencies' emphasis on jobs.   They tend to work more with firms that will provide the most jobs.   A small business can take up a lot of the time of a small staff straining to cover a lot of complex activities in a large territory.   Further, some do not feel qualified to deal with small businesses or help them with their business plans.   This study cannot evaluate how well small business's needs are being met, but it does suggest that the question needs to be asked.   Another related question must also be answered at the same time.   How can we decide how much public money and effort should be put into endeavors with such a high failure rate, and how do we decide what efforts will cut down that rate sufficiently to justify the costs?

Summary

The primary task of the local development organizations is to assist business in the creation of jobs.   It does so by performing a wide variety of tasks, a different assortment depending on local resources and needs.   Thus the organizations vary not only in structure, but in their activities.   It is evident from the last chapter's description of relations with government and this chapter's description of contacts with business that the local development organizations are information centers and coordinating organizations. In dealing with business the good developer is entrepreneurial, imaginative, quick to act, innovative. He is autonomous, responsible, and as theory predicts, gives off an aura of liking his job. Thus in their day-to-day activities, in their informal structure, the local development organizations act in ways business understands, and meshes with its needs.

Chapter 10

The Wider Network of Development Organizations

In addition to county level economic development organizations there are many others that work on a larger or smaller territorial basis. The way state and federal aid reaches business is through a wide and complicated network of agencies operating from regional, county, city, and town bases. Examination of what they do, where they do it, and, above all, their interrelations will give a picture of great complexity. It will enable us to describe cooperation among agencies, the specialization that develops among them, and how services grow if the demands of an area outstrip the original organization's effort. A substantial part of any developer's time is spent in contact with this network of public and private organizations.

It is tempting to think of regional organizations, county, and city, and town organizations as if these were three levels of organization nested in an hierarchical manner with authority and dependency relations from level to level and a definite division of labor among them. In fact, this is not the case. Organizations operating on a wider than county level may be unique to a certain area, may cover some arbitrarily large area, or may cover the state systematically. They may perform the same functions as county, town, and city organizations, or very different or additional ones. They typically work with and support local development organizations in various ways. But none of them have any authority or control over local organizations, nor do the latter depend on them. Town and city organizations may perform the same functions as the county organization, especially in the larger cities. Many of the former lack staff, however, and these typically rely on the county organizations. Of those with staff, many are preoccupied mainly with various kinds of downtown rehabilitation, face lifts for streets or buildings, remodeling buildings, building parking garages, and the like, but some are deeply involved in industrial development.

Let us look at some of the agencies that work on a supra-county level and at a sub-county level, and then see how the network of organizations function together. While we mainly concentrated the study on county organizations as a comparable group, we also interviewed a number of multi-county organizations, including at least a couple of each type, and a number of sub-county organizations. Let us first look at the multi-county organizations.

The New York State Department of Economic Development maintains ten regional offices that cover the whole state. These regions are based on economic factors, and hence do not coincide with other state regions, such as those used by the Department of Labor. In their systematic coverage of the whole state, they fit the idea of regional organizations. They do not have authority over county, town, or city organizations, but they offer many of the same services as the latter. With the change of Department of Commerce to the New York State Department of Economic Development, the regional offices are acquiring additional staff and new functions. However, we will describe them as they have been functioning in 1987 and early 1988. One function is to act as ombudsman for businesses with state agencies of all kinds. They act for the Department of Labor for training. They help the JDA with loan applications and are responsible for interviewing management and helping process applications. They use the resource data bank in Albany for information for companies wanting to find a company to do or provide something to them. Their international division provides leads on foreign business and information on export problems.

In addition, however, they do many of the things that the county economic development organizations also do. They try to intercede with organizations that might leave, sometimes arranging leveraged buy-outs of branch plants by local management. They help with site selection, expansion, all kinds of training programs, and financial packaging of loans for buildings and machinery. They spend a good deal of time traveling over their regions, keeping in touch with all businesses in it on a systematic basis. Their emphasis, as in the case of the local economic development organizations, is on retaining what business they have. They respond to calls for help and tend to give extra help in rural counties that may not have staff of their own. They work with local development organizations on projects, and they help provide information and assistance to new local staff people until they are able to function on their own. They have a good reputation among local developers and business people, but they have few people per office and their efforts are spread thin over wide territory.

Another set of regional offices that cover the state systematically are the Regional Planning Offices. As the name indicates, they are mainly planning offices, but they enter into and give support to economic and industrial development. There are eleven of them in the state, and they are funded 75 percent by federal funds (Economic Development Administration and Appalachian Regional Commission), and 25 percent by local funds. They, first of all, are involved in long-range planning and impact assessment in their areas, and focus on all economic sectors and varied problems. They are involved in such general multi-county issues as conservation, rail service, airports, water and solid waste disposal, housing, and energy. They collect and analyze systematic information on their areas that they provide to local governments and other agencies. They are involved in marketing the area, developing brochures and visual materials, and some even conduct trade missions to Canada. They may help on a project such as an industrial park. They do not work directly with business, and only go into a county with the blessing of the government and local agencies. They, too, tend to be asked for and provide more assistance to rural counties. Large cities and urban counties with large staffs of their own seldom call on them for direct help. They keep in close touch with local organizations, may meet with them on a regular, formal basis or serve on their boards of directors, that, in turn, serve on their own. In addition to backstopping local organizations with research and information, they also may provide technical assistance when needed, as well as help in securing grants. They also operate revolving loan funds provided by EDA and matching local money which local developers can assist local business in applying for.

Another group of organizations that operate on a wide territorial basis are the public utilities and Conrail. The utilities work in the areas to which they provide service. Thus they cover wide areas, but not in any neat way. New York State Electric and Gas serves parts of forty-three counties, not all in a single contiguous group. Occasionally a county will be served by two or three utilities. The utilities got into economic development because they want to market electricity, but their economic development departments, while heavily emphasizing marketing, have as their goal economic development. They realize that in the long-run the latter is more likely to accomplish their purpose. They do a vigorous marketing job and specialize in site location, for which they have natural advantages since they can keep track of available buildings. But they also put great effort into helping existing companies to remain and expand. They often work with large corporations on location of a new plant, and a large project can take from three to five years to complete. As with the local development agencies with whom they cooperate closely, they work on any problem a corporation may have, and try, too, to be a one-stop shop. An example is given in a brochure distributed to business by Niagara Mohawk. In it they ask why Owens-Corning chose its location in their service area, and answer this question as follows:

> Perhaps most important, our Economic Development Department bore the primary responsibility for helping Owens-Corning find an acceptable location. And we stayed with them to a successful conclusion.
>
> We helped coordinate their associations with many agencies – Federal agencies, like the FAO, FAA, EPA, OSHA and ICC. State agencies like the DOT, two divisions of the Department of Labor, the Public Service Commission, plus the Department of Environmental Conservation in consideration of water, air, solid waste and noise. Regional agencies. County agencies.
>
> And, Town of Bethlehem agencies – the Town Board, Planning Board, Board of Appeals, Building Inspector, and Water Department.
>
> Then, we assisted them at every step – We formed a site selection committee, issued site reports, helped initiate site testing, helped present the proposal to Bethlehem, assisted in public meetings, and helped Owens-Corning obtain zoning changes, variances, and building permits.
>
> Today the plant employs 250 people, and serves the entire northeast with insulation products.
>
> And though it's been several years since we began our relationship, Niagara Mohawk and Owens-Corning remain in close contact.
>
> According to an Owens-Corning spokesman, "Niagara Mohawk's professional assistance was the major factor in Owens-Corning's decision in locate in Bethlehem, New York."

Conrail's territory is very large – the whole Northeast and Midwest, and going into Quebec. For the eastern half, headquarters are in Selkirk, New York. The organization is interested in recruiting customers for its rail services, and in this interest helps companies plan their transportation, provides special trains on order, and provides storage and truck connections. Their economic development division also works with industry in order to develop the area in which it operates. It tries to know a great deal about the industries it deals with so that it can make intelligent suggestions about planning, strategy, and expansion, about new trends coming up in an industry that a corporation may utilize. It works with local economic developers and real estate people to maintain a large industrial site inventory and also works with them to get sites developed that an industry may need. They help, too, on all aspects of getting an industry located and underway, and a large project may again take three to five years to complete. They work with counties to develop industrial parks, work with corporations for "piggy-back" needs, or related activities corporations can develop, and they do site searches.   They put emphasis on keeping in touch with a large network of involved agencies and companies. Only a small number of the prospects they develop are expected to come to fruition, and their staff are expected to deal with any problem impeding the project, such as a sewer problem. As they say, they may not be able to fix it, but they do try to deal with it. Their attitude is to be proactive, and not wait for prospects to call on them, though a large portion do so.   They put great emphasis on knowing the industries and industrial trends and innovations, and on knowing the regions and resources. Thus while these companies are trying to sell their services and they emphasize marketing and recruitment, this is done in a broader context of economic development. Many are staffed by people who have had experience in local development agencies. They therefore get into the same issues and activities as other types of agencies.

The New York State Science and Technology Foundation also funds eight regional organizations. One such, for example, is the Northern Technology Council, covering the north country: Clinton, Essex, Franklin, St. Lawrence, Jefferson, and Lewis counties, on or close to the Canadian border. It is not long underway and encourages business-university cooperation, regional marketing, and the like. Its executive director is also an executive of the Northern Advanced Technology Corporation, a local not-for-profit organization whose members are Clarkson University, SUNY Potsdam, the village and town of Potsdam, and the St. Lawrence County IDA. NATCO operates a high-technology incubator and is in the process of developing a research park.

In addition to those types of multi-county organizations, which are repeated in various parts of the state, there are a number unique to a particular area.   One such is the Western New York Economic Development Corporation.   It is a subsidiary of the Urban Development Corporation and was created by the governor "to plan, finance, and manage major development projects in Erie, Niagara, Chautauqua, Cattaraugus, and four other western New York counties, and coordinate the state's economic development activities in the region."   It is headed by a former New York State Commerce Department Commissioner who also had been head of the JDA and of the New York State Science and Technology Foundation.

It is engaged, first, in strategic planning for the region including economic planning and also such issues as health care, the airport, forest products, and business services.   An aim is economic diversification.   It also has a minority business development program including a professional office incubator, loan funds, and technical assistance. It specializes in accessing state economic development loan programs for all kinds of development.

Its special effort for industry is its Industrial Effectiveness Program in cooperation with centers and departments of SUNY Buffalo.   The plan of work is that a team meets with the top management and labor leaders of a company or branch plant seeking help.   This is followed by a review of the company by the Center for Industrial Effectiveness of SUNY Buffalo, from which an organizational development strategy is developed and agreed upon.   The Western New York Economic Development Corporation then pursues needed funding and proceeds with the action recommended, using consultants and specialists from a variety of sources as needed, placing them in the factory if this is called for.   The process should take one to two years and is evaluated eleven months into the project when plans are revised, if necessary.   They have begun with six corporations.   In these they have done such things as to provide technical training for management and labor, introduce a flexible manufacturing system, and consolidate and reduce space, resulting in economies.   The aim is to prevent further closures among the 500 large companies still in the region, an older industrial area where closures have been taking place.

An additional effort in this direction is assisting in a number of management buy outs of branch plants.   The agency has also participated in a number of other projects such as creation of an industrial park, a "spec" building, a trade center housing twenty small businesses, the SUNY Buffalo Center for Regional Studies, an Earthquake Center, and a high-technology incubator. They, together with other agencies, worked on the projects helping them to secure a variety of state funds. They operate two revolving loan funds of their own. They envisage a future project in the field of international trade. The Western New York Economic Development Corporation was intended as a possible model for other state regional organizations. So far, however, it is unique.

There are a number of state commissions and authorities, part of whose task is economic and industrial development. These include, for example, the Adirondack Park Association, the Tug Hill Commission, the St. Lawrence-Ontario Regional Commission, the Development Authority of the North County, and many others like them in other parts of the state. All of these have more general programs than economic and industrial development. Most engage in planning activities, have obligations for conservation, and work with local governments in various ways, but all have some economic development activity and focus. One authority that engages more heavily in industrial development is the Ogdensburg Bridge and Port Authority. In addition to operating the port and bridge, railroad and airport, a sizeable responsibility in itself, the authority operates industrial parks and an incubator for Canadian firms and markets its facilities in Canada.

There are also a number of private agencies operating on a multi-county level. One such organization is the Adirondack North Country Association. This organization covers the fourteen counties north of the New York State throughway, from Oswego east to Washington County and north to the Canadian border. It is a not-for-profit association with dues-paying individual, corporate, and institutional members. All over the area people talk of the North Country, so this concept is not one invented by the association. ANCA has existed for several decades but took on a new lease on life a few years ago when it moved to Lake Placid to a new building, hired a new executive director, and adopted a nine point program. For two years it was given a block of money by the state legislature. This resulted from the efforts of a group of leaders from the Adirondack and North Country counties who went to Albany and organized a meeting with their legislative delegation. It has used this block of money to make grants to various projects, and is now discussing using further grants for a revolving loan fund. The nine part program includes agriculture, tourism, forestry and natural resources, crafts, education and museums, health and human services, international cooperation, and economic development. It reflects the nature of the region with its forests, parks, its diversity, its poverty, and its Canadian border. Much of the territory is within the Adirondack Park Association area and is constrained by its zoning rules. The ANCA's industrial emphasis is on the small entrepreneur. They have helped a rug business, a boat building business, wood products, canvas bags, leather, and concrete businesses.

But they have, more importantly, acted as a focus for a rising sense of regionalism in these fourteen counties, and through their meetings and conferences, as a center for exchange of information and mutual reinforcement among governments and agencies in the area. As the interviewer traveled the area, many developers mentioned the organization and its regional leadership and the contact and cooperation it makes possible. Many of these regional organizations are relatively new and their program descriptions focus more on intended functions and aims that may not yet be realized.

Another set of actors not usually thought of in connection with economic development are large corporations. Their activities vary greatly. In many cases, their activities relate closely to their own business interests. They may spin off small companies by licensing products or otherwise authorizing use of products generated by their research and development or internal innovation programs that they do not wish to manufacture themselves. Sometimes they finance such companies or invest in them, or place their employees on the small company's board of directors.

Another way in which they encourage growth is through buying out products or services formerly produced in the company. This trend has been increasing due to the adoption by companies of a just-in-time inventory policy, that cuts inventory way back, and by consolidation of corporate activities resulting in buying out of products that a company cannot produce itself as economically. The corporation may work closely with a subcontractor on quality control. They may urge them to develop other customers. But they are not responsible for the fate of such companies, even though the latter may depend on them heavily.

A broader effort is sometimes made. One such example is Corning Glass, through its Corning Enterprises. Under this latter subsidiary is grouped all of Corning's non-manufacturing interests: land, an airport, a tourist business, its retail trade, a museum, downtown buildings, a race track, and a hotel. In addition, Corning Enterprises, in order to make its headquarters city more attractive and livable, has cooperated in community development, such as rehabilitation of the town of Corning. But its interest goes beyond such rehabilitation to regional development. Its most recent interest, along with Alfred University, is in establishing two ceramic incubators, one in Corning and one at Alfred University, which specializes in ceramic studies. The aim is to stimulate the development of a ceramic corridor east to west from Corning to Alfred University. This is by no means a complete list of all agencies and actors operating on a multi-county basis, but reflects the variety of organizations, actors, and programs, public and private, around the state.

In some few counties, especially those with larger cities, one or several city agencies may exist that are very active and have a number of staff members. Such agencies may have expanded their activities to cover a metropolitan area. If they do not, they will typically cooperate with various county agencies on projects. Many towns also have agencies of their own.

Town and city agencies often are involved in various kinds of urban renewal designed to attract business to the area, including remodeling of buildings, face-lifts of neighborhoods, parking garages, shopping malls, and the like. They also carry on many of the same activities that county agencies do but in a smaller area. These include working with businesses on all of their problems, establishing industrial parks and incubators, and revolving loan funds. They may also, as do other agencies, provide unique services, such as maintaining an inventory of government contracts for which a business may bid.

Most cities, and some towns, have such an agency. Which ones? Large cities tend to have them. For towns, there is no single answer, and we have not surveyed town agencies and cannot speak with certainty. But there are clues. Some areas where there has been metropolitan expansion have active town agencies. Even in urban counties that are doing no more than holding steady economically, some of the newer types of business prefer suburban locations – small, clean industries, back office operations of banks and insurance companies, and especially warehousing and distribution operations find access better outside of large cities. Amherst, in Erie County, has seen such development. It grew from being entirely residential to having several hundred businesses within a few years. The town of North Greenbush in Rensselaer County has been activated by the growth of the Rensselaer Polytechnic Institute industrial research park. The whole of Orange County has seen growth of warehousing and distribution operations, and several county and town agencies are very active. These represent examples of metropolitan expansion and integration of outlying areas made possible by modern transportation and communication, and in these areas town agencies are active. The Town of Hornell in Steuben County has an agency that has been very active since the Southern Tier Expressway connected it with the east and west. Relative isolated before, it has seen an explosion of development activity in recent years.

Those city agencies we have interviewed tend to work closely with other agencies in the area. Town agencies vary from not existing to being nominal to being very active, depending on particular local needs and opportunities. An additional reason for the existence of some is that they may constitute the only economically depressed areas, pockets of poverty, in a county, and thus qualify for federal and state aid not available to the county as a whole, which may be a great deal more prosperous. In some cases towns or cities whose agencies lack paid staff have acquired funds through means, for example, of the repayment of a HUD loan and used it to establish a revolving loan fund. In such a case the county agency may be asked to manage the fund for the city. Thus there are many links between multi-county, county, city, and town agencies.

Now that we have thrown the whole issue of town, city, county, and multi-county agencies into confusion, let us see what sense we can make of how the several agencies in a county work. Do they work separately, compete, cooperate, or what are their relationships? Let us look at a few counties and see how the networks of agencies operate.

Several things should be kept in mind. For one thing, a minority of counties have more than one county-level agency, though many have town agencies, and all come within the influence of more than one regional agency. In this respect, the counties we shall discuss are not typical but they lend themselves to discussion of how the network of agencies can work together. The cases discussed illustrate the different strategies used by counties to meet different economic problems and opportunities. While each situation is comprised of a unique set of economic pressures, many of these various economic pressures are shared by a number of other counties each with its unique assortment of pressures. Similar pressures evoke similar responses. A core characteristic of developers is that they know their own county very well with its unique set of problems and opportunities, and they tailor their programs to these. Therefore, in the cases to be described, we should look for strategies devised in response to various pressures common to a number of counties as well as the set of activities designed to respond to the county's unique situation.

Erie County

The City of Buffalo and Erie County have been undergoing drastic changes in economic structure, with the decline of heavy industry and the closing of steel mills in 1982. In this respect it is similar to many counties in the older industrial areas of the state. In a recent upswing in the economy of the state, the county's high unemployment rate reduced to the national average, assisted by reduction in population that migrated to more prosperous areas. However, while its economy seems to be turning around, its problems stimulated a good deal of organizational activity in the county as it pulled itself together to meet its problems and utilize new opportunities. Agencies are now working to stabilize the economy, retain industry, diversify it, strengthen new trends, and to help its industry establish local roots. It is widely thought in the area that one of its problems has been that it is a branch plant area and is therefore more vulnerable to outside economic shifts. Therefore, it would like to increase local ownership so industry will have local loyalties and local roots. It also wishes to do what is possible to hold what industry it has, though it feels less threatened now since none of the remaining large industries compare in size of employment with the several thousand employee steel plants that shut down. It also wishes to continue to diversify its economy and industry, including attracting Canadian companies. In recent times a regional consciousness has been growing. Agencies formerly confined to the City of Buffalo are now concerned with a wider area. The city's mayor and his development agency cooperate with local and regional agencies and take the position that they have a common fate. What happens in the city, the county, and the region are related. In its simplest form, people commute in and out of the city. This is not unlike other areas of the state where agencies, for example, have developed multi-county marketing teams. Let us look at the economic development agencies that exist, what their division of labor is, and how they relate to each other.

The Erie County Industrial Development Agency was organized in 1970, the oldest in the state. The agency has a strong professional staff of thirteen or fourteen people. A study was commissioned by Battelle Institute that recommended that they needed space for start up companies, so they developed incubators. They also bought land and developed a shell building. As of 1984, Erie County has eighteen publicly owned or assisted industrial parks and twenty private. Various agencies assisted with the public industrial parks, an important activity of industrial development agencies. The agency has a staff position for visiting existing industries. It has two revolving loan funds. It puts a great deal of emphasis on helping industries develop financial packages and on issuing bonds. In one year prior to the interview (early 1987), they issued sixty million dollars worth of Industrial Revenue Bonds for which they charge a fee ranging from one-half of 1 percent to 1 percent. They only intervene after a business has gone to commercial banks. They then help fill the gap if the private sector finds the project worthy of support.   They have also participated in management buyouts of branch plants.   Collectively, the various agencies have assisted in a considerable number of these as branch plants threatened leaving or closing.

One division of the agency also deals with Canadian companies and the Foreign Trade Zone along with company visitation. A second deals with land development, technical assistance for private companies and municipalities for industrial park development as well as grant application work. The financial division, the largest, deals with bonds.

The administrative division also takes responsibility for coordinating with other economic development agencies in the county. They meet regularly, on a weekly basis, with the Chamber of Commerce, the Western New York Economic Development Corporation, and the Greater Buffalo Development Foundation to coordinate referrals and activities.

The Chamber of Commerce has a Business Development Group structured as a nonprofit membership organization, including both Erie and Niagara County Chambers of Commerce. It was formed in 1961 to process Job Development Authority loans and that was its sole function until this year. Its present director, on the job for less than a year, is on the board of the Erie County IDA and was formerly employed by it. He is a vice president of the Chamber of Commerce. The Chamber of Commerce specializes in business information and in marketing. They have a staff member who concentrates on Canadian business.

The Greater Buffalo Development Foundation has existed for thirty-five years. It is a nonprofit private organization, and until 1987 it has mainly been concerned with physical development of the City of Buffalo. Most of its financial support comes from the largest corporations in western New York. In 1987 it hired a new executive director and expanded its area of interest to eight counties of western New York. It has broadened its interests to social and physical infrastructure, and its 1987 projects included: central city revitalization, providing management advice and analysis to cultural arts institutions, cooperating with other regional agencies to plan and implement economic development, strengthening health care, improving local government effectiveness, and building regional cohesion. It aims at providing the underpinnings for development rather than dealing directly with business.

The Western New York Economic Development Corporation was created recently by the governor. Formally, it comes under the jurisdiction of the Urban Development Corporation. It is the only public regional development corporation in New York State and, as has been stated, it also works in the eight western counties. It works on several fronts: regional strategic planning with the Center for Regional Studies at the University of Buffalo; tourism; minority business development; economic project funding, specializing in accessing state economic development programs of all sorts; and industrial effectiveness. As we have described, the latter program works with the remaining large corporations in the area to try to improve their functioning, to keep them in the area and progressing. They work on each company's peculiar problems. They too have cooperated on leveraged buy outs and on urban projects such as the new baseball stadium. The program includes two loans funds, one for minorities.

The City of Buffalo also has an economic development organization, the Buffalo Enterprise Development Corporation. Their program has also been directed at retaining larger industries, but has mainly concentrated on stimulating new business. It has worked on industrial parks and has a large lending program for small industry and neighborhood business from Housing and Urban Development Block Grants. It does not issue bonds but leaves this to the Erie County IDA. It works with this organization on loans. It is interested in Canadian industry coming into the area, but leaves recruitment to the Chamber of Commerce. Another of their activities is federal procurement assistance for small companies. They too participate with other agencies on leveraged buy outs. These require large amounts of money, from ten to twenty million dollars a project, and much effort. They work on various projects with the Western New York Economic Development Corporation, and all of the agencies work with various centers at SUNY-Buffalo.

The Town of Amherst, in Erie County, east of Buffalo, has previously been mentioned as a former residential community which now has several hundred businesses operating there, including distribution and warehouse operations, back office operations, and small clean industries. It too features the advantages offered by SUNY-Buffalo in its recruitment literature. Its clients do not tend to need financial help as much as management help of various kinds, and it runs a number of workshops and seminars for business. It does, however, issue bonds, and in recent times a number of taxable bonds which cost less to issue than tax-free, and therefore can be issued in smaller amounts.

It is evident that in Erie County there is a division of labor among the agencies. While there is a great deal of coordination, keeping in touch, regular meetings, overlapping directorships, agencies have worked out specialties for each agency which other agencies do not replicate. We will later ask the question, why so many agencies rather than one large one?

In addition, of course, the area is part of a regional planning district, a Department of Commerce region, and a Small Business Administration region. It is also served by public utilities and their development teams. In this area, as in others, the SBA takes care of a large proportion of counseling and guaranteeing loans for small firms, and they, like other SBA offices, utilize SCORE members to counsel small firms. SCORE organizations are composed of retired executives who donate their time.

Monroe County

Monroe County is a prosperous county whose main city, Rochester, has several large high-technology industries, including Eastman Kodak and Xerox, and a number of smaller ones. When Eastman Kodak recently reorganized and reduced its labor force by several thousand jobs, this was not perceived as a county economic crisis, in contrast with the steel mills shut down in Erie. The developers did not so regard it, and the unemployment rates did not increase. This county is served by a county IDA, a Chamber of Commerce, and a Rochester city economic development agency. At the time of the original interview, the county government had recently hired an assistant for economic development who thus far had worked on a variety of publications useful to business, on zoning, permits, financing and the like. In this region, we also interviewed the regional planning office and the office of Rochester Gas and Electric, the public utility serving the region.

Not only is county industry growing, but in this area, too, it is spreading out from the county to the East and South. The explanation for the direction of spread that was offered is that affluent residential neighborhoods were located to the east of the city and summer homes on Canandaigua Lake, southeast. Therefore, when executives wanted to move or expand their businesses, they went out beyond their residential area or went south and east to an area of weekend homes. In this prosperous area, there are no public incubators, but there are industrial parks, some owned by the City of Rochester.

In this county, agencies divided the tasks differently than Erie County, partly, it was suggested, because companies are expanding and the economy is doing well, and partly because of a conservative tradition toward private enterprise. When we interviewed, the county had an IDA that confined its work to the issuing of bonds. The county took the money earned in this way and contracted with the Chamber of Commerce to do much of the work the IDA does in other places. The Chamber not only worked on marketing and relocation, a typical Chamber of Commerce task, but worked on a Foreign Trade Zone and included international trade in its mission. It assisted individuals with loan applications, with information, helped with zoning and regulations, and operated a loan fund. It spent most of its effort on retention of existing business, like most development organizations in New York State. Because of its status as a Chamber of Commerce, like most other Chambers it is active in lobbying and legislation of interest to business. The city also has an economic development agency with a large staff that conducts a loan program also and a facade program.

Our hypothesis about why, in some counties like this, the Chamber of Commerce did the main development job rather than an independent government-sponsored agency, like the IDA, was that these counties were conservative, and businessmen took the lead in county affairs, both politics and business. And businessmen would prefer private over government control. Some months after the initial interviews, an election replaced Republican officials with Democratic in the county. With this turnaround came another. The county dropped its contract with the Chamber of Commerce to do development work and organized a greatly expanded economic development organization under county control to carry on all of the work, also abolishing the small office that formerly issued Industrial Revenue Bonds. In this one case, at least, our original hypothesis is supported by the change that took place. The leading role the Chamber of Commerce took under a Republican regime was supplanted by a leadership role taken by a county economic development agency under a Democratic regime.

In this area we also interviewed the Regional Planning Office and the economic development office of the Rochester Gas and Electric. One developer spoke of cooperation in terms of a confederation of organizations. As in other areas, the Regional Planning Office backstops the agencies of the region with information, data, and public relations materials. It also helps with loan applications. It does research and it networks with other agencies. It tries not to work one-on-one with communities without the consent of the county agency. It operates a loan fund with money from the Economic Development Administration and matching local funds. It has also worked on such projects of regional interest as the airport and solid waste management. It tends to be called on for assistance more frequently by rural counties in the area.

Rochester Gas and Electric works on regional planning in nine counties, and on advertising and recruiting. They say they call on all small businesses: "little businesses have to be here to sell to the big." The area is also served by a regional state Department of Economic Development office and a regional Small Business Administration office.

As industry spreads to the Southeast, it is expanding into Ontario County which is also prospering and mainly because of this spread. The IDA there does a great deal of what can be called facilitating of industrial location, functioning and expansion. This growth can be viewed as an expansion and change in this metropolitan area.

In Monroe County we see a division of labor among agencies again, but a different one. In Erie County the IDA is large and has a very active and complex program in addition to issuing bonds, while the Chamber of Commerce is mainly responsible for marketing. In Monroe, the county contracted with the Chamber of Commerce for carrying on all of the program activities that the IDA does in Erie, while the Monroe County IDA had only a single staff member and confined its efforts to issuing bonds. But now that the Democratic party dominates public offices, the Chamber of Commerce is no longer the lead agency for county economic development.

Orange County

Orange County is a SMSA county just outside of the New York City standard metropolitan statistical area, and is feeling the effects of metropolitan expansion, especially in the last couple of years. Its residents are beginning to commute into New York City – several bus and train loads a day. It is also enjoying the growth of distribution and warehousing businesses and is beginning to get new manufacturing companies also.

The county has an IDA, a county planning office that is active in economic development, two Chambers of Commerce that divide the county geographically, and the Orange County Partnership, a nonprofit countywide organization recently formed, and it has two cities with economic development staff. It is also served by various regional agencies, along with a special Urban Development Corporation office located there to operate Stewart Field, a state airport, and its industrial park.

The county planning department leads in planning and information and sees its main role as an information center, though it processes Economic Development Administration grants. The county IDA has a part-time staff, consisting of a lawyer who works out of his office, and confines its efforts to issuing bonds. The two Chambers of Commerce both process Job Development Authority loans, help small business, and have regular business contact programs. Marketing is now mainly done by the newly established not-for-profit county agency, the Orange County Partnership, which is funded by the county and the IDA, with representatives on its board from the two Chambers of Commerce.

The agencies coordinate through interlocking directorates and say "we see each other every day," "our offices are very close." The two cities with agencies are poorer than the county as a whole and are eligible for funds the county is not. In addition to the normal complement of regional offices, the county is also served by two utilities, each with an economic developer. Before the Orange County Partnership was formed, the various agencies cooperated in subscribing to a study by a consulting firm that thought the county appeared to be too fractionated and recommended the formation of a countywide agency. This recommendation resulted in the new Orange County Partnership. This agency is responsible for marketing and site selection for the county, and it works closely with the other agencies when the prospects it has recruited visit the county. The county has enjoyed a very low unemployment rate for two years, at the time of the interview—but it is still making a major recruitment effort. If the period of prosperity lasts over the long haul, the county may develop a new and different set of problems than in the past when it was mainly concerned with unemployment and jobs. It is fast becoming part of the

New York City metro area; it may face labor shortages, and it will need to think about and plan for these new forces impinging upon it. Again in this county, the same activities are carried on as in the others, but there is a still different division of labor among agencies. Note that marketing, frequently a task carried on by the Chamber of Commerce, here is done by a special not-for-profit agency.

St. Lawrence County

St. Lawrence is a large rural county bordering on Canada with five small equally sized communities. It has a county IDA and two town/village IDAs. In this county, the Chamber of Commerce confines its efforts to tourism and retail trade, and has a good reputation for serving these sectors in a county where they are of some importance. It also has two special regional agencies peculiar to this region: one is a public authority, the Ogdensburg Bridge and Port Authority, and another a not-for-profit originated by a consortium of two universities and the county, a village, and a town for the purpose of technological industrial development called NATCO, Northern Advanced Technology Corporation. In addition to these, the normal complement of regional agencies serve the county.

The IDA was started in 1972 and now has several staff. It does marketing, issues bonds, and helps with grant applications and financial packaging. It also houses the county Private Industry Council, unlike most counties. It has loan funds of its own. It owns a spur railroad, some buildings, and an industrial park. It has investments in some businesses. But it mainly knows every business in the county and tries to meet every need. If a business has trouble with health regulations, for instance, a staff member will learn what he needs to advise and help out. The agency has a hands-on philosophy and believes in the importance of day-to-day work and contact.

Potsdam, one of the village agencies with a part-time staff member who also works in village administration, is active in downtown development and is starting a loan fund. The village loan funds are developed from Housing and Urban Development loan pay back. The other village, Messina, does not issue bonds, leaving this task to the county IDA. It became active in 1979, and its main project at present is the development of an industrial park.

The Ogdensburg Bridge and Port Authority is a state authority located in the county that operates a port, airport, and bridge, in addition to an incubator, industrial parks, and a railroad. A main goal is to attract Canadian business and it has a Canadian marketing program. It has the right to issue bonds and would do so if necessary, but lets the county do this. It works with the City of Ogdensburg and with the county IDA. It has municipal powers, like the IDAs, and in addition to that of bond issuance, has, and has exercised, the right of eminent domain, though rarely and with caution. Though authorized by the state, it must earn its own way through its activities.

NATCO, the Northern Advanced Technology Corporation, sponsored by the two universities in the county, along with the county IDA and local governments, runs a high-technology incubator whose main purpose is to foster business resulting from various university research efforts in Clarkson University, an engineering university, and SUNY-Potsdam, which has a strong computer department. A related organization aiming at a multi-county clientele is Northern Advanced Technology, operated in conjunction with NATCO, sponsored by the New York State Science and Technology Foundation and is trying to encourage high-technology industrial development in a wider multi-county area.

Again, in this county, the various agencies speak of each other, try to avoid stepping on each other's toes, try to cooperate in mutually helpful ways. This county also gets help from the normal complement of regional agencies, in addition to a technical assistance center based at SUNY-Plattsburg (outside the county) that, among other activities, helps agencies in the region with small business referrals. This agency is supported jointly by the EDA and the University. In this county the Chamber of Commerce has a traditional role (helping retail business), and industrial development is the work of several other agencies.

Jefferson County

Jefferson County has large rural areas with rivers, lakes, and forests that have given rise to state commissions and authorities in response to public concerns. It also has one good-sized city, Watertown, and a major military installation, Fort Drum, currently undergoing major expansion that affects a multi-county area.

The county IDA was formed in 1971. Recently it has been controversial because it issued a number of bonds for retail and commercial establishments, rather than industry, but it argues that these provided a lot of employment for women especially, and this is a group in need of jobs in this county, many wives of servicemen. Further, it is also argued that it keeps retail trade in the county, rather than going to Syracuse in Onondaga County. In addition to issuance of bonds from which it has earned large amounts of money in fees, it operates an industrial park with a Foreign Trade Zone, an incubator, and two loan funds. At the time of the interview it was about to launch an enlarged marketing program in response to public pressure.

The Chamber of Commerce takes care of small retail business. The county is also served by a Regional Planning Office, a Department of Commerce regional office, and a Small Business Development Center. In addition, there are two regional commissions operating in the county area and a wider regional authority.

The Tug Hill Commission was organized because of threatened land sale in 1972. It covers a number of townships in several counties. It now has a large staff, mostly of planners, who help with planning and problems of local government functioning in the multi-town area it covers. It also has a small economic development staff who work on rural economic problems.

The St. Lawrence-Ontario Regional Commission has a main purpose of conservation and development of the region's many areas along lake and river shores, again in a multi-county area. They assist local governments in the area bordering these waters with land, water and shore problems of preservation and of economic development at local request, work on tourism in the area, and they do research on area resources. It dates from 1969.

A regional multi-county state authority, the Development Authority of the North Country, was established in 1985 to deal with expansion of Fort Drum at the behest of local officials. It has held local hearings and has contracted with outside consulting firms to develop a master economic strategy for its area. It also is currently dealing with problems of infrastructure, and in particular with water and sewers serving the fort as well as surrounding areas.

All of these agencies with their different functions speak of cooperating with each other. One of the commissions talks of asking the IDA for help with projects and technical assistance in preparing loan applications.   The other talks of concern with the military installation and of working with several other organizations.   Their geographic territories and their functions are quite clearly separate, but they know each other's roles and coordinate.

Steuben County

Steuben County was faced with a disastrous flood in 1977, which brought federal relief funds to the area. The crisis and its aftermath of reconstruction is viewed as a watershed for the county, and from that date economic development agencies became very active.

There are three principal agencies in the county, the county IDA, a city agency, the 3 Rivers Development, and an organization owned and sponsored by Corning Glass, Corning Foundation Inc. Enterprises. The IDA issues bonds and helps with major industrial projects, mostly in rural areas. They also built and own a 35-mile spur railroad and have helped improve the airport. The IDA markets an industrial park owned by a private developer. The agency is also interested in promoting tourism and agriculture. The developer works closely with business, sitting down and reviewing all their needs. He does very little general marketing of the county.

The 3 Rivers Development Foundation, Inc. consists of three private organizations under one roof with the same staff. They do marketing of the city area. They work on community development projects in the city such as housing and zoning. They work on business development but only in the city. They own an industrial park, and help the city government with the revolving loan fund it has accrued from Housing and Urban Development pay back funds. They work closely with Corning Enterprises and are also linked by board of directors membership.

Corning Enterprises takes care of some of its corporate projects and properties, land, its airline, its retail and tourism business, but also takes an interest in development of the city and, indeed, a multi-county area.   It has worked on tourism and on main street commercial development and rehabilitation. It has developed a parking garage, hotel, office building, and motel with the help of the 3 Rivers Development Foundation. Its aim was to help create jobs in the area as well as to improve the quality of life and make the area attractive to its many employees. The corporation's former head is also active in the 3 Rivers and now serves on the staff of the Congressman for the district to advise on economic development. The various organizations are all interested in completion of Route 17, the Southern Tier Expressway, which is the four lane throughway that is near the city. They sometimes advise local business on seeking financing. The three county agencies meet once a month; "they can maintain secrecy." They are working with two nearby counties on a regional marketing program. They will be assisted with a marketing plan by the Regional Planning Office that also operates a loan fund as well as backstopping the efforts of other agencies in the area.

In addition to other regional organizations, NYSEG (New York State Electric & Gas) the public utility that covers the area is active, especially in marketing, but will also work with local agencies and businesses. It covers a very large region, however. In this region, the local Congressman is personally very active in economic development in his large district and meets regularly with all the economic developers in the district. He maintains an office in Corning.

In addition, in the western part of the county is an extremely active local IDA in the town of Hornell. It shares quarters with the town Chamber of Commerce and is active in downtown rehabilitation, water and waste management, and highway development. It works with local companies on expansion, operates four industrial parks, and runs training programs. It helps develop financial packages, and has an active marketing program using its own airplane to travel around the country. The director is active in state economic development organizations and takes an active interest in state policy formation. Thus, the county organizations cooperate and work together a great deal, though they have worked out geographic and functional divisions of labor, as in other counties, but here again somewhat differently.

Regionalism — Conclusions

There are a number of other counties with several agencies. With those described, they share several features. There is a recognized division of labor among the agencies which differs from county to county. The various agencies make efforts not to compete and they refer clients to the most suitable agency for the problem. The division of work can be along geographic lines, and we have described two different divisions. Or it can be along functional lines, of taking responsibility for different tasks.

Another common feature is that the several agencies typically keep in close touch informally, they may have regular formal meetings, they frequently work together and cooperate on projects, and they may serve on each others' boards of directors.

They rarely, if ever, contemplate amalgamation. Why not? First, they are subject to different types of authority, have different charters, staffs, and, as we have pointed out, different functions. But we can also offer a sociological explanation. We have mentioned the hypothesis that small organizations can maintain greater flexibility. And flexibility is an earmark of local development organizations. Their separate and independent nature provides the developers with autonomy, flexibility, and the capacity to respond quickly and in innovative ways without working through bureaucratic lines of approval. But the network of agencies and agents nonetheless maintain the capacity to work together when it is necessary. In additional, all of them have networks of government and business contacts throughout the county and constantly relate to each other as well. One might argue that if amalgamated, they would lose autonomy, flexibility, ability to react quickly and to use initiative. They would become bureaucratic, strive for regulation and standardization, and spend a good deal of staff time on such concerns that do not impede them at present. Thus close network relations are essential for effective functioning of the various agencies. Their wide contacts with business and government and with each other, and their information-processing role mean that these economic development organizations can correctly be characterized as open systems.

Chapter 11

Development Projects

As we have discussed strategies and program content of the local development agencies, we have not conveyed the nature of projects, their complexity, or the array of services, sources of financing, or the degree of cooperation among agencies required for the completion of many projects. Nor do we get a sense of how large and complex some projects are, or how small and simple others. As we present a number of projects as illustrations, let us not forget that not all projects that are undertaken succeed. Sometimes many months of effort are invested and a project may fall through, perhaps through delays on the part of one of a number of sources of funding involved. But often the lack of significant projects indicates that a developer has assessed his county and does not find the probability very great of filling an industrial park or inducing business. Or he realizes the county lacks technically skilled labor needed for certain types of industries. Or his own organization lacks the time or professional staff needed for certain types of projects. But perhaps one element in success is realizing the limitations of the situation.

The following examples do not represent any kind of sample, for we have only project descriptions from brochures or annual reports of some of the agencies. Therefore they are simply illustrative. But they are nonetheless useful in understanding how activities and agencies come together in behalf of business. First are a number of examples from annual reports of the Erie County Industrial Development Agency, the oldest in the state, followed by examples from a number of other county agencies.

New Companies

Mobile Diagnostic Testing, Inc. (1985)

Two important sectors of Western New York's diversifying economy - medicine and electronics - were merged in 1985 with the formation of **Mobile Diagnostic Testing, Inc.**, (MDTI).

MDTI provides medical diagnostic testing and screening services for area hospitals and physicians using a mobile laboratory van to reach patients in suburban and rural areas where technological resources or trained staffing are not readily available to provide such state-of-the-art outpatient testing and examination as echocardiograms and Holter monitoring.

Headquartered in the Town of Clarence, MDTI was provided $12,000 in start-up financing through the Erie County Business Development Fund (ECBDF) loan program administered by the ECIDA's Buffalo and Erie County Industrial Land Development Corporation. The ECBDF is a small business revolving loan fund capitalized by Erie County's community development consortium communities and designed to meet the working capital and equipment financing needs of expanding businesses in that area.

Norstar Bank, N.A., provided term financing and a line of credit accommodation to the company which anticipates the creation of nine new employment opportunities over the next three years.

Iimak (1984)

The Buffalo-Erie County area's image as a leader in the printing and printing-related products industries was further enhanced in 1984 as **International Imaging Materials, Inc. (Iimak)** commenced operations in the Town of Amherst.

Iimak, the sole U.S. and Canadian licensee of the Fugi Kagakuski Kogyo Company headquartered in Osaka, Japan, manufactures and sells thermal ink transfer recording products used with microcomputer systems for printing black and color type and graphics. Thermal transfer coatings are produced by the firm on both polyester and paper offering a unique, direct electronic printing process providing excellent print quality and high speed production capabilities.

The decision to locate Iimak's operations in Western New York was partly business and partly personal. Robert H. Downie, company founder and current president, recognized Western New York's assets as a printing center - the industry is the area's second largest employer following automotive component manufacturing - and, building on both his knowledge of the area while employed the Moore Corporation and the close association he had developed with the president of Fugi, Mr. Downie set his sights on establishment of Iimak as a leader in its field serving the North American marketplace.

Following nearly two years of negotiations to arrange for the licensing agreements and the completion of a successful private placement offering in early 1984, area public financing agencies joined with Marine Midland Bank to provide an attractive financial arrangement to secure the establishment of the company's operations in Erie County. Marine Midland purchased $2.5 million in industrial revenue bonds issued by the Amherst Industrial Development Agency, and the ECIDA's Regional Development Corporation provided a $500 thousand loan for a portion of Iimak's working capital requirements.

In July, the company held a grand opening celebration at its new, fifteen thousand square foot facility in the Audubon Industrial Park where Iimak projects its work force to total 120 employees by mid-year 1986.

Cyber Digital, Inc. (1985)

The continuing growth of the high technology-electronics industry in Western New York was evidenced during 1985 as **Cyber Digital, Inc.**, a Long Island-based firm engaged in the research and development of the MSX microswitch system, chose the Erie County town of Amherst as the site for establishment of its primary U.S. manufacturing facility.

Commercial production of the MSX, a digital switching unit capable of providing users with the capacity to integrate, transmit and receive data and voice communications over standard telephone lines in a single integrated system, is slated to begin at the company's Amherst

International Business Park location in Spring, 1986. Over 150 new jobs are anticipated to be created during the next two years.

A $1 million loan from the ECIDA's Buffalo and Erie County Regional Development Corporation (RDC) leveraged $7 million dollars for the project in the form of new equity capital contributions and term and line of credit financing made available through Buffalo-Based Empire of America, FSB. Loan guarantees from the federal Economic Development Administration and the New York Job Development Authority were instrumental in securing the bank financing. The Town of Amherst Industrial Development Agency issued $780,000 in tax-exempt industrial revenue bonds for Uniland Development Company's construction of Cyber Digital's 23,700 square foot facility and provided the RDC with a $200,000 loan for the project. The ECIDA previously secured, in 1983, an $850,000 federal Urban Development Action Grant (UDAG) from the U.S. Department of Housing and Urban Development for Uniland's advancement of the international business park project.

Expansions And Changes

Nitzer Machine Corporation   **(1985)**

Nitzer Machine Corporation commenced construction of their new 14,000 square foot manufacturing facility at the Fire Tower Drive Industrial Park in the Town of Tonawanda. Fifteen new positions will be added to the company's precision metal fabricating operations work force.

The combined resources of the ECIDA's Industrial Tax-Exempt Mortgage (ITEM) and Town of Tonawanda Business Incentive Fund (TTBIF) financing programs were secured for the company's expansion with a $420,000 bond for land acquisition and building construction purchased by Chemical Bank and a $50,000 working capital loan approved by the Buffalo and Erie County Industrial Land Development Corporation (ILDC) to meet the company's working capital requirements.

The ILDC, a member of the ECIDA Financing and Development Group, administers the Business Incentive Fund in association with the Town of Tonawanda Development Corporation. The fund provides equipment and working capital resources for expanding firms in the Town's manufacturing, wholesaling and transportation industries sectors.

Hi-Tech Robotics, Ltd. (1983)

A new location in a plant that had been vacant for two years, a new name reflecting the company's emerging product lines and a new financial base obtained through a public common stock issue are expected to result in a tripling of employment during the next two years at Hi-Tech Robotics, Ltd.

Through 1982, the firm known formerly as Wilton Metal Manufacturing Company, Inc., generated the bulk of its business through the design, fabrication, manufacture and installation of automation and material handling systems dedicated to user specific applications. Building on its experience and utilizing new technologies available through computerization, Wilton Metal was readied for a new era and the development and sales of new products involving robotic controls, computer circuitry and programming, and other support equipment for "turnkey," total systems solutions to customer material handling needs.

In order to attract new customer interest in its products and establish an identity suited to the investment market, Wilton Metal become Hi-Tech Robotics in early 1983. The result was a successful stock issue and the negotiation of a purchase agreement to acquire a 70,000 square foot plant on Harlem Road in Cheektowaga.

Financing for Hi-Tech's new facility was completed through a $375 thousand Manufacturers Hanover Trust Company, N.A. bank mortgage and $300,000 New York Job Development Authority second mortgage loan. The ECIDA-affiliated Buffalo and Erie County Industrial Land Development Corporation provided a $300,000 interim loan to facilitate the company's mid-year acquisition and renovation of the building in which an estimated 65 persons will be employed within the next two years.

Gibraltar Steel Corporation (1984)

It was a decade ago when the ECIDA first issued a $995 thousand tax-exempt bond for the expansion of the **Gibraltar Steel Corporation**. Gibraltar, at the time, employed 120 persons and projected the addition of nine new jobs at its Walden Avenue strip steel and strapping production facilities.

Ten years and 300 additional employees later, Gibraltar Steel continued, in 1984, its commitment to the growth of its Western New York operations with a multi-million dollar modernization program at the Cheektowaga plant and the expansion of the firm's Seneca Steel Division located at the municipal boundaries of the City of Buffalo and the Town of Tonawanda.

In June, the ECIDA issued $3.8 million in bonds to finance the installation of state-of-the-art gauge control equipment at the Walden Avenue plant; increasing milling capabilities and improving quality control systems necessary to meet higher customer product specifications. And, by year end, an additional $1.6 million bond issued by the ECIDA enabled Gibraltar to expand its Seneca Steel Division operations on Military Road to meet added space and material handling requirements and upgrade sheep processing lines with the installation of microprocessor controlled shearing and resquaring devices. The bonds, purchased by Chase Lincoln First Bank, will allow Gibraltar to store higher levels of inventory on site and improve operational efficiencies necessary to maintain a competitive market position.

Gibraltar's three Western New York plants process steel - slitting, leveling, cold reducing, edging and annealing - for more than one thousand companies in a wide variety of industries with sales in 40 states and Canada. The company projects its area work force to total nearly 450 workers within the next two years.

Shur-Line on Solid Ground in
Lancaster Village Industrial Park (1984)

A sixty-three thousand square foot manufacturing facility and office complex in the Lancaster Village Industrial Park will become the new headquarters for Lancaster-based, Shur-Line Manufacturing Company,

Inc., as a result of a complete financing arranged through the ECIDA Financing and Development Group during 1984.

Shur-Line, a thirty-one year old manufacturer of foam and flat-pad paint application tools, acquired a 7.5 acre site at 2000 Commerce Parkway for the $2.25 million facility financed with industrial revenue bonds issued by the ECIDA and purchased by Liberty Norstar Bank. The Buffalo and Erie County Regional Development Corporation provided a $200 thousand permanent working capital loan in conjunction with bank line of credit financing and the Village of Lancaster allocated $61,000 in community development block grant funds for site preparation to assure the retention of the firm in the Lancaster area.

Shur-Line's project, expected to result in an increase in the company's work force from its present 86 employees to 110 persons over the next two years, is the third business expansion into the Lancaster Village Industrial Park since the site's development in 1981. The first phase, 35-acre tract was developed by the village with technical assistance from the ECIDA and is expected to facilitate ten to twelve companies when fully occupied.

McCauley/Phoenix Acquisition   (1984)

The newly formed Town of Tonawanda Business Incentive Fund and the Buffalo and Erie County Regional Development Corporation joined, during 1984, to provide near-equity financing for the acquisition of Tonawanda-based **McCauley Metal Products, Inc.** and Buffalo-based **Phoenix Die Casting Company**;local manufacturers of stainless steel, fabricated metal products and alloy castings.

The purchase of the firms from the estate of the McCauley family by current company president, James M. Downing, allowed for continued operations and returned the businesses to active ownership management with a projected increase in employment from the present combined work force of fourteen to forty-three persons within the next three years.

McCauley, founded in Buffalo in 1922, manufactures handlebars, fenders, kick stands and chain guards for the bicycle industry and other products for electrical, automotive and appliance manufacturers.

Formed prior to the turn of the century, Phoenix produces low temperature alloy castings for a wide variety of industries from railroad product to medical and dental equipment manufacturers.

A $725 thousand financing was arranged through the ECIDA Financing and Development Group with the Buffalo and Erie County Industrial Land Development Corporation's Town of Tonawanda Business Incentive Fund providing $50,000 for working capital and equipment acquisition at McCauley's 40,000 square foot, Woodward Avenue, Tonawanda plant and the Regional Development Corporation closing an additional $100,000 working capital loan for J.M. Downing Industries, Inc., the corporation formed to acquire the two concerns. The Permanent Savings Bank provided $525,000 in term and line of credit financing.

Buffalo Specialty Products, Inc.   (1983)

A complex $7.96 million financing was arranged by the ECIDA during 1983 for the acquisition of Bethlehem Steel Corporation's Specialty Steel Products Division by Buffalo Specialty Products, Inc.

Buffalo Specialty, a newly-formed subsidiary corporation of the H.J. Williams Company, Inc. of York, Pennsylvania, purchased 16 acres of land, three buildings totaling 189,000 square feet and machinery and equipment at the Town of Hamburg facility which had been scheduled for shutdown as part of Bethlehem Steel's phase-out of Buffalo-area steelmaking operations.

M&T Bank provided the primary private sector lending participation including the purchase of a $4.4 million ECIDA-issued industrial revenue bond and a $2 million line of credit accommodation. Subordinate lending included a $1.76 million New York Job Development Authority loan and a $500,000 working capital loan from the Buffalo and Erie County Regional Development Corporation; the ECIDA's revolving loan fund program.

Financing for the project, which is expected to retain 40 positions and create 100 new jobs during the next two years, was completed just three days prior to the first anniversary of Bethlehem Steel's announcement to discontinue steelmaking in Lackawanna.

The former Specialty Products shop with its capacity for shearing, press-braking and roll-forming construction materials used in building, highway and bridge work will provide products for its parent company's primary general contracting business and to other construction industry end users.

The following example comes from the Allegany County IDA, 1987:

Combustion Engineering   (1987)

The Office of Economic Development was instrumental in the delivery of a financial incentive package to Combustion Engineering management which identified $2.1 million dollars to be reduced from the overall projected cost of the consolidation at Wellsville. This package was a key in the selection of Wellsville as the site for operations.

This office's role was to offer input and coordination of activities among the various agencies and elements which supported the incentive package. Among the elements of the package were investment tax credit, a freeze on real estate assessment increases, economic development incentive rates by utilities and development of an employment training program to put 125 new hires to work. Funds to support training efforts have been generated by a 17 member group known as the Allegany County Training Consortium (ACTC). Through this process a close working relationship has been developed between this office and the Allegany County Private Industry Council. Both offices collaborated in developing a successful REDS Application for a $200,000 training grant for CE Air Preheater.

Operation Oswego, Inc.'s 1985 report offers an example of preservation of an abandoned factory for further use and helping a company develop a product line.

Operation Oswego, Inc.

Operation Oswego County, Inc. coordinated the negotiations between **Niagara Mohawk, Robertson Paper Company** and **North End Paper Company** to maintain heat for the closed plant while purchase offers were being formulated. If these arrangements had not been successful, the equipment at the papermill would have been rendered useless and the future buyout would not have been feasible.

General Foods

At the request of General Foods' Fulton plant management, Operation Oswego County prepared a special report for their use in attempting to secure and attract a new product line. Efforts were successful and the Fulton plant will be adding around 150 new jobs after the plant is converted.

They also helped a number of other companies with expansion, rebuilding, pollution control, new buildings, acquiring an existing company, and with working capital.

Blount Lumber Company of Lacona completed a 25,000 square foot expansion to their flush door division. The $600,000 expansion created 38 new jobs. A HUD Small Cities Grant was secured to provide a $150,000 low interest loan to help finance this project.

A $16,800 Rural Development Loan was secured from the New York Job Development Authority to assist the **Parish Red & White** in rebuilding, 7 jobs were retained. The total project cost was estimated at $135,000.

Miller Brewing Company received $12.5 million in tax-exempt industrial development bonds through the Oswego County IDA for pollution control abatement facilities.

Black Clawson Converting Laboratory, Inc. built a new $3.2 million laboratory facility in Fulton. The Oswego County IDA issued $1.9 million in tax-exempt industrial revenue bonds for this project which will create 95 new jobs.

Acro-Fab Ltd. of Hannibal received a $12,000 loan from the Oswego County IDA to help finance the acquisition of a new building. The $50,000 expansion helped to retain 10 jobs and will create 6 new jobs.

Pontiac Photo Engraving & Press, a 48-year old printing firm in Oswego, was acquired and a $5,000 working capital loan through Operation Oswego County was provided. The project created 2 jobs and helped to retain an existing business.

A $21,000 short-term working capital loan was made to **The Arrowhead Group** of Phoenix. The loan, made jointly by the IDA and Operation Oswego County, helped to retain 45 positions at the La-Del facility.

The 1986 Oneida County Industrial Development Corporation report described the work of developing a business park and acquisition of a Massachusetts-owned company of a local firm.

One of the most exciting and important projects ever worked on by OCIDC was the Allied Bendix/Utica Business Park development. The project involved the purchase of the 80 acre Utica College Golf Course by the City of Utica for development of a business park and developing an approach through which Allied Bendix would be the Park's first tenant.

OCIDC was rightfully referred to as the "catalyst" in this effort. The project's importance is profound. It stabilizes the presence of Bendix in the area and within the City's boundaries while reclaiming area jobs. It will result in an investment of $5-$7 million by Bendix which will lead to the creation of over 200 new jobs. And, it demonstrates the ability of the economic development agencies to satisfy the needs of a major employer. OCIDC and the City worked together in outstanding fashion to make this project a reality.

This project cost $10 million and involved participation of the county IDA, the City of Utica, the state and federal government.

Another significant 1986 project was the acquisition of Burgess, Inc., a Massachusetts firm, by D.B. Smith, an Oneida County firm, and the relocation of Burgess to Oneida County. The project will immediately result in 80 new manufacturing jobs and improve D.B. Smith's position to grow in the future. OCIDC made a significant contribution to the project by structuring the approach to financing the acquisition. The package included sizable loans through the New York Job Development Authority and the State Urban Development Corporation. OCIDC also joined with Mr. Eugene Romano, the owner of D.B. Smith, and Linda Roman, his attorney, in making presentations to the respective state agencies. All in all, it was a solid team effort toward winning one instead of losing one.

This project cost $5.2 million and involved the county IDA, the City of Utica development organization, JDA, and bank funds.

The Metropolitan Development Association of Syracuse (1985) described a very complex long-range project of converting Hancock Field, a military air field to commercial use. While such a project is not carried out every day, such complex long-range tasks are not unusual.

Hancock Air Base

The activities of the Community Committee on Hancock Field, which was created and is staffed by the MDA, continued through 1985. Robert E. Wehrle is Chairman of the committee, which focused on the need to create a plan for reusing the base, since military uses are limited. The 152nd TAC unit of the Air National Guard, which includes 20 full-time members and 150 part-time Guardsmen, moved to the base in October, 1984. The Department of Defense also announced plans to locate another 100 people in the former SAGE complex, in addition to the Northeast Telecommunications Switching Center (NETSC), which handles all of the military messages for the defense of the Northeast at that facility. Congressman George Wortley led the effort to secure these new missions for the base, as well as to provide high level contact with the federal agencies that could address base redevelopment.

The major civilian reuse of the facility is for the expansion of the adjacent Hancock International Airport. The Aviation Department retained the engineering firm of Calcerinos and Spina to update the airport's master plan and to develop plans to construct a third runway, 9,000 feet long and parallel to the main existing east-west runway at the airport. This would make Syracuse the only airport in Upstate New York with simultaneous operation capability under all weather conditions. The New York State Department of Transportation and the Federal Aviation Administration studied and endorsed the plan for the development of the third runway.

The firm of Hueber, Hares and Glavin, working under contract to the Metropolitan Development Foundation, prepared a reuse plan for the base. The MDF also retained the firm of Coopers and Lybrand to undertake a financial feasibility study for creation of the industrial park and reuse of the base housing. The MDF has obtained significant federal and state funding to undertake these plans.

In May, 1985, the Department of Defense sponsored a "pre-disposal" conference to discuss the planned federal disposition of the base. As the disposal of the base land moved forward, the firm of Pomeroy Appraisal was retained to complete an appraisal of the base property. This will be used for negotiations with the GSA. MDA counsel, Don Denton of Hancock and Estabrook, began work to draft the by-laws and articles of incorporation for a not-for-profit entity to manage the base lands that lie outside the clear zone of the airport.

Since the airport industrial park will not be developed until the early 1990's, the community committee developed a short-range strategy to lease the existing base buildings. Many local firms expressed interest in locating at the base. The MDF began negotiations with the Air Force to permit these manufacturing and commercial firms to locate at the base.

At the same time, two new public users began operations at the base: 1) The Onondaga County Sheriff's Department has opened its first substation at the base entrance, and 2) the Town of Cicero operated the officer's club for recreation activities during the summer. The Syracuse Area Interreligious Council obtained a license for the use of the gymnasium to establish the first foodbank in Central New York. This will be a warehousing facility to allow the centralized distribution of food to the needy in the region.

The MDA approached New York State to request funding for building rehabilitation at the base. This proposal is now being considered by the state. It is anticipated that negotiations for the acquisition of the base will be underway during 1986.

The Genesee County IDA 1986 Report describes a somewhat different type of project.

Genesee Center for Industry

Background

In 1982, N.L. Industries decided to close its Doehler-Jarvis Die Casting facility in Batavia, dislocating approximately 175 workers. N.L. Industries sold the facility and equipment to Mill Street of Batavia Industrial Park, Inc., principal owners being Wilbur-Ellis Corp. and Stetter Machinery Corp.

Upon taking title to the property in October of 1982, the Mill Street Corporation undertook the liquidation of machinery, equipment and furnishings. Many of the items were sold at auction while others were disposed of through individual transactions over the next 2-1/2 years. During this period little attention was given to the maintenance of the property with utility services eventually being terminated.

While the real interest of the Mill Street Corp. was in liquidating the equipment, the company indicated a desire to work with the Industrial Development Agency in trying to lease or sell the property to industrial firms. On several occasions prospective clients were brought to the Mill Street group with viable purchase offers. Due to the lack of cooperation to negotiate in good faith, the deteriorating condition of the building, and non-payment of property taxes, the Agency had to cease its promotion and marketing of the property.

Recognizing that the property was becoming a liability to both the owners and the community, the Industrial Development Agency put forth a proposal to accept the property as a donation. To accomplish this, the Wilbur-Ellis Company acquired 100% interest in the former Doehler-Jarvis building and donated it to the City of Batavia. After forgiving $71,000 of back taxes due, the City transferred title to the Industrial Development Agency. As part of the agreement, Wilbur-Ellis also made a $40,000 contribution to the Agency to help defray some of the clean-up and carrying costs of the building.

Plan for Reuse

Prior to accepting the "donation" of the industrial building, the Agency began to formulate a plan for the facility's eventual use. Having already experienced a great deal of difficulty in marketing the 275,000 square foot facility, the Agency's plan was to demolish the 80,000 square foot "mid section," subdivide the property into two parcels, renovate the front 125,000 square feet and sell the remaining 69,000 square foot building on Ganson Avenue. By doing this the Agency would have a multi-tenant leaseable facility to attract new companies and to offer locational incentives for hiring dislocated workers.

It was recognized early on in the formulation of this plan that it was going to cost a great deal of money to renovate a building for eventual use as a multi-tenant industrial complex. To that end, the Agency began to apply for and eventually received over $1.2 million of Federal and State funds for the renovation activities.

Acquisition and Renovation

Immediately after the Industrial Development Agency took title to the property in April 1985, its plan for reuse was implemented. Based on the strategy already devised, the Agency commenced the environmental clean-up of the property, contracted for the demolition of the 80,000 square feet of foundry and casting areas, subdivision of the property, marketing the 70,000 square foot Ganson Avenue building and detailed engineering of the 125,000 square foot multi-tenant building.

Renovation of the former Doehler-Jarvis facility commenced with a conceptual plan of dividing the building into seven tenant areas, each individually metered for electric and gas services. With the awarding of Federal and State grants for renovation work, the Agency was able to commence the general construction activities in June of 1986 and roof repairs in October of the same year. Improvements to the facility included the replacement of windows with insulated wall panels, fire rated tenant walls, partitions and doors, new plumbing, electrical and heating systems, roof repairs and an elevator for the two-story building. With substantial completion of the renovation work already accomplished, the project is scheduled for completion in early 1987.

Marketing

According to the reutilization plan developed by the Agency, it was going to market both leaseable industrial building space and the sale of the 69,000 square foot Ganson Avenue property. Knowing that the multi-tenant facility was to require more time for renovations, the Agency started with the marketing of the Ganson Avenue property.

In marketing the Ganson Avenue facility, the Agency was promoting the property as a shell building since all utilities had been disconnected. Varying degrees of interest were shown until Exceltronic Computing, Inc., a Canadian electronics manufacturer, submitted a purchase offer. For six months the Agency worked with the company in formulating a financial package, job training assistance, identifying engineers and contractors, and a range of other forms of assistance needed by a new company. The day before the legal papers were to be executed for the property and loans, the company, based on the advice of its Canadian bankers, decided not to proceed with the project.

Shortly thereafter, Ronald Viele, of Viele Construction Company, submitted a proposal to purchase and renovate the facility for lease to companies he was negotiating with. The sale of the facility was concluded in November of 1986, thereby, putting the property back on the tax rolls with the prospects of new jobs forthcoming.

When assessing the viability of acquiring, renovating and operating a multi-tenant industrial facility, the Agency recognized the unique inducement this would make in attracting new companies, but also realized the potential risk involved. As the Agency was applying for the grants to renovate the building, it began to identify prospective tenants. One firm, Surbond Lubricants, Inc., expressed an early desire to locate in the building once the renovation work had been completed. With the construction work to the two-story building having been substantially completed in November, Surbond Lubricants, Inc. executed a lease and started to locate its operations in this structure. This occupancy by an industrial tenant has begun generating additional interest among prospective clients and is expected to increase as the marketing program intensifies.

Genesee Center for Industry

Throughout the Agency's involvement with the former Doehler-Jarvis complex, the connotation of a metal casting foundry had a tendency to dissuade prospective individuals from looking at the facility. Having spent $1.5 million on the complex, the Agency felt it could ill afford to discourage interest in the building because of its name. In an effort to better reflect the community and the facility's use, the Agency christened it the "Genesee Center for Industry."

The Genesee Center for Industry, once a vacant and deteriorating building that was rapidly becoming a hazard to public health, is now being put to more productive use. It will once again be a focal point for jobs and will foster the location and growth of new industry. This has been a community-wide effort with contributions from the City. Town, County, State and Federal governments, and the Genesee County Industrial Development Agency accepting the challenge and seeing it through to a positive community result.

This was a $1.2 million project with funds from three sources including state and local loans.

Ulster County counted among its 1985 projects an expansion of an industry and a rehabilitation of the Adirondack Transit Lines.

KTB Associates participated in a $5,700,000 bond issue to purchase property and equipment and construct a 60,000 s.f. printing facility in the Town of Saugerties. The new facility and state of the art equipment will allow for an additional 26 jobs to be created, and 125 jobs to be retained in the Saugerties area. This is the second bond issue for KTB, the first allowed for an expansion and the purchase of new equipment at their Simmons Street location.

Adirondack Transit Lines needed to construct a new garage and office complex, and to purchase additional Trailways buses. This $1,500,000 project in the City of Kingston will result in the construction of a new 32,500 S.F. building, the purchase of 4 new buses and the creation of at least 10 new jobs. The new facility is located on property sold to the company by the City of Kingston.

The Schenectady County Development Corporation (1985) described the rehabilitation and use of an empty plant and of a former Naval depot.

The old 43,000 square foot Pepsi Plant on Freemans Bridge Road has stood empty for years. Now underway is a $2 million rehabilitation of this structure by Retired Persons Services Inc. for its regional mail order pharmaceutical operation. They expect to start hiring in the spring of 1986 and when fully staffed will employ 125 people including 25 registered pharmacists. The County IDA issued bonds to make this project a reality and the Town of Glenville expedited all the zoning and permit processes. This company, a subsidiary of the American Association of Retired Persons, is a first class company that selected Schenectady County over a number of other upstate locations because of our aggressive and helpful approach to making it easy to do business here.

In June of last year, a strong competitive effort by the County IDA, the City in securing UDAG funds, and the Town of Glenville made the Galesi Group's $12 million rehab of the old Scotia Naval Depot possible. This provides the Community with 1.3 million square feet of space to recruit new industry into. Three of the 100,000 square foot buildings are being used by Galesi's warehousing company. Two of the buildings will be used for expansion by Adirondack Beverages and Sofco.

We are working with the Galesi Group in aggressively marketing the remaining space. Our second 100 plus new company of 1985 was a result of that activity. American Safety Closure is a start-up plastics manufacturing company that has a patented process on a new soda closure. The company, after looking at numerous cities in several states, settled on Schenectady because they felt we had the resources, staff and team effort needed to put together the $9 million financial package they need. This is a complicated financial deal that involves a $3-1/2 million bond issue, a $3 million public stock offering and a $2-1/2 million UDAG. While there is a lot of work left to bring this deal to a successful conclusion, it is significant that they chose Schenectady. If successful, this company could employ as many as 250 people in the next several years.

The Adirondack Economic Development Corporation, a private organization, serves several townships in two counties, Franklin and Essex. Its operations are on a smaller scale than many examples given but, again, not unusual. Their report is more detailed than many that deal with problems of smaller businesses, and therefore useful for comprehending problems that may not be as complex or expensive but nonetheless vital to the companies involved. These are from its report on 1985 and 1986. They list the company name, type of assistance, and a synopsis of what was done.

(1985/1986)

Diversified Area; September 1985; Business plan. 5 employees; Aircraft Maint. & Repair, fixed base operator. Coordinating sea plane base operations and customs service.

Snapshot Photo; Site Location Business Plan. 2 employees; 1 hour photo service. AEDC-SBDC/TAC provided feasibility study.

Riverside Bakery & Shoppe; October 1985; Site Location, Feasibility Study. 5 employees; Bakery, catering service. AEDC reviewed financing and SBDC/TAC provided technical assistance.

American Village; September 1986; Business Plan, Market Study. 4 to 6 employees. AEDC provided information on financing and with SBDC/TAC assisting on market study for drive through dry cleaning.

Burger King; September 1986; Business plan, Market Study, Permit applications, Technical Assistance. 76 employees. As an independent franchise utilized the full resources of AEDC to put first store in Tri-Lakes.

Bionique Laboratories; September 1986; Financial Assistance, Technical Assistance. 20 employees; Provided assistance for a successful $280,000 expansion project for a Bio-Medical facility. 2nd consecutive use of Job Development Activity (JDA) monies <1st use of in either Franklin or Essex counties> and Regional Economic Development Partnership Program. Efforts recognized by visit from Governor of New York State.

Big Tupper Ski Area; September 1986; Technical Assistance. Jobs preserved; Provided technical assistance for $175,000 "Aid to Distress Localities" grant in conjunction with Town of Altamont.

Nason's Carpets; June 1986; Financial Assistance, Business Plan. 3 employees; AEDC in conjunction with SBDC/TAC assisted with business plan and currently formulating financial assistance for expansion.

Finally, to get an idea of the functioning of one agency in one year, let us look at the Overview from the Jefferson County IDA's 1985 report.

Jefferson County Industrial Development Agency

Overview

The year 1985 reflects another milestone in the slow and steady emergence of the Jefferson County Industrial Development Agency as lead Agency in the Economic Development of Jefferson County.

For the purpose of this report, the years 1983 and 1984 have been assessed to get a better understanding at where we have come from and to project a better approach towards future direction.

Economic Development without specific infrastructure and programs as tools, is Economic Development without purpose. In understanding this, the Jefferson County Industrial Development Agency (JCIDA) in 1983 began a 20 month project to create the Jefferson County Foreign Trade Zone. Presently, the Foreign Trade Zone has three specific sites. First the New York Air Brake Co., second the Jefferson County Industrial Park, and lastly the refurbished Dexter Sulphite Mill in Dexter. Also in 1983, JCIDA worked closely with Frontier Housing Corporation to obtain a $400,000 New York Job Development Authority loan to complete construction and renovation of the Sulphite Mill for ultimate use as a Foreign Trade Zone.

The Industrial Park in early 1984 underwent some careful planning to further develop the Industrial Park's infrastructure. JCIDA applied for and received funding through the U.S. Economic Development Administration to double the capacity of our sewage system from 10,000 GPD to 20,000 GPD. (Our sewage system presently carries no user charges and is considered an incentive to locate in the Park.) The same $369,000 grant also included funding for a 250,000 gallon water tower, which not only serves the Park, but also enhances to a degree the entire water district. The local share of funding to obtain this grant came from the Watertown Trust, Jefferson County, and JCIDA.

In 1984 and again in 1985, an unprecedented need for small business expansion surfaced. These expansions were in the $50,000 to $200,000 range where Industrial Revenue Bond financing can be too costly to be effective. JCIDA responded by applying for, two separate Community Development Block Grants which were funded to the amount of $1,400,000. These monies are now capitalizing a revolving loan fund for the needs of Small Business in Jefferson County.

Besides Small Cities funding in 1985, the Agency came to the aid of the Black River St. Lawrence Regional Planning and Development Board, with the help of the Jefferson County Board of Supervisors. The IDA in essence leveraged $370,000 in U.S. Economic Development Administration funds by granting the Regional Planning Board $130,000 from a long term $250,000 note we have with Jefferson County. The Board of Supervisors helped by extending the note by nine (9) years, thereby allowing the Agency to invest the remainder of the note and still remain liable to the County for the $250,000 face amount. This important project could not have been completed without the support of the Jefferson County Board of Supervisors.

Also in 1985, the Agency issued bonds for eight projects totaling $92,025,000, increasing the Jefferson County tax base by approximately $68,170,000. These specific bond issues directly effected 1500 jobs, both new positions and retainage of existing jobs.

Conclusions

These examples of projects from a few counties are not unlike those from many others, both large and small. We cannot call them typical because each agency works on such a range of businesses and problems, and each in its own way is unique. However, they illustrate several important points.

Many projects require continuing effort over a long period of time, and a company may, after its first problem is solved, come back for help with expansion or change.

Many require cooperation among a number of regional, county, city, and town agencies where they work together, each contributing in its own way. Occasionally business people or state organizations will comment on competition among local agencies. These and many similar projects show that there exists a great deal of cooperation. We also hear a lot about the several agencies in an area meeting regularly, keeping in touch, and referring clients to each other. We cannot claim that competition does not exist, though we have not heard much about it. Actually it is difficult to imagine what form it would take.

Certainly agencies can fail to cooperate, but we have evidence that there exists a great deal of cooperation among agencies and a great deal of appreciation of each others' abilities and specialization.

Many projects require a number of different types of help to succeed and a variety of organizations provide these including site selection, building and remodeling, change of production methods, development of products, pollution control, training and recruitment of employees, tax incentives, permits, and credit and working capital as well as loans.

A successful project thus means that agencies often tackle a variety of related problems needed to complete the project. Among cooperating agencies a variety of skills and a wide range of knowledge is required.

Projects cover a great span of complexity and cost, from very complicated multimillion dollar undertakings to small ones with no financial involvement, but assistance on management problems of various kinds.

In short, developers will tackle any size or type of problem and work with many other people and agencies over whatever period of time it takes to complete it.

Chapter 12

Pressures On Counties — Similarities
and Differences in Programming

Despite similarities in structure and programs, the organizations from various areas differ in emphasis. I have pointed out that they are very aware of their local problems and resources and very responsive to these. Therefore it is not surprising that they tailor their programs to their own regional opportunities and pressures.

One trend affecting a number of counties is metropolitan expansion. For whatever reasons, the various problems of city development or the desire for open space, outer areas beyond the Standard Metropolitan Statistical Areas are becoming part of metropolitan economies. Modern transportation and communication has made this possible. In at least two regions, distribution and warehousing firms are becoming established in such areas. They also attract back office operations. And of course, people are commuting what formerly seemed like great distances into the cities. In some cases, suburban residential development has attracted industry to or beyond such areas. No one wants to live next to a smokestack industry. But the small clean industries and back office operations with their attractive buildings and landscaped grounds do not depress the quality of the residential environment, and they are convenient for executives who live in the area to commute to work. Therefore, they are intermingling in heretofore purely residential communities.

Sixty percent of Rensselaer County commutes to Albany. The Albany spread extends up the Northway to Saratoga, and other nearby counties also supply workers to Albany and are becoming part of the metropolitan economy, with new business moving in or starting up. Therefore, the counties out beyond the metro regions are preparing for the spillover and are busy facilitating the economic growth they are realizing, putting emphasis on servicing the businesses that are coming in, providing infrastructure and a variety of intangible helps. In some of these, marketing of the county is a lesser emphasis, as is financing of business, than in slower growing areas. Agencies help with settling in, with management information. What they soon will be facing is the threat of labor shortages.

Another regional pressure is location on or close to the Canadian border. Border counties are establishing Foreign Trade Zones and conducting marketing programs in Canada to attract branches of Canadian firms that market their products in the United States. Location in a Foreign Trade Zone permits a firm to choose whether to pay a tariff when it imports parts or materials or when it ships out a finished product, thus saving money. The developers' idea is that Canadian firms are eager to expand into the vastly larger United States market and locating here facilitates this. Developers at first expect warehousing and distribution, and hope to move companies from that to manufacturing. Agencies with such an interest try to supply material and intangible help to firms they attract. This situation will, of course, change with changing Canadian trade relations.

Some of the older, traditional industrial areas of the state face similar problems with similar remedies. These areas have lost and continue to lose the industries that made them grow: steel, automobiles, apparel, and textiles. This is due largely to national changes in industrial structure and to regional changes in the United States that cannot be prevented by local efforts. For example, chemical industries of importance in some counties have a finite life. Apparel and steel have been going off shore. Many firms in such areas have been branches of multi-plant corporations. Therefore, one effort common in such areas is to arrange local buy outs of branches still deemed viable that are threatening to leave, in an effort not only to keep jobs but also to indigenize the economy, to have manufacturing firms with local roots that have a vested interest in the area.

Another effort in such areas is toward diversification of their local economies. They want and encourage through their assistance efforts more different types of business and smaller ones. They would not turn down a large company, especially if it were clean and nonpolluting, but they prefer more and smaller companies of different types, and this is where they place their efforts. They assess their present strengths and current trends and encourage the high-technology industries for which their universities can give support. They try to attract back office operations of banks or insurance companies, for example, that no longer need to be in the great metropolitan areas.

They look at their labor force and its skills. For example, one such county developer described their workers as having diagnostic skills, of knowing what to do if things are not right, of being able to read plans, of having mathematical skills, of being fabricators. They do look at supplying their own areas, but more at attracting custom from outside, for tourism and recreation, or by exporting local products. They look at the structure that has been developed in the past and that now can serve different purposes _ research capability, management strength, educated and skilled labor, transportation access _ and see what needs to be added to these to make new enterprises flourish. What is happening in such areas may not be apparent in the usual statistical indicators. Jobs may not be increasing in number, but new jobs are replacing old. In many such areas they feel their economies have bottomed out, that they have turned around and used their strengths to diversify into new endeavors. But they may believe they still are "running to stay in place" or "treading water." Such areas often need to deal with labor problems, such as helping unions with a new perspective, retraining older workers, and training new, and helping with such problems in new ways, with universities offering cooperative programs, by developing or redeveloping industrial properties for new activities, and by attracting and providing help to new locally developed firms. "We have a lot of old buildings in this area." This often involves a major restructuring and updating of urban infrastructure, amenities and institutions. Developers sometimes use the word recycling. And it involves an effort to target the types of business for which they have special strengths, an effort to see what these are and put buildings to new use. What has not had sufficient recognition, on the part of those who predicted the demise of the rust belt, is the heritage left, the institutional structure developed by the old economy, still in place and available for new activities: the research institutions, educated and skilled labor force, transportation systems, financial institutions, management abilities, local governments used to dealing with business, and a lot of relevant and usable physical infrastructure. Such areas also have developed a diversity of manufacturing and service industries and a large dense population at which to target retail business. Their educational, health and welfare institutions not only train workers but attract people and business.

Another large factor in regional differences is location and natural endowment. Regions with parks such as the Adirondack Park or the Catskills, or on rivers or lakes have natural resources that offer opportunities but also problems of development with preservation of these resources. This takes the form of rules, permits, constraints, zoning. They have opportunities for tourism and recreation and also, if properly managed, for lumber and wood products in forested areas, for power plants using energy from the St. Lawrence River, and some of these areas have valuable minerals. Therefore, in such areas, there are limits to types of manufacturing desirable and more emphasis on resource-dependent businesses. But even in such circumstances, these areas do not want to be solely dependent on tourism, notoriously vulnerable to economic and weather changes. They, too, want to diversify, encouraging agricultural development, certain types of manufacturing, and non-tourist service industries, such as medical and biological research. The Adirondack North Country Association's nine point program illustrates such multifaceted interests.

Another aspect of geography providing opportunity or constraint is access and proximity to cities and to the rest of the country. Despite the north-south highways, such as the Northway, many of the Adirondack-North Country counties are in the main difficult of access to New York City and the West, and are more accessible to Ottawa and Montreal. In fact, they get a good deal of Canadian tourism and retail trade. Even in the western part of the state, location away from Route 90 or 17 (the main east-west arteries) is a problem, and location on one of these, especially if it also is a crossing of one of the north-south highways, is an asset in the eyes of developers. The construction of Highway 17, the Southern Tier Expressway, opened up an area of the state heretofore undeveloped industrially, agriculturally, or for tourism.

In a state crossed by such a network of four lane highways and throughways, there are nonetheless rural counties that are remote because they lack such access. Such remoteness is clearly a component of the economic distress experienced in such counties, where unemployment can be nearly double that of the state as a whole. Solution of their problems is not easy since their lack of development means lack of funds to launch a development program or hire an experienced full-time staff. The main town may be small and the population scattered and social services and infrastructure lacking.

Such counties usually have thin development programs and tend to lean more heavily on regional organizations that may find it difficult to fill the gap. Many counties prospered along with the nation as a whole. And took off when interest rates fell. But not all ships have risen with the rising tide, and there are great regional disparities, exacerbated recently by the recession.

The region's degree of prosperity or level of development also constrains present efforts. Because of its economic past, a county may have a well-developed infrastructure, land developed for industrial use, an alert and active government and organizational structure, a skilled work force, and good educational and research capacities. Or it may lack all of these. Where it lies between these extremes establishes the basis and boundaries for present efforts. It may have to find investment for such infrastructure or supporting institutions before it can expect much new business – development for sewers, local transportation, or education of workers. Or it may need to renew, reorganize, modernize, rehabilitate. The past level of development and past type of economic structure must be dealt with and helps or constrains present efforts, and the activities of developers in different areas reflect this. Some are tending to basics. Others are helping prosperity to roll over the county. But each county and region has not only a different level of past development but a different array of economic institutions based on past use of resources and opportunities.

In some areas of the state there is an emerging sense of regionalism. In the Adirondacks and North Country this is reflected in widespread support of ANCA; in the western counties are two regional organizations, a two-county Chamber of Commerce, and a city mayor with a broad perspective. One of the two agencies is created by the state, and this signals another aspect of regionalism. The state agencies have been encouraging such development also. So regionalism appears to be developing from the bottom up and the top down. In other regions developers have organized a cooperative marketing effort. Sometimes agencies in adjacent counties will cooperate. Legislators often hold meetings of the developers in the region they represent to seek opinion on legislative issues. The new New York State Department of Economic Development has tried to strengthen its regional staff and offices and broaden their mission. This might be the right time for such an effort that would give support to indigenous regional organization.   Why regional consciousness has grown in recent years is problematical.   One can speculate as always that it comes from a sense of "hanging together or hanging separately" or, more practically, that some necessary activities could profitably take place only on a multi-county basis.   When regional consciousness develops, it brings with it the realization that it is more important for counties and communities to cooperate in order to compete successfully with the rest of the world instead of with each other.

Another difference with a basis in past regional activities and institutions is whether counties are targeting and developing high- or low-technology industry.   Those that are increasing high-technology industries have an institutional basis for this.   They may have large cities, technical and research universities, or a high-technology government installation, such as the Rome Air Base that is the technical center for the Air Force.   Another such influence is a large high-technology industry that attracts scientists and technicians to the area, subcontracts with smaller firms or job shops, or spins off smaller companies.   Such areas offer not only a labor pool, a source of knowledge, but also opportunity.   Other areas not so endowed realize this.   They may try for apparel or other industries that can use experienced sewers.   Or they may eschew the idea of starting an incubator, but encourage small retail business or new agricultural enterprise or a strong tourism program.

Thus regional economic history, resources, institutional endowments, access and transportation, level of prosperity, location and many other factors present problems and opportunities that lead to very different programs and activities.   Developers have to constantly update and expand their knowledge of their counties and relate this assessment to regional and national economic pressures.   Developers talk of "changing atmospheres" and constantly have their feelers out, probing and questioning.

In addition to regional differences, we should mention the effect of national economic shifts.   In 1984 and 1985 there was a sudden expansion of dormant organizations, changes in direction, new programs, and new agencies all over the state. The analogy that comes to mind is the effect of rain on the desert where suddenly flowers bloom after many dry years.   This economic revival was nationwide and economists are still looking for explanations. But this seemingly spontaneous turn of fortune in localities all over the state was clearly responsive to national economic shifts.

How do program differences relate to regional differences? In the older industrial areas we have mentioned the preoccupation with management buy outs. They also work at finding new uses for old buildings, remodeling, retooling, revitalizing, and trying to carve out adequate industrial space in urban areas.

The expansion of the reach of metropolitan areas has led to continued suburban economic development. Counties heretofore beyond urban reach are linking in. We find industry blending into what formerly were exclusively residential areas. They are trying to develop industrial land, sometimes including infrastructure. They are marketing to try to increase the flow. Some are spending a lot of time facilitating the settling in of new industry that is taking hold, that needs not funding but management help. They are helping the new kinds of businesses that are coming to these outer areas, distribution and warehousing, back office operations for banks and insurance companies and small clean industries.

Some of the more prosperous areas are beginning to concern themselves with labor shortages or problems of housing workers. Some counties concentrate efforts on coping with a major local change, such as the decline of a major employer or the expansion of Fort Drum. The counties within reach of the Canadian border are busy recruiting Canadian business and establishing Foreign Trade Zones. They, of course, try to find ways to use local resources, be these attractive outdoors, wood from forests, or a major technical university or facility. The poorer counties are still in need of basic infrastructure, sewers, local transportation, education of the unemployed and the like. Thus the developers try to match local problems and resources to opportunities, attempting to knit their economies into the larger one. In this way each county chooses from an array of possible activities and adds a few efforts peculiar to itself to try to develop a unique program suitable to the local situation.

Rural Areas

Rural counties can in principle do all of the things urban or suburban counties can. But in actuality they suffer disadvantages. If they do not have access to a four lane highway or throughway, they correctly believe themselves to suffer. Wherever they are located, they are remote.

If they lack a large city, they have several problems.   Their population may be scattered and lack public transportation. They may be on the average less well educated.   Because of lack of public transportation people are not accessible to social services, health services, education or employment.   The area may not offer potential employees with technical skills or training.

A poor rural county cannot afford the specialized economic development staff a large city or prosperous county can. Yet the problems of development may be more difficult, and activities, such as issuing a bond, as complex and expensive as in counties that are better staffed. They tend to lean on regional agencies that up to now have not been set up to provide these services on the level needed. Regional staff do not live and work in the county and at best cannot perform the day by day, hands-on job that most developers think necessary. In looking at the geographic distribution of various development activities, certain rural counties lack many of these.

In addition, they lack the density and variety of urban business activities that spawn new ones, and they lack a large industry or university that can stimulate economic activity. They also can have limits on what is possible because of conservation problems and restraints.   It is not difficult to argue that strengthened regional organizations and perhaps special funding should be made available to them. Many federal and state programs are basically targeted at urban poverty and should be. But urban areas are not the only ones that can be depressed.   Depressed rural areas have many interconnected problems that even the worst cities lack and therefore some attention to basic services, education, infrastructure and transportation may be necessary before more direct economic development efforts can be successful.

Conclusions

Regional disparities are due to urban or rural structure and location, geographic access or remoteness, natural endowment of rivers, lakes, forests, minerals, or agricultural land, past types of economic activities, and levels of poverty or affluence. All of these call to mind the complex job of the development organization to constantly assess a county's endowments and weaknesses, and tailor efforts to using these to link the county with the national economy as it undergoes change. In some counties developers first have to work on basic infrastructure or even social services as a prelude to action. In others, they assist in reaping the rewards of a fortunate endowment and luck in location. Therefore it would be difficult to judge a local development organization's efforts except against the backdrop of the county's resources and problems. Equal efforts cannot be expected to yield equal results.

Chapter 13

How the Public Entrepreneurs Work

Most of the local development organizations were started in response to federal and state funding opportunities and according to requirements laid down by law, though a number of private agencies exist performing similar functions. These formal charters made organizations eligible for and responsive to various financial opportunities. Nonetheless from the outset they had many variations in formal organization, some achieved by establishing parallel organizations not controlled by government. The organizations varied in types of control and authority, office location, relations to local government and source of funds. In all of these respects they appeared to distance themselves from the local government that often had given rise to them. They changed over time in many respects. We can especially see this by examining organizations originally set up to deal with a local crisis. These typically changed and broadened their missions and continued to function long after the initial crisis had passed.

An hypothesis suggested by Stinchcombe (1965) on organizational formation has had currency, namely that the nature of society at the time of founding influences organizational form, and that therefore organizations take the same form if founded at the same time and do not change even when social structure changes. This is very evidently not the case with these local development organizations. From the outset they took different forms and continued to change over time.

The formal organization, often dictated by requirements of legislation or funding agencies is, therefore, not only qualified to deal with government agencies but, because of its formal structure, government connections, and public accountability, it inspires confidence on the part of government agencies that often use it as a conduit for local help and as a mediating agency, even when not required to do so. Thus the local development organizations have one face turned toward federal, state, and local government.

The local development organizations also face in another direction, toward business. Their directors are entrepreneurial in nature – they are public entrepreneurs, facilitators, helping business avail itself of government help. The variety of help business calls for and the unique nature of every business and problem require imagination and flexibility. The agencies have to respond quickly with appropriate help, and this requires not only knowledge of government resources, but of the resources, needs, and business in their own counties. The day-to-day operations and the activities and programs undertaken by the agencies are not laid down in their formal charters and are varied, changing, and responsive. They have many of the same activities, but no two agencies have identical programs and few, if any, activities are common to all. They deal with each case on an individual and comprehensive basis. They try to be one-stop-shops, providing the assortment of help needed to solve each problem. Though they commonly have marketing programs to induce outside business to locate in the county, they spend most of their time helping local and existing business: start up, site location, buildings, equipment, expansion, remodeling, recruitment and training of employees, and a variety of unique problems. They try to keep in touch with all the businesses in the county. They believe that they should not do for business what it can do for itself, and of course this varies from place to place and case to case. But they give nothing of a material nature; they give advice, intervene in governmental contacts and problems, and help businesses avail themselves of various types of government loans or bonds that of course carry tax benefits, reduced interest rates, or easier pay back terms. When they undertake a business project of their own, such as rehabilitating and inducing business into an old factory, they do so as the business of last resort. If anyone else will do it, they will not. Their actual activities, then, comprise the informal organizational system.

An important part of the day-to-day job of the county development organization is working with the wider network of development organizations and other agencies. These include branches of state and federal agencies, and regional organizations, public and private. Some are unique to an area; some cover the whole state systematically or large chunks of it such as do the public utilities. They also include city and town agencies and in some cases other county agencies. These various city, county, and regional agencies do not nest. They are not hierarchical and have no formal ties or dependency relations. They all may perform many similar tasks. They cover greater or lesser geographic areas. They often also divide up the tasks to be done, some specializing in one, some another, referring clients to the relevant agency for the problem at issue. The way they divide the tasks is different in different counties. In one county the Chamber of Commerce may provide the services that the Industrial Development Agency takes responsibility for in another. Nor do counties have similar arrays of agencies. One county may have two active chambers of commerce, an Industrial Development Agency, a county government unit concerned with industrial development, a private local agency, and several town/city agencies. Another will have a similar number but a different assortment. A small or rural county may have only one.

In addition to having a division of labor acknowledged by all, the various agencies tend to keep in touch on a regular basis, sometimes by regular formal meetings. They also often cooperate to solve a complex problem or launch a large project, putting the various shoulders to the wheel over a considerable period of time. The several cooperating agencies may each list such projects in their annual reports and mention it as one of their achievements. And the reality may be that the effort of each of the several was necessary for success.

When a county has a number of development organizations, why do they not amalgamate into one large organization? Wouldn't that be more effective? In the first place, the array of local development organizations in a county often come under a variety of jurisdictions and authorities, public and private, and derive their funds from different sources. This would make amalgamation inconvenient though not impossible. Organization theorists of all persuasions agree that as organizations grow in size, they become more bureaucratic. They standardize tasks and codes of behavior and rules of operation. Decision making often involves layers of consultation and periods of time. Divisions of labor may have sharper boundaries. Innovation may become more difficult once rules and regulations have specified tasks to be performed and methods of operation. Response is no longer speedy. It is difficult to deal with unusual problems for which precedent or rules do not provide ready-made solutions. But the essence of the local development organization is flexibility, risk taking, quick decisions taken by personnel on their own, quick response, and ability to deal with a succession of unique problems. That is, the essence is innovation, imagination, and entrepreneurship. Each agency is a communication center, and one could also argue that communication with the variety of public and private organizations and persons necessary is facilitated by having a number of communicators, each with complex network ties, rather than if communications were funneled through one in-take person or department of a larger organization. Developers deal with unique problems in new ways and can contrive new solutions for new problems. They cooperate and communicate when they need to, and they do not spend a lot of time in bureaucratic dealings and staff meetings. Their role as communication and information centers and their wide and varied ties mark their openness.

The diversity of problems local development organizations deal with and the cooperation required for solutions is illustrated by a number of cases. Problems range from very large to very small. A long period of time is often required. Many are projects that are not likely to be undertaken by private persons in the area or at the time: industrial parks, infrastructure, building remodeling or reuse, malls. In addition to tasks frequently undertaken, such as expansions, start ups, retooling and remodeling, they also have included pollution control, loans for working capital, labor problems, organization of Foreign Trade Zones, acquisition of existing companies, and management buyouts. Very large and long-range problems such as developing and realizing a plan for reuse of Syracuse's Hancock Field are sometimes undertaken.

We have emphasized the important role of the agency in knowing and fitting its program to local resources, needs and pressures. Without taking account of these, it is difficult to say what an agency should or should not have done. The fire that melts the butter hardens the egg. Among widely shared regional pressures are the economic expansion of metropolitan areas; the opportunity of Canadian border location; and the region's economic past, its heritage, good and bad, left by declining industries of a former era. Natural endowments also create pressures such as access to cities and the rest of the country. Forests, parks, lakes, and rivers provide both opportunities and constraints. The remoteness and complexity of problems of the most rural areas comprise another set of problems including poverty, lack of infrastructure, and lack of a skilled labor force. All counties do not start from an equal basis; they differ in past affluence or poverty and all that implies. Activities needed, possible, and undertaken are all influenced by such differences.

In some areas there seems to be an emerging sense of regionalism, coming from within the region, a growing sense of a common fate resulting in agencies working on wider geographic areas and in cooperation with other counties. It is sometimes assisted by efforts of state agencies that want to encourage regional cooperation.

In addition, the whole state and all agencies and counties can be affected by national ups and downs that we do not pretend to predict or understand.

Another kind of evidence also bears on the roles of local development organizations in industrial development. We have argued that the local development organizations act as intermediaries between business and government, especially in the matter of accessing federal and state funds and issuance of bonds for industrial development. Quantitative information on the distribution of these various funds among counties shows that all of the five types of funds studied are distributed proportionally to total employment in a county. Together these facts suggest that the local development organizations have become institutionalized, every county has and needs such an agency performing these specialized duties. In studying the allocation of proportions among the five types of funding within a county, it is possible to discern the interplay of county characteristics and funding policies. The role of the local development organization is in fitting funding opportunities to local needs, and in performing the broader job of helping development in many complex ways beyond accession of funds, which is only one step in the development process.

Theoretical Implications

What is most important about local development organizations is the new public-private partnership they have forged. Whatever the theoretical orientation, state-society or government-economy relations are regarded as confrontational or at least uneasy. Questions take the form of how much government should regulate business, or tax business. Businesses of different types lobby government. Deals between government and business, such as defense contracts, are subjects of often justifiable suspicion. Government-operated businesses, state-owned businesses, such as in the USSR and China, tend not to run well, to run into awkward problems at best. At the one extreme, state-run businesses are often inefficient because of the lack of normal market pressures, such as a realistic price system, and also abnormal government intercession. At the other extreme of no government regulation, we often find cutthroat competition and harmful exploitation. Therefore a new type of local organization which negotiates and mediates between government and business successfully and peacefully, and on a local basis, is new and suggests a new type of state-society relationship. Of course, government-business relations have always been complex, and those who study the matter point out that in recent times the edges are blurring in a wide variety of ways, such as the flow of business executives into government service and the flow of cabinet members into business. And we still do preserve distinctions. There are lines to be crossed. Despite changes, therefore, there is a real function for these new small agencies to perform.

Organization theory developed for large complex organizations still helps to focus our attention on aspects of structure of these small organizations which make their integrating role possible: a formal structure consonant with government requirements of public supervision, public accountability, and consistency over time; an informal method of operating that is flexible, responsive, innovative, entrepreneurial, and makes sense to business; an openness, as a center for information, open to and in touch with a wide variety of federal, state, and local organizations, public and private, which facilitates coordinated action on a local level not otherwise possible. Their informational role calls to mind Simon's (1957) concept of bounded rationality, and the limits on a given businessman's capacity for absorbing information needed for availing himself of outside help. This is supplied by the local development organization. Their small size makes it easy to preserve their entrepreneurial nature and their open quality.

We should take account, however, of the constraints within which they operate. They do have some funds and property of their own that they use in their work, but they mainly help business draw on other public and private resources. Getting these means that a business has to fulfill requirements of a variety of lending agencies. All help is in the form of loans; the agencies have nothing to give of a tangible nature. It is within these constraints that agencies have to be responsive and find solutions to problems. The fact that the financial packages they help pull together have to be approved by other, often by several other, organizations is also an element in both their success and failure. It effectively keeps them and the businesses they help from many kinds of failure, for they will not find funds available for businesses that cannot stand careful scrutiny.

Three widely shared values circumscribe their programs, and have much to do with focusing their efforts and limiting their roles. One is tying their efforts to job creation. This is also a requirement of most state and federal funding. This goal means that businesses are not viewed as profits, products, or productivity, but as jobs. It means some selecting of businesses to be aided, inevitably with less emphasis on very small ones. A second constraint is that they want only to do for business what business cannot do for itself. What business can do varies from place to place and business to business. It sometimes means undertaking tasks no business can do for itself, such as getting a sewer system established. It also means doing things in one area, such as establishing industrial parks, that private developers do in another, but it is a criterion of acceptable effort always kept in mind. Developers do not want to run businesses, but to help a business to manage itself more successfully. This constraint keeps the organization in the middle between government and business.

The third value, that each agency should be a one-stop shop, coordinating and integrating various helps and avoiding confusion, is an extremely important element in any success they have and diametrically opposite to what the common man thinks of as bureaucratic narrowness, confusion, and refusal to accept responsibility. It is a value which keeps the role of the local development organization carefully separate from that of the government agency.

A further perspective widely shared is the necessity of adapting efforts to local resources and needs. This again differentiates the ways these organizations work from government agencies that try to, or at time by law have to, administer similar programs in similar ways on a state- or country-wide basis.

The whole system of state, regional, and local organizations would not work without an acknowledged if rough and ready division of labor and an equally acknowledged readiness to cooperate with other agencies. Since problems differ from time to time and place to place, a good deal of flexibility in both the divisions of labor and integrated efforts are needed rather than rigid rules and lines of demarcation.

All of these observations are the general, normal, desirable case, and do not imply that there are no failures, exceptions, or rough edges. But without a general prevalence of such values and ways of work, the system could not function at all effectively.

Many people think of local development agencies as mainly engaged in recruiting business from outside the area to move in or establish branches, or, as the developers speak of it, in marketing the area. The actuality is that marketing take a small share of the time and resources of most agencies. Rather they spend most of their time helping existing and local business, helping in start up, change, expansion, in meeting problems, and surviving, and in working on any problem necessary for this, such as a change in infrastructure. Indeed, what agencies do emphasize is what most of us think of as a proper development effort and what many unjustifiably accuse them of neglecting. In doing this, because of their own typical lack of material resources, they are not simply pouring money on problems, which is what public agencies are often accused of. Their main contribution is analysis of problems and opportunities, planning an integrated approach, and coordinating management of solutions. All funds extended to business have to be paid back.

This leads to a question of what we mean by industrial development. Should it be something deeper, broader than jobs? If so, what form should it take? As we have described them, developers might be judged to be opportunists in the best sense, living and responding from day-to-day. The other extreme would be a rigid three or five year plan. Developers actually are mostly in what is probably a healthy middle ground. They typically know their area very intimately and within it track change all the time. More than that, many, if not most, have a good sense of direction about where they would like to see the county go and think it can go. We call this healthy since we have seen the failure of so many elaborate county-level development plans that such plans now have acquired an aura of fantasy. We cannot document this specifically, but we believe many developers do look forward, have long-range plans, flexible ones, a sense of direction that guides their efforts. Some, of course, do formulate explicit development goals and plans with the help of their boards of community members, but most have at least a well-formed sense of direction. Development should be something more than jobs, and focus on a restructuring of the economy. If agencies succeed in reshaping the environment, this process goes beyond what the Stinchcombe (1965) hypothesis envisions. In fact, they exist in order to transform their environment.

While most developers share the view of doing only for business what it cannot do for itself, there are a range of views about how influential business or government roles in the agency control should be. Most agencies have predominantly chosen businessmen for their boards. Differences among counties appear most explicitly in the different division of labor among agencies. In counties where the lead agency is the Chamber of Commerce, rather than the Industrial Development Agency, explanations for this take the form of local conservatism, the influence of business in government, and a history of business taking the lead locally in a well-developed chamber of commerce.

From all of the foregoing it should be clear that evaluation of the work of these agencies is anything from difficult to impossible. Virtually every county has such an agency. Therefore the simplest approach does not exist, namely comparing counties with and without agencies to see which fare better. Even if this were possible, we would still have the problem that what an agency in county A ought to do is not necessarily what the agency in county B ought to do. In fact, success is different from place to place. In some areas where older heavy industry has declined, developers who are very active and who initiate many projects say they are "running to stay in place," or "treading water." In other places developers need to be less aggressive but simply facilitate the prosperity that is washing over the area. Many agencies cite jobs created, as do state agencies, as evidence of success. But in many cases we have no way of knowing whether these jobs would have come without agency assistance.

Our impression after talking to so many developers at such length is that the agencies do make a difference, and in support of this opinion we could cite many examples of projects that contributed to development that no private person would have undertaken. But beyond this, more difficult to document is a general process of helping that one perceives as new, different, and important. One test will be to see whether these efforts survive whether local economies have been strengthened to better survive recessions. Of course, if every county has such an agency developing programs, activities, and properties as needed, and supplying information, any county without such an agency would be at a comparative disadvantage. Therefore perhaps if not essential initially, they have become so, and are well on their way to being institutionalized.

Do organizations compete with each other? Again, we can offer no proof. But we have heard a great deal about cooperative projects, networking, keeping in touch, referring clients to each other. There seems to be enough work for all, and their way of work is one of being careful not to step on others' toes. We also do hear, of course, of competition among counties for new business from outside, even as we hear about cooperative multi-county marketing efforts, multi-county cooperation on problems, and multi-county agencies.

Another issue is the nature of the developer. As we went from agency to agency, the incumbent developers seemed much alike, entrepreneurial. We thought of their similarity to chess pieces; if you changed places of two, they might not do exactly the same thing in the new place, but the styles of operation would be very similar. The thought is that certain types of organizations call for certain types of personnel. Someone not suitable, in this case, without entrepreneurial skills and enthusiasm, would not last long.

Implications for Public Policy

We have offered the opinion that the local development organizations perform an essential role in making a variety of public and private help available to a businessman. Most businessmen have a fair education and also have experience. They are clever, hard-working, and eager to succeed. Yet they need help in gathering information and putting together an integrated program to solve their problems.

If this is the case, perhaps the sick, the poor, those on welfare, the homeless, the aged, children living in distress also need a one-stop shop that could help them find and apply for a complex package of public and private help to solve their problems. Most government programs operate on a principle that reminds one of garments labeled "one size fits all." All but me! No one program solves all of the problems of anyone. Yet the ill, the poor, the aged, the problem-ridden do not have any advocate to assist them in finding the help they are entitled to and get it working for them. Only a proportion of those eligible apply for food stamps. Why? Perhaps local organizations and representatives of state and federal agencies need to coordinate their efforts on a local level so that a person with problems need only go to a single lead agency that would put together an appropriate package of help from various sources.

There are still regional disparities in New York State and different types of regional problems. There is still a double-digit rate of unemployment in some rural areas, while some metropolitan areas until recently faced labor shortages. Often the rural poor do not have the training to fill urban jobs even if they could move. Rural areas often cannot afford to establish and adequately man and finance the kinds of local development organizations that they need. Issuing a bond is just as complicated in a rural areas that does it infrequently as it is in a thriving area. And rural problems can be more intractable. Developers tell us that their work requires day-to-day effort, yet regional organizations that do help in such areas do not have enough manpower to make such intensive effort.

A major policy issue facing the various agencies involved in economic development is what effect the end of tax-free bonds will have on their programs or even on their survival. Because of changes in the law, the number of bonds issued in New York State has declined radically in recent years: in 1985, 600 bonds were issued; in 1986, 250 bonds; and in 1987, 37 bonds; and the program was scheduled to end in 1989 but is still alive. Two factors enter into this question. One is the availability of taxable bonds that nonetheless bring benefits and cost less in legal fees to issue. Therefore, they can be issued in smaller amounts, costing a few thousand dollars in legal fees instead of fifty thousand. And they can be issued for smaller businesses.

The other factor is that the more successful agencies have developed broad and diverse programs and sources of funding. Organizations often twist and turn and change their purposes and programs, and they do seem to survive. Organizations are notoriously reluctant to close their doors even when all signs point to this solution for their problems. At least changes in strategy will be called for.

Can local development organizations survive recessions, and will they help counties better meet problems of recession? They seem to survive at least. The local development organizations have undoubtedly benefited from the success they have enjoyed in times of prosperity. Will their efforts pay off in harder times?

The new United States-Canada trade agreement will affect efforts in border counties to attract Canadian business. A number of such counties have been making serious efforts to attract Canadian industry. With the new trade agreement, Canadian business may not regard such a move as necessary for their marketing program. Other changes with policy implications include the spread of metropolitan areas out to surrounding counties, and also growing tendencies to regionalism. Together, all of these changes could lead to a restructuring of economic development organizations and programs. If some local agencies find it difficult to carry on, perhaps regional agencies can be reinforced to substitute for their efforts. Or perhaps some agencies may be absorbed into government departments, but this raises questions about autonomy, flexibility, and rapid decision making.

Metropolitan areas have had economic influence over widening regions, and what were rural economies in the past are now parts of a wider metropolitan area of influence. This presents both problems and opportunities, and developers are very much aware of this process and thinking how to deal with it to the benefit of their local areas. Warehousing, distribution, back office operations, and light industry are moving out to areas beyond the metropolitan regions, and people are commuting long distances to jobs. There is even talk of the region from Albany to New York City ultimately tying together into a single metropolitan region; as of now there are few counties in that area not tied to either sphere of economic influence.

In the older industrial areas of the state, it has been pointed out that progress has sometimes consisted of standing still, or not losing jobs.

This has meant a good deal of upheaval in such areas – rehabilitating and making old areas and buildings suitable for new use, developing new areas for growth, retraining workers, and diversifying the economy while trying to keep older industries going, where possible, by modernization or by promoting local ownership of branch plants. This whole set of activities constitute a turnaround process, with older enterprises declining and newer ones coming along, and all of them requiring a great deal of help. Such drastic changes of direction, of the restructuring of the economy are not always reflected in employment statistics in a way to make one appreciate the turmoil, the amount of change and its complexity. Standing still requires an immense amount of change in these cases, and very diverse programs and skills to cope with it in agencies in such areas.

How do present agencies work? They work on a one-to-one basis with each business, and day by day. Their approach is highly individualized, and they try to provide comprehensive help for each business they deal with; they use the expression a one-stop shop. They have to be willing to get into any problem that arises, to be decisive and to respond quickly. The agencies that exist appear to have much agreement on their approach. Therefore any program that is not going to deal with each business in such a manner, to keep in close touch on an ongoing basis, needs to give thought to what it can accomplish if it sees its task differently. Can regional agencies keep in close enough touch? Do classes, seminars, workshops that deal with specialized problems have a real contribution to make, and under what circumstances? Can groups of businesses be dealt with together?

A second problem for a new program or agency is the need to mesh with the network of existing organizations, to avoid duplication of effort, competition, to cooperate, and to find useful functions and a clientele not already being well served by an existing organization. And of course the pattern of what will work differs from county to county. Statewide agencies may not find that the same programs and policies work in different parts of the state. How can new agencies and programs find a proper role to play in local development?

Another quality required is consciousness of change, knowledge of the county, and how its needs and resources fit into what is going on in the rest of the world. Not only is detailed knowledge of one's own back yard necessary, but it is also necessary to put this knowledge into perspective in order to know what is possible and what may not be.

Flexibility, the requirement for quick decisions, the emphasis on cutting red tape, of using different federal and state programs together to accomplish a task mean that an economic development agency cannot operate like a normal bureaucracy that goes according to rules and guidelines laid down and observed by all, that is slow to innovate or change, slow to move and works through levels of authority and responsibility. This is a basic reason why such agencies function best as quasi-governmental or privately run. The executive needs autonomy and elbow room, and the chance to try new things and change directions, sometimes quickly.

The complex set of arrangements, services, and finances a business might need indicate how difficult it could be for a business to deal with the multiplicity of federal, state, and local programs to which it is entitled to apply for help. Sometimes a matter is simple and direct. More often, with so many agencies, changing rules and programs, it takes a local expert to put together the complex package of help needed. The agency not only needs to know the county and the business but also the helping agencies and programs and to keep in touch and know whom to call.

The efforts agencies make to acquire revolving loan funds and the rules constraining use of federal and state funds suggest that discretionary funds are needed at a local level for immediate or flexible use, to cover needs not taken care of by standard programs, or for businesses that may not qualify for them. Working capital is in especially short supply. Sometimes a good new business has a cash flow problem.

While the Small Business Administration, the Small Business Development Centers, and local agencies expend effort on small business, their needs for help, especially with business management, exceed the supply. How help for them should be, can be, strengthened is not an easy, or perhaps cheap, problem to solve.

Another reason for added staff and discretion over funding at a regional level is the great differences in resources, existing economic structures, labor, and needs in different regions of the state. Rising tendencies toward regional consciousness, whether introduced by state agencies or springing up locally, or, often, a combination of the two, indicate that local and regional agency staff might be able to exercise better judgment about use of funds in ways that would solve local problems and promote local development than state and federal agencies. Strengthening of regional offices with staff and funds may be indicated, and these same moves could also help regional staff to give added help to rural areas that are falling behind.

In short, the new public-private partnership made possible by the work of the local development agencies might provide the means of reshaping of local economies; they may be organizations that participate in changing their environments in a continuing process which is flexible, user-friendly, and adapted to local differences in a way that national or state-administered programs cannot be.

The contributions agencies can make is limited by social, economic, and political forces bearing down on the counties: the national economy, natural endowments, location, their own economic history. A large part of what is possible is a result of these broad economic forces and constraints. But it is easy to believe that there is at least a small, but important, part determined by local efforts, including those of economic development agencies. In this part, the agency makes a difference. It facilitates or makes up for trends, but still within the constraints imposed by broader forces. Therefore, because of their facilitating nature and readiness to deal with problems, because of their apparent success in making things happen, this new public-private enterprise is, in at least some form, here to stay.

Chapter 14

Conclusions

We have presented two types of organization that are in a constant process of change; manufacturing firms and economic development agencies. About 35 percent of the small manufacturing businesses get a government loan, 45 percent apply for one. Therefore business and government are intertwined. The economic development organization's purpose is to change their environment. All economic development organizations began differently and they changed over time. The small manufacturers are also flexible. A high proportion of them custom manufacture, which means a steady stream of different products. We are told that a new product lasts 5 years, but the firm is constantly working on the next one. Nearly all small firms grow over time. Both sets change constantly. Much of economics is based on the assumption that economic organizations are stable, they stay the same over time. Large corporations, judging by the press, also change. They buy or shed branches, they change chief executives officers and products, they grow or shrink. But to admit to change would complicate theory and measurement. Nor does it help to consider SIC's together; we have shown that some firms in an SIC innovate and others do not, as Schumpeter suggested. But who is in charge of these highly changing organizations? They are run by entrepreneurs. By this we mean that they are run by independent people who make decisions, take chances and are responsible for what they do. If a businessman fails, he is out of business. If an economic developer blunders he is accountable to the community and solely so since he makes the decisions.

Both are embedded in constant change. The economic developers' job is to change their environment. They all have a vision of this and work for progress. The small business world is constantly introducing new products, specializing and changing specifications on old products. About one third innovate. Fifty percent of them use computerized processing of one kind or another. They all - economic developers; and business people - interact with a wide network of people; business people interact with suppliers, with customers, with rivals and subcontractors and with government agencies. The economic developers interact with a wide array of local, state, and federal agencies and with every business in the community.

Both types of organization are members of networks, the manufacturing business in a network of small and large firms that buy from and sell to each other; the economic development organizations are part of a network of local, regional, state and national agencies and the businesses in their locality. Therefore any change in the network can affect all of them.

The economic development organizations deal with new businesses, current business and businesses that are closing down. They deal with a large variety of changing government projects and cooperate with other organizations. They take on any duty they need to in order for their environment to challenge, be it a new sewer, an industrial park or health regulations.

Most small businesses are growing. They are innovating and adopting high technology processing and changing products, diversifying, changing specifications, making things to order, hiring new employees and moving the firm to a new location. None of them stand still. We have described the way both types of organizations are members of networks. The business nearly all sell locally, but a high proportion export from the state and nearly half from the nation. The economic developers spend most of their time on local business, but all participate in programs of recruitment of business from outside the county, often with a network of other organizations.

The entrepreneurs who run these organizations are very independent. An economic developer quickly sheds his framework by developing multiple organizations with different functions and capacities that give him room to do what he wants, to make decisions and take action quickly. The entrepreneurs in small business start their own companies, finance themselves, work long hours and grow gradually. They both have few pressures aside from the goals of the organization itself; the economic developers try to change their environments; the business men produce a changing product and keep afloat financially.

Neither job is one for timid souls or super conservative people. They take risks and if their decision fails, only they are responsible. Thus organizations and businesses work within framework that sets the stage but does not hamper them. No choices are forced on them. They all decide for themselves and take the consequences.

The small manufacturing businesses are part of a network of firms that buy parts and sell them to larger companies. The large companies are essential parts of the network. The small firms ensure themselves of any catastrophes by diversifying their sales out of state and to other companies. But if a large factory to which they sell fails, can they stand the loss of, say, twenty percent of their business? They adopt high technology production programs and innovate constantly. Eighty percent of the sample had been in business ten years or more. Thus they are not left behind large corporations technically.

They are supported by the web of local and regional organizations that draw on state and federal funds. Twenty-seven to 38 percent of firms in three areas get these loans and 45 percent apply for them. They also get a great deal of advice and help aside from financial from these organizations: site selection, buildings, equipment, personnel and a variety of unique personal problems. Developers tell us that once a business has called on them for help with a problem, it tends to return with others. The organizations were still running five years after the initial interview and a couple of new ones started up. The organizations soon develop auxiliary organizations and cooperative programs that help them burst out of their framework.

The small manufacturing business all have competitors. They keep in touch, even learn from them. Their network positions give them information which, if used, will help them to stay afloat. Both they and the economic development organizations are always looking for ways to change and improve the business. We have seen that most businesses have grown since they were started, that is those that are still alive.

Both economic developers and small firms have contacts outside the community and keep in touch with what is going on in the world and adapting to it. The developers' programs are adapted to the needs and resources of the region, but adapted in terms of what they can provide to the wider world. Most of the small firms export from their state and must be in touch. Both are intertwined in the social networks. Thus an elaboration of the Romo et al hypothesis seems to be true. They are all embedded in networks that are closely related to the large concentrated firms in their county and mostly also look outside of the county.

Why has this country supplied the loose but supportive framework that permits these organizations and firms to be independent, responsive, to produce fast, make decisions, innovate and change? In the countries formerly under Soviet domination free enterprise did not work well. Well, neither do small suppliers work independently in a super conservative country like Japan. In the United States entrepreneurship is a tradition since the immigrants settled in the East and started their own farms or businesses and gradually moved West, creating as they went. They were very independent and very much alone. They gradually developed a constitution of protection but of noninterference, maintaining the essentials that they started with. People are free to start a business and are free to fail. Developers are free to launch new plans and are free to have them not pan out. It is the essence of this society and other societies like it. It is difficult to invent out of whole cloth in a society that has no experience in independence, entrepreneurship and individual responsibility, and no support for it.

Bibliography

Abernathy, William J., and James M. Utterback. 1978. "Patterns of Industrial Innovation." *Technology Review 80* (June/July):41-47.

Alderman, N., and M.M. Fisher. 1992. "Innovation and Technological Change: An Austrian-British Comparison." *Environment and Planning* A, v.24:273:288.

Aldrich, Howard E. 1979. *Organizations and Environments.* Englewood Cliffs, NJ: Prentice-Hall.

Amin, A. and Robins, K. 1990. "The Reemergence of Regional Economies? The Mythical Geography of Flexible Accumulation." *Environmental Planning D* 8:7-34

Aoki, M. 1984. *The Economic Analysis of the Japanese Firm.* North-Holland, New York.

———. 1986. "Horizontal vs. vertical information structure of the firm." *American Economic Review* 76:971-83.

Aoki, M., Reingold E. and Shimomura, M. 1986. *Made in Japan.* Dutton, New York.

Aoki, R. 1991. "R&D Competition for Product Innovation: An Endless Race." *American Economic Review* 81:252-6.

Armington, D., C. Harris, and M. Odle. 1983. *Formation and Growth in High Technology Business: A Regional Assessment.* Washington, D.C.: Brookings Institution.

Averitt, R. T. 1968. *The Dual Economy: The Dynamics of American Industry Structure.* Norton, New York.

Beesley, M.N., and R. Rothwell. 1987. "Small Firm Linkages in the United Kingdom." Pp. 189-200 in Roy Rothwell and John Bessant (eds.), *Innovation, Adaptation and Growth: An International Perspective.* Amsterdam: Elsevier.

Birley, Sue. 1985. "The Role of Networks in the Entrepreneurial Process." *Journal of Business Venturing* 1:107-117.

Blau, Peter and W. Richard Scott. 1962. *Formal Organizations*. San Francisco, CA: Chandler.

Blauner, Robert. 1960. "Work Satisfaction and Industrial Trends in Modern Society." Pp. 339-60 in Walter Galenson and Seymour Martin Lipset (eds.), *Labor and Trade Unionism*. New York: John Wiley.

Castells, Manuel. 1989. *The Information City: Information Technology, Economic Restructuring and the Urban Regional Process*. Oxford: Basil Blackwell.

Christopherson, S. and Storper, M. 1989. "The Effects of Flexible Specialization on Industrial Politics and the Labor Market: The Motion Picture Industry." *Ind. Lab. Rel. Rev.* 42:331-47.

Doeringer, Peter B., David G. Terkla, and Gregory Topakian. 1987. *Invisible factors in Economic Development*. New York: Oxford University Press.

Dosi, Giovanni. 1988. "Sources, Procedures, and Microeconomic Effects of Innovation." *Journal of Economic Literature* 26: 1120-71.

Feller, Irwin. 1975. "Invention, Diffusion and Industrial Location." Pp. 83-107 in L. Collins and D. F. walker, eds, *Locational Dynamics of Manufacturing Activity*. New York: Wiley.

Felsenstein, Daniel, and Raphael Bar-El. 1989. "Measuring the Technological Intensity of the Industrial Sector: A Methodological and Empirical Approach. *Research Policy* 18:239-52.

Fiedler, Fred E. 1964. "A Contingency Model of Leadership Effectiveness." In Leonard Berkowitz (ed.), *Advances in Experimental Social Psychology*. New York: Academic Press.

_____. 1971. "Validation and Extension of the Contingency Model of Leadership Effectiveness: A Review of Empirical Findings." *Psychological Bulletin* 76 (August):128-148.

Florida, R. and M. Kenney. 1990a. "Silicon Valley and Route 28 Won't Save Us." *California Mangement Review 33(1)*:68-88.

_____. 1990b. "High-technology Restructuring in the USA and Japan." *Environmental Planning A* 22:233-52.

_____. 1991b. "The Transfer of Japanese Industrial Organization to the US." *American Sociological Review* 56:381-98.

_____. 1991b. "W(h)ither Flexible Specialization." *California Mangement Review* 33(3):143-6.

Freeman, C. 1991. "Networks of Innovations: A Synthesis of Research Issues." *Research Policy* 20:499-514.

Freeman, Christopher. 1982. *The Economics of Industrial Innovation*. Cambridge, Mass.: MIT Press.

Friedman, Milton. 1962. *Capitalism and Freedom*. Chicago: University of Chicago Press.

Gellman Research Associates, Inc. 1976. *Indicators of International Trends in Technological Innovation*. Report prepared for the National Science Foundation. PB-263-738, april. Washington, D.C.: U.S. Department of Commerce, National Technical Information Service.

Gertler, M.S. 1984. "Regional capital theory." *Progress in Human Geography* 8:50-81.

_____. 1988. "The Limits to Flexibility: Comments on the Post-Fordist Vision of Production and Its Geography." *Transactions Insitute of British Geographers* N.S. 13:419-32.

_____. 1989. "Resurrecting Flexibility? A Reply to Schoenberger." *Transactions Insitute of British Geographers* N.S. 14:109-12.

_____. 1992. "Flexibility Revisted: Districts, Nation-States, and the Forces of Production." *Transactions Insitute of British Geographers.* N.S. 17:259-78.

Gibbs, D.C., and A. Edwards. 1985. The Diffusion of New Production Innovations in British Industry. Pp. 132-163 in A.T. Thwaites and R.P. Oakey (eds.), *The Regional Economic Impact of Technological Change.* New York: St. Martin's Press.

Glasmeier, Amy K., Peter G. Hall, and Ann R. Markusen. n.d. *Recent Evidence on High Technology Industries' Spatial Tendencies: A Preliminary Investigation.* Berkeley: University of California, Institute for Urban and Regional Studies.

Gould, Andrew, and David Keeble. 1984. "New Firms and Rural Industrialization in East Angolia." *Regional Studies* 18: 189-202.

Granovetter, M. 1973. "The Strength of Weak Ties." *American Journal of Sociology* 78(1):360-80.

Harrison, Bennett (ed.). 1994. *Lean and Mean: The Changing Landscape of Corporate Power in the Age of Flexibility.* New York: *Basic Books.*

Herman, E.S. 1981. *Corporate Control: Corporate Power.* Cambridge, U.K.: Cambridge University Press.

Hull, Frank, and Jerald Hage. 1982. "Organizing for Innovation: Beyond Burns and Stalker's Organic Type." *Sociology* 16: 564-77.

Jaikumar, R. 1986. "Postindustrial manufacturing. *Harvard Business Review* 64:69-76.

Jevons, F. R. 1976. "The Interaction of Science and Technology Today, or, Is Science the Mother of Invention?" *Technology and Culture* 17:729-42.

Kenney, M. and R. Florida. 1989. "Japan's Role in a Post-Fordist Age." *Futures*, April, pp. 136-51.

_____. 1992. "The Japanese Transplants: Production Organization and Regional Development." *Journal of American Planning A* 58:21-38.

Kent, Calvin. 1984. *The Environment for Entrepreneurship.* Lexington, MA: Lexington Books.

Kirchhoff, Bruce A. and Bruce Allen. 1994. *Entrepreneurship and Dyamic Capitalism: The Economics of Business Firm Formation and Growth.*

Kirchhoff, Bruce. 1994. Entrepreneurship and Dynamic Capitalism. *Frontiers of Entrepreneurship*, Babson College, Wellesley, Massachusetts.

_____. 1989. "Creative Destruction among Industrial Firms in the United States." Small *Business Economics* 1(3):161-173.

Leibenstein, Harvey. 1976. *Beyond Economic Man.* Cambridge, MA: Harvard University Press.

_____. 1978. *General X-efficiency Theory and Economic Development.* New York: Oxford University Press.

Lloyd, P.E., and C.M. Mason. 1984. "Spatial Variations in New Firm Formation in the United Kingdom: Comparative Evidence from Merseyside, Greater Manchester and South Hampshire." *Regional Studies* 18:207-20.

Lorenzoni, Gianni, and Oscar A. Ornati. 1988. "Constellations of Firms and Ventures." *Journal of Business Venturing* 3:41-57.

MacPherson, Alan. 1985. "Role of Technical Service Linkages." *Economic Geography* 61:(1):63-75.

_____. 1991. "New Product Development Among Small Industrial Firms: A Comparative Assessment of the Role of Technical Service Linkages in Toronto and Buffalo." *Economic Geography* 67 (2):136-146.

Malecki, E.J. 1980. "Corporate Organization of R and D and the Location of Technological Activies." *Regional Studies* 14:219-34.

McArthur, R. 1990. "Replacing the Concept of High Technology: Towards a Diffusion-Based Approach." *Evironment and Planning A*, 22:822-828.

Meyer, John W., and Brian Rowan. 1977. "Institutionalized organizations: Formal Structure As Myth and Ceremony." *American Journal of Sociology* 93 (September):340-363.

Miller, James P. 1990. *Survival and Growth of Independent Firms and Corporate Affiliates in Metro and Nonmetro America.* Washington, DC: USDA, Economic Research Service, Rural Development Research Report No. 74.

Morris, Michael, and Gordon W. Paul. 1987. "The Relationship Between Entrepreneurship and Marketing in Established Firms." *Journal of Business Venturing* 2:247-259.

New York State, Department of State. 1980. *A Step-by-Step Guide to Resources for Economic Development.* 2nd Edition. Albany, NY: New York State Urban Development Corporation.

New York Times (The). 1997. "Bowing to the `Great Yellow Father'." *The Metro Section*, Sunday, November 16, 1997.

Oakey, R. P. 1984. "Innovation and Regional Growth in Small High Technology Firms: Evidence from Britain and the USA." *Regional Studies* 18:237-52.

Oakey, Ray. 1984. *High Technology Small Firms: Regional Development in Britan and the United States.* New York: St. Martin's Press.

OECD Employment Outlook. 1994. Ch. 3 "Job Gains and Job Losses in Firms," pp. 103-135.

Pfeffer, Jeffrey, and Gerald R. Salancik. 1978. *The External Control of Organizations*. New York: Harper and Row, Publishers.

Phillips, Bruce D. and Bruce A. Kirchhoff. 1989. "Formation, Growth and Survival; Small Firm Dynamics in the U.S. Economy." *Small Business Economics* 1(1):65-74.

Phillips, Bruce D., Bruce A. Kirchhoff and H. Shelton Brown. 1991. "Formation, Growth and Mobility of Technology-Based Firms in the US Economy." *Entrepreneurship & Regional Development* 3:129-144.

Piore, M.J., and C.F. Sabel. 1984. *The Second Industrial Divide: Possibilities for Prosperity*. New York: Basic Books.

Pratten, Cliff (ed.). 1991. *The Competitiveness of Small Firms*. New York: Cambridge University Press.

Rees, John, Howard Stafford, Ronald Briggs, and Raymond Oakey. 1983. *Technology and Regional Development in the American Context*. Lazenburg, Austria: International Institute for Applied Systems Analysis.

Reynolds, Paul. 1987. 'Economic Development and New Firms: Policy Implications of the Birth and Development of New Firms." Paper presented at the 82d annual meeting of the American Sociological Association, Chicago, August.

Reynolds, Paul, and Brenda Miller. 1988. *1987 Minnesota New Firms Study: An Exploration of New Firms and Their Economic Contributions*. Publication no. CURA 88-1. Minneapolis, Minn.: Center for Urban and Regional Affairs.

Riche, Richard, Daniel E. Hecker, and John V. Burgan. 1983. High Technology Today and Tomorrow: A Small Slice of the Employment Pie. *Monthly Labor Review* (November):50-58.

Roberts, Edward B. 1968. "A Basic Study of Innovators; How to Keep and Capitalize on Their Talents." *Research Management* 11:249-66.

Roberts, Edward B. 1991. "The Technological Base of the New Enterprise." *Research Policy* 20:283-298.

Romo, Frank P., Hyman Korman, Peter Brantley, and Michael Schwartz. 1988. "The Rise and Fall of Regional Political Economies: A Theory of the Core." Pp. 37-64 in *Research in Politics and Society*. Vol. 3, Greenwich, Conn.: JAI Press.

Saxenian, A. 1990. "Regional Networks and the Resurgence of Silicon Valley." *California Management Review* 33:89-112.

Sayer, A. 1989. "Post-Fordism in Question." *Int. J. Urban Regional Research* 13:666-95.

_____. n.d. "New Developments in Manufacturing: The Just-In-Time System." *Capital and Class* 30:43:70.

Sayer, A. and R. Walker. 1992. *The New Social Economy: Reworking the Division of Labor*. Blackwell: Cambridge, MA.

Schoenberger, E. 1988. "From Fordism to Flexible Accumulation: Technology, Competitive Strategies, and International Location." *Environmental Planning D* 6:245-62.

_____. 1989. "Thinking about flexibility: a response to Gertler."Transactions Institute of British Geographers *N.S.* 14:8-108.

Schumpeter, Joseph A. 1934. *The Theory of Economic Development*. Cambridge: Harvard University Press.

_____. 1939. *Business Cycles*, Vol. 1 New York: McGraw Hill Book Co., Inc.

_____. 1947. *Capitalism, Socialism and Democracy*. New York: Harper and Brothers.

Scott, A.J. 1988. *Metropolis: from the Division of Labor to Urban Form*. University of California Press, Berkeley.

_____. 1990. "The Technopoles of Southern California." *Environment and Planning A*, 22:1575-1605.

Scott, W. Richard. 1981. *Organizations: Rational, Natural, and Open Systems*. Englewood Cliffs, NJ: Prentice-Hall, Inc.

Shapero, Albert. 1979. *The Role of Entrepreneurship in Economic Development or the Less-Than-National Level*. College of Administrative Science, The Ohio State University, Working Paper Series 79-10.

Shapero, Albert, and Lisa Sokol. 1982. "The Social Dimensions of Entrepreneurship." Pp. 72-90 in Calvin A. Keist, Donald L. Sexton, and Karl H. Vesper (eds.), *Encyclopedia of Entrepreneurship*. Englewood Cliffs: Prentice Hall.

Sheppard, Harold L., and Neal Herrick. 1972. *Where Have All the Robots Gone?* New York: Free Press.

Simon, Herbert A. 1957. *Administrative Behavior*. 2nd Edition. New York: Macmillan.

Smith, N.R. 1967. *The Entrepreneur and His Firm: The Relationship Between Type of Man and Type of Company*. Ann Arbor: Michigan State University.

Smitka, M. 1989. Competitive Ties: Subcontracting in the Japanese Automotive Industry, Ph.D. Dissertation, Yale University.

Special Task Force to the Secretary of Health, Education and Welfare. 1973. *Work in America*. Cambridge, MA: The M.I.T. Press.

Stevens, Candice. 1997. "Mapping Innovation." Pg. 16-19. The OECD Observer #207 (August/September).

Stinchcombe, Arthur L. 1965. "Bureaucratic and Craft Administration of Production: A Comparative Study." *Administrative Science Quarterly* 4 (September):168-187.

Storper, M., and R. Walker. 1989. *The Capitalist Imperialist Territory, Technology and Industrial Growth.* New York: Basil Blackwell.

Thompson, Wilbur. 1962. "Locational Differences in Inventive Activity and Their Determinants." Pp. 253-71 in Richard R. Nelson, ed, *The Rate and Direction of Inventive Activity.* Princeton: Princeton University Press, for the National Bureau of Economic Research.

Thomas, Morgan D. 1985. "Regional Economic Development and the Role of Innovation and Technological Change." Pp. 13-35 in A.T. Thwaites and R.P. Oakey (eds.), *The Regional Economic Impact of Technological Change.* New York: St. Martin's Press.

U.S. Office of Technology Assessment. 1984. *Technology, Innovation and Regional Economic Development.* Washington, DC.

Utterback, James M. 1979. "The Dynamics of Product and Process Innovation in Industry." Pp. 40-65 in C.T. Hill and J.M. Utterback, eds, *Technological Innovation for a Dynamic Economy.* New York: Pergamon.

Whittington, R. C. 1984. "Regional Bias in New Firm Formation in the UK." *Regional Studies* 18:253-56.

Williams, K., T. Cutler, J. Williams and C. Haslam. 1987. "The End of Mass Production?" *Economy. & Society* 16:403-39.
Williamson, O.E. 1985. *The Economic Institutions of Capitalism: Firms, Markets, Relational Contracting.* The Free Press: New York.

Woo, Carolyn, Arnold C. Cooper, and William Dunkelberg. 1991. The Development and Interpretations of Entrepreneurial Typologies." *Journal of Business Venturing* 6:93-114.

Young, Christopher H. and Ruth C. Young. 1995. "Innovation, Technology and Employment Growth." Presented at the Eastern Sociological Meeting, Boston, Massachusetts, March 29.

Young, Ruth, George L. Rolleston, and Charles C. Geisler. 1984 "Competitive Structure and Fiscal Policy." *Social Indicators Research* 14:421-52.

Young, Ruth C. and Joe D. Francis. 1989. "Who Helps Small Manufacturing Firms Get Started?" *Rural Development Perspectives* 6 (October):21-25.

Young, Ruth C. and Joe D. Francis. 1991. Entrepreneurship and Innovation in Small Manufacturing Firms. *Social Science Quarterly*, 72(March)1:149-162.

Young, Ruth C. 1993 Serendipity and the Network of Manufacturing Firms. *CaRDI, 19 Innovation in Community & Rural Development*, October 1993.

Young, Ruth C. 1993 Small Manufacturing Firms and Regional Business Networks. *CaRDI,* 1,1, February 1993.

Young, Ruth C., Joe D. Francis and Christopher H. Young. 1993. Innovation in Small Manufacturing Firms. *CaRDI,* 1, 4, October 1993.

Young, Ruth C., Joe D. Francis and Christopher H. Young. 1993. Flexibility in Small Manufacturing Firms and Regional Industrial Formations. *Regional Studies*, 28, 1:27-38, July.

Young, Ruth C., Joe D. Francis and Christopher H. Young. 1993. Innovation, High-Technology Use, and Flexibility in Small Manufacturing Firms. *Growth and Change*, 24, pp. 67-86, Winter.

Young, Ruth C. and Joe D. Francis. 1994. The Role of Self Help, Private Help, and Community Assistance for 1994 Small Manufacturing Firms. *CaRDI* (Cornell Community and Rural Development Institute), 2, l.

Young, Ruth C., Joe D. Francis and Christopher H. Young. 1994. Small Manufacturing Firms and Regional Business Networks. *Economic Development Quarterly*, 8, 1:77-82, February.

Young, Ruth C. and Joe D. Francis. 1997. "Secrecy as a Factor in the Spread of New Technology: Photonics in the Rome Labs." *American Geographical Society: Focus*, 44 (1): 7-9.

Index

Community Development
Block Grants, 104, 105,
130, 148, 168, 199-200;
Urban Development Action
Grant Program, 104, 105-6,
182
Small Business
Administration, 104, 226;
resources and services
provided, 151-53
United States rust belt:
arrangement of firms in,
10-11, 59; two kinds of
industry, 57-58

Viele, Ronald, 194

Walker, R. See Storper and
Walker
Wehrle, Robert E., 190
Western New York Economic
Development Corporation,
160-61, 167-68
Williamson, Oliver, theories
of, 9-10, 11; undermining
of, 33-34, 73, 75
Wortley, George, 191